CHINA'S LATER DYNASTIES

SUZANNE STRAUSS ART

PEMBLEWICK PRESS
Lincoln, Massachusetts

To Dick Upjohn

With deep appreciation for his support of my writing projects, and with great respect for his lifelong dedication to developing the minds and spirits of the students of the Fay Upper School

Illustrations are by the author.

Other Books for Middle School Students by the Same Author

EARLY TIMES: THE STORY OF ANCIENT EGYPT
EARLY TIMES: THE STORY OF ANCIENT GREECE
EARLY TIMES: THE STORY OF ANCIENT ROME
EARLY TIMES: THE STORY OF THE MIDDLE AGES
*WEST MEETS EAST: THE TRAVELS OF ALEXANDER THE GREAT
*QUINTET: FIVE LIVELY PLAYS FOR KIDS
*THE STORY OF THE RENAISSANCE
*ANCIENT TIMES — THE STORY OF THE FIRST AMERICANS, BOOK I
*NATIVE AMERICA ON THE EVE OF CONQUEST — THE STORY OF THE FIRST AMERICANS,
          BOOK II
*THE STORY OF ANCIENT CHINA

*Available through Pemblewickpress.com.
Others can be obtained through waysidepublishing.com.

CONTENTS

To The Teacher

The purpose of this book is to introduce middle school students to the exceptionally rich civilization of China, focusing upon the last four imperial dynasties — the Song, Yuan, Ming, and Qing. It is the second book in a series that began with THE STORY OF ANCIENT CHINA. However, this book can be used independently, since the first chapter presents a comprehensive overview of the major achievements of earlier times.

It is very important to begin your study of China with a thorough grounding in geography. Have sufficient copies of a good atlas on hand. Have your students make relief maps of China's physical features and locate the major regions and important cities. Chapter 1 is tightly packed with information covering a long time span, so go slowly. Understanding what happens in the rest of the book depends upon being familiar with such ancient traditions as Confucianism, Daoism, Buddhism, the concept of the Mandate of Heaven, and the mythology of god-like superheros. Devote plenty of time to discussing these topics as you encounter them in the reading. It's a good idea to have a copy of *The Analects* of Confucius and *The Way and Its Power* by Laozi on hand in the classroom for easy reference. Since the early dynasties will be referred to frequently in the later chapters, it is worthwhile for students to make posters or timelines for each of them.

As you proceed through each of the later chapters (2 through 6), have your students keep lists of the major figures of each dynasty and their contributions to Chinese culture. You might want to develop mini-units on such topics as poetry, porcelain, the novel, landscape painting, or Chinese symbols. Always do a class timeline at the end of a dynasty, and encourage your students to tackle as many enrichment projects as time allows.

You should have a wide variety of written materials on hand — books on Chinese history, poetry, art, literature, and calligraphy, with as much primary source material as possible. (See Suggested Readings at the end of this book.) Do take advantage of the many excellent movies that are now available on Video Cassettes and DVD's. *The Last Emperor* is a good example of a carefully researched history feature film, and companies such as Time-Life, Discovery Communications, and Schlesinger Films offer outstanding documentaries. Use the Internet. Particularly recommended websites are asiasource.org and askasia.org. Visit Edsitement.neh.gov for additional resources and lesson plans.

Consider doing a Chinese unit with other specialists in your school, such as the art, music, and drama teachers. Visit museums in your area and invite Chinese members of your community to visit your class. Most of all, have fun learning with your students about the fascinating history and culture of ancient and imperial China!

Tips on Pronounciation

Chinese is written with characters, which represent ideas rather than specific sounds of the alphabet. The pronounciation of these characters has been transcribed into Western languages using sound systems compatible with Western manners of speech. In 1956 the Chinese government introduced a system for the transliteration of Chinese into English known as *Pinyin*. It is the system most commonly used today. Below are a few rules from the Pinyin system that will help you pronounce the Chinese names and general terms that appear throughout this book.

Most of the letters used in Pinyin are pronounced as they are in English. However, the following consonants have a different pronounciation:

c	pronounced like ts
zh	pronounced like dj
q	pronounced like ch
x	pronounced like sh
z	pronounced like dz

Vowels are usually pronounced in the following manner:

a	ah as in father
e	usually like eh as in get
i	usually like ee in sheep
o	au as in author
u	usually like oo as in too
ai	ie as in pie
ei	ay as in day
au	ow as in how
ou	oe as in low
but...	

i written after z, c, or s is pronounced like uh
i written after sh, zh, or ch is pronounced like ur

Syllables in Mandarin (the official dialect of China) always end in vowels, n, or ng. The family name of a person is written before his given or Christian name. This is the opposite of the way names are written in English. (If an English name were written in this manner, it would appear as Smith John or Hamilton Mary.) The most common family name in China is Li.

Important Dates

Beginnings

Paleolithic/Neolithic Periods	c. 600,000 — c. 2000 BCE
Xia Dynasty	c. 2299 — c.1750
Shang Dynasty	c. 1750 — c.1027
Zhou Dynasty	c. 1027 — 256

Early Imperial China

Qin Dynasty	221 — 206
Han Dynasty	206 BCE — 220 CE
Period of Division	317 — 589
Sui Dynasty	581 — 618
Tang Dynasty	618 — 907
Five Dynasties/Ten Kingdoms	907 — 960

Later Imperial China

Northern Song Dynasty	960 — 1127
Southern Song Dynasty	1127 —1276
Yuan Dynasty	1271 —1368
Ming Dynasty	1368 —1644
Qing Dynasty	1644 —1911

Introduction

As the 21st century begins to unfold, China is emerging as a superpower of the modern world. It is a vast country, the third largest in the world, with a gigantic population — nearly one out of every four people on the planet live there. Although China lagged behind the major industrial nations in the last century, it now has a burgeoning economy. It is also a major player in global politics.

Being a superpower is nothing new for China. Three thousand years ago, a remarkably rich civilization was already flourishing there. Two centuries before Augustus ruled the Roman Empire, China's first emperor had established a form of centralized government that would endure, with some alterations, until modern times. When Europe was just awakening from the Dark Ages, China's capital, Chang'an, was the wealthiest and most sophisticated city in the world.

The Chinese called their country the Middle Kingdom, convinced that it was the center of civilization. In many ways, it was. Throughout most of history, China's closest neighbors were nomadic tribesmen. When more advanced civilizations to the West learned about China through the traders of the Silk Road, they were dazzled by the country's "wonder products" — silk cloth, paper, lacquerware, and, later on, porcelain, tea, and gunpowder. Over the centuries, foreign ambassadors flocked to China's imperial court. In the 18th century, Voltaire, a famous French philosoper, described the Chinese bureaucracy as the ideal form of government.

Written records of China's history extend back to the 2nd millennium BCE. Studying such a vast scope of events sounds like an impossible task, but the Chinese scholars made it easier by dividing their history into dynasties, during which generations of one family ruled the country. Most major dynasties lasted several centuries. You will be learning all about the last four dynasties, each of which brought important changes and innovations to Chinese civilization. But first, it is important to know something about the country's unique geography and the major achievements made in ancient times, so our study will begin there.

By the time you've finished this book, you will have encountered a wide panoply of characters — warriors, philosophers, poets, artists, bandits, novelists, actors, merchants, courtiers, concubines, alchemists, and, of course, a great many fascinating emperors. Are you ready? Then let's get started!

CHINA

Chapter 1
Early Times
An Overview of Ancient China

Any study of Chinese history must begin with a close look at the country's geography. China is slightly larger than the United States and occupies much of the eastern third of Asia. The landscape varies widely — from the Siberian-like wastelands of northern Manchuria to the lush tropical rainforests of the southern provinces. The western highlands are bounded by vast deserts and ranges of towering mountains.

The heartland of China, known as Inner China, lies in the rich lower valleys and floodplains of the country's two largest rivers — the Yellow River and the Yangzi. The rivers originate in the Tibetan Plateau and, like all Chinese rivers, flow eastward. Inner China comprises only 10% of the country's area, although most of the nation's huge population lives there today. It was in this fertile region, isolated from the rest of the world by the rugged terrain and vast oceans, that Chinese civilization evolved.

Look at the map on the opposite page. Notice how the Yellow River cuts a wide loop before beginning the final leg of its journey to the sea. This is where it enters Inner China. The river gets its name from the yellowish soil it picks up in this region. The soil, known as loess (luss), is made of finely ground minerals that have blown here from the Taklamakan and Gobi deserts over the millennia. Loess is extremely fertile and ideal for farming, but when it is carried by the river it gradually settles to the bottom as silt, causing the riverbed to rise. This has caused the Yellow River to flood so many times that it is known as "China's Sorrow." There are few trees in this northern part of Inner China. They were all cut down long, long ago for fuel. Winters are cold and blustery, and summers can be very sizzling hot. The climate is dry, with most of the rain arriving in the spring.

The Yangzi River flows about three hundred miles south of the Yellow River in

Highlights of This Chapter

The Geography of China
China's Stone Age
The Xia
The Shang Dynasty
The Zhou Dynasty
The Great Philosophers
The Han Dynasty
The Period of Disunion
The Tang Dynasty
Five Dynasties and Ten Kingdoms
The Founding of the Song Dynasty

Inner China. It is a deep, fast moving river, and it passes through some of the most scenic landscapes in China. In its eastern reaches, the Yangzi flows through a beautiful lake district before coming to its delta at Shanghai. A network of smaller rivers and canals makes it easy to travel about this region by boat. The Yangzi valley is much warmer and wetter than the north, and the mountaintops are often shrouded in mist.

The Sichuan Basin lies in the southwestern portion of Inner China. Millions of years ago this was the site of an inland sea. Today, the Yangzi and three of its tributaries flow through the flat and fertile farmland of Sichuan. The West River is the longest river in the southeastern section of China. It is joined by the Pearl River and forms a delta near Guangzhou.

Beginnings and

As early as 25,000 BCE, bands of primitive tribesmen inhabited the river valleys of Inner China. They hunted deer, fished in the rivers, and gathered edible plants, nuts, and berries. By 6,000 BCE, people living near the Yellow River had discovered how to grow millet, a grain similar to wheat. This revolutionary discovery enabled families to settle down in one place. Archaeologists refer to the period when primitive people first became farmers as *Neolithic*.

Over the years, numerous settlements were established along the Yellow River. By sharing their labor and tools, the farmers were often able to produce a surplus of grain. This freed up some of the more creative members of the group to devote their time to tasks like making tools and pottery. Such a division of labor is an important step in the development of a civilization. The early settlers also raised pigs and dogs — for food. (Even today, dogmeat is often consumed in certain parts of China.) As farming spread further south, rice became a second major crop. The rice-growers domesticated the water buffalo to help them plow their fields.

Over the centuries, a number of distinctive cultures arose in the valleys of the Yellow and Yangzi Rivers. The best known of these are the Yangshao and Longshan, who are particularly noted for their pottery. The Yangshao decorated their pots with geometric designs and animal figures. Some were marked with a primitive form of writing. The Longshan, who were the first to use a potter's wheel, produced black ritual vessels as thin as eggshells.

By 2000 BCE, the Chinese had learned how to make silk cloth. Silk comes from the cocoons spun by a moth caterpillar, known as a silkworm. Most likely, silk was discovered when an ancient villager accidently dropped a cocoon in water and noted that its threads could be unraveled. Once the connection was made between the cocoon and the silkworm, villagers began gathering bunches of the voracious caterpillars and feeding them mulberry leaves. After the silkworms spun their cocoons, they were collected and dropped in pots of hot water. This drowned the pupating moths and loosened the sticky material that held the strands of silk together. Several strands were spun into thread, which was then woven into cloth on wooden looms. Many of the pieces of silk cloth were used for shrouds, which were placed on the bodies of local leaders. As you will see, the production of silk would later become a major part of the Chinese economy.

The Xia (c.1953- 1750 BCE)

By around 1900 BCE, a fairly advanced society known as the Xia (Shee ah) was flourishing on the banks of the Yellow River. The Xia were farmers, who lived in walled cities and were defended by an elite class of warriors. They were ruled by a king, whose authority spread over a fairly wide area. Xia craftsmen worked with molten bronze to fashion weapons, tools, and objects for religious ceremonies.

For a long time, historians believed that the Xia existed only Chinese legend. However, excavations at Erlitou, a site in the Yellow River valley, revealed evidence of the buildings (including a large palace), tombs, and artifacts of this ancient culture.

The Shang (1750-1027 BCE)

The Shang (Shawng) were a warlike people who conquered the Xia around the year 1750 BC. Theirs is the first dynasty for which we have a written record. Archaeologists have discovered examples of picture-writing incised on animal bones, like the fragment shown below. These were apparently used to predict the future.

Here's how it worked. The king would ask a diviner (a sort of fortune-teller) a question. Would he win a war? Would it rain soon?

Would there be a good harvest? The diviner made a groove on the back of the bone and then placed a hot rod in the groove. This produced a series of cracks, which were believed to represent the answer to the question sent by ancestral spirits. The diviner interpreted the patterns of the cracks to give the king his answer. In many cases, the question and the answer were carved on the bone itself. The simple drawings of animals, the sun and moon, and other aspects of the natural environment that made up this system of picture-writing are the origins of the characters that comprise the modern Chinese written language. Because they were used to predict the future, the bones incised with these writings are called "oracle bones." Thousands of them were discovered at the site of the last Shang capital at Anyang.

Among the roles of the Shang king was that of high priest. He led his people in the worship of their ancestral spirits. Later kings interpreted the cracks of the oracle bones. Shang craftsmen were the first to cast molten bronze in clay molds to produce metal pots. They made elaborate cauldrons with handles and "feet," so they could be placed among the coals of the fire. These ornate vessels were used to heat wine for religious rituals. Many of these were inscribed with writing similar to that on the oracle bones. Shang bronze vessels are considered among the finest made anywhere in the world.

The major cities of the Shang were square in shape and surrounded by massive earthen walls. They were carefully aligned with the four points of the compass. This layout reflected the ancient belief that the world was a square. Priests determined the directions by observing the movements of the sun, moon, stars, and planets. All major buildings faced south, the direction associated with warmth and energy. The square shape, the south-facing orientation, and the thick earthen wall would characterize most major Chinese towns and cities until modern times.

The Zhou (1059 – 221 BCE)

In the middle of the tenth century BCE, the Shang were overthrown by the Zhou (Joe). They established a new dynasty with a capital at Chang'an, a site on the Wei River near its junction with the Yellow River.

The Duke of Zhou, a founder of the dynasty, was the first to mention the con-

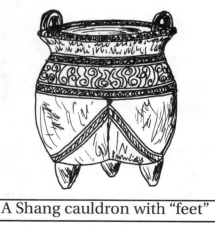

A Shang cauldron with "feet"

cept of the Mandate of Heaven. A mandate is a command or authorization. Heaven (*Tian*) was the main deity of the Zhou. In a speech, the Duke announced that Heaven had been displeased with the Shang king, who had acted immorally (he implied that he was a drunk), and had withdrawn from him the mandate to rule. His own people, on the other hand, had proven themselves worthy of leadership, and the mandate had been passed on to them. Beginning with the Zhou, the Chinese ruler was considered the Son of Heaven and the possessor of the Mandate. This power held certain moral obligations. If a ruler failed to meet them, Heaven would express anger through such natural calamities are floods or earthquakes and the people would rebel. Eventually, someone qualified would come along to claim Heaven's Mandate.

The Zhou dynasty lasted for about 800 years, longer than any other. Historians divide the dynasty into two periods known as the Western Zhou (a relatively peaceful time) and the Eastern Zhou (a time of constant warfare).

The rulers of the Western Zhou established the precedent of keeping records of important government activities. Decisions were written on bamboo strips, which were tied together with pieces of silk cord like the one pictured above. These were history's first books. Before long, nonofficial writings were also appearing on

bamboo strips. In fact, three works that would become important classics throughout the rest of Chinese history were written during this time. These are *The Book of Documents*, *The Book of Songs*, and *The Book of Changes*. They deserve a closer look.

The Book of Documents is China's oldest history chronicle. It contains legends that had been handed down for centuries about the mythical founders of China and descriptions of actual rulers, including the debauched last king of the Shang and the founders of the Zhou dynasty. It also includes speeches given by kings and other political leaders. (This is where the speech about the Mandate of Heaven appears.)

The Book of Songs is the earliest collection of Chinese poetry. It contains 305 ancient folk songs, political poems, and ceremonial odes dating from as early as the 10th century BC. Most are written in four-syllable lines that rhyme.

The Book of Changes is a manual for predicting the future. It uses a complicated system of trigrams, which represent the basic elements of the natural world. (A trigram is an arrangement of three lines, which can be broken or unbroken. There are many possible combinations.) The

The symbol for *yin* and *yang*

manual is based on the ancient belief that human destiny is closely linked to the ever-changing relationship between the dual forces of nature, *yin* and *yang*. (They are represented in the symbol above.) These forces are not opposites; they are complementary. *Yang* (the white half of the symbol) represents everything that is male, bright, warm, active, and joyful, while *yin* is everything female, dark, cold, passive, and melancholy. Everything in nature is composed of both, but at a given time one is dominant over the other. (Notice how in the symbol each force contains a part of the other.) In an unending series of cycles, one force predominates for awhile and then gives in to the other until it, too, diminishes — and so the pattern continues. To understand the concept, think about how summer slowly gives way to winter, which in turn leads back to summer. In a similar vein, a person can be enthusiastic and joy-ful at one time and brooding at another. Isn't human life filled with highs and lows, excitement and tranquility? According to *The Book of Changes*, *yin* and *yang* are closely connected to certain elements of nature. For example, *yang* is linked to the sun and the mountains, while *yin* is associated with the moon and water. Each of the trigrams in *The Book of Changes* represents a certain combination of elements, which , in turn, symbolize a human state. For example, a combination of wind and water might indicate stormy times ahead. A diviner would randomly arrange a bunch of sticks into trigrams and then "read" them to predict changes in a person's life.

Zhou metalworkers cast large vessels of bronze. Many of these bear lengthy inscriptions, which provide fascinating clues about life during the early years of the dynasty. Zhou artisans carved small statues and circular disks (symbols of Heaven) out of jade. This stone was valued not only for the beauty of its greenish hues but for the resilience of its surface. (Only a diamond is harder than jade.) Since Neolithic times, the Chinese have associated the unyielding qualities of jade with immortality. The Zhou often buried their dead with an amulet carved from the stone, hoping it would enable the deceased to live forever in the next world.

Zhou craftsmen knew how to coat carved pieces of wood or bamboo with heated lacquer, the sap derived from a tree that grows in central and southern China. When the lacquer cooled and hardened, it formed a surface that was resistant to water, heat, and even corrosion by acid. It was the plastic of the ancient world!

In 771 BCE, the Zhou were driven from their capital by an alliance of nomadic tribesmen. They reestablished their court further east, at Luoyang, and thus began the period of the Eastern Zhou. The kings never regained the power their predecessors had held earlier. In fact, their territory was restricted to the region around Luoyang. Much of Inner China was now ruled by warlords, who were constantly fighting for supremacy with weapons of iron and the latest invention, the crossbow.

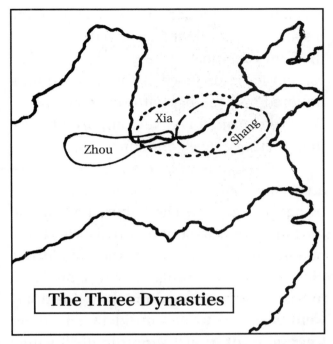

The Three Dynasties

The Great Philosophers

Despite the political turbulence, or perhaps because of it, this was a time of considerable intellectual activity. China's most renowned philosophers, Confucius and Laozi, lived in the later part of the Eastern Zhou.

Confucius spent his early years as a petty government official. He had received a good education, which at that time meant that he had learned to read and write Chinese characters and had closely studied *The Book of Documents*, *The Book of Songs*, and *The Book of Changes*. Confucius was very concerned about the political unrest of his times, and he wondered how peace might be restored. He found his answer in the structure of Chinese society. The family was the basic unit of this society. Each family was headed by the father. His authority

Although historians traditionally list the Xia, Shang, and Zhou dynasties in chronological order, these cultures actually overlapped one another. Their "succession" to power was simply a matter of one becoming dominant in central China at a given time. It is also important to know that other cultures were flourishing at the same time they were. Sichuan, for example, was the heart of a culture that produced a number of bronze masks and unique tall bronze statues of gods and rulers with bulging eyes and pointy ears.

was never questioned, but it was his moral responsibility to be sensitive to the needs of the family members. When he died, his eldest son took his place as family head and honored his memory with ritual sacrifices. For this reason, it was very important for a man to have at least one son.

The family was organized as a hierarchy, a person's ranking being determined by age and gender. The father, the head of the hierarchy, was superior to his wife, both parents were superior to their children, older siblings to younger siblings, brothers to sisters. Those in dominant positions were expected to be considerate in their treatment of their subordinates, while those in subordinate positions owed their superiors respect and obedience. Everyone knew his or her place and acted accordingly. Respect for one's parent, known as *filial piety*, was the highest social virtue and the cornerstone of stability in China.

Confucius believed that government could be run in the same way. The king was like the father of the extended Chinese family. It was his duty to live in a moral way, setting a good example for his people while remaining sensitive to their needs. He performed sacrifices to the ancestral spirits of the dynasty on behalf of his subjects. The people, in turn, should honor him and obey his commands. If everyone followed the rules, society would be orderly and peaceful. Confucius considered this a realistic

goal. He believed that people were basically good and needed only to be taught how to live in a virtuous way. Of course, if the king did not conduct himself in the proper manner, his subjects would have every reason to reject him and support a new leader. This approach to government tied in nicely with the concept of the Mandate of Heaven.

Confucius became a teacher. He welcomed any student showing intellectual promise to his school, regardless of his social background. This was an unconventional idea, since education had been limited to the sons of wealthy men. Confucius looked back in history for models of good government. He considered the early days of the Zhou a "golden time" when China was ruled by virtuous men. He instructed his students to study the great writings of the Western Zhou. These books would become part of the Five Confucian Classics. (The other two were *The Book of Rites* [a collection of documents describing ancient rituals and court ceremonies] and *The Spring and Autumn Annals* [a chronicle of events written in the philosopher's home state of Lu].) You'll be hearing a lot about the Five Classics in the chapters that follow.

Confucius hoped that his students would become government officials and bring the ideals of earlier times to the present rulers. He himself traveled from court to court, hoping to convince the local governors of his views. Although he failed to achieve this goal in his lifetime (he died a disappointed man), his teachings would become the basis of the Chinese political and social structures for centuries to come. After his death, many of his teachings were written down in a collection known as *The Analects*. Among them is a concept that is probably familiar to you: "Do not impose on others what you yourself do not desire."

Laozi (Low tzuh) was a contemporary of Confucius. He had a totally different approach to dealing with political disharmony. It consisted mainly of ignoring it! Laozi believed that the key to social order and personal contentment lay in observing the patterns and rhythms of nature. Rather than protest an action or resist an obstacle, one should submit to it, or "go with the flow." So in place of a highly structured social organization, Laozi proposed having none at all. By doing nothing, something positive — peace — would be achieved.

Laozi's main ideas are described in his short book, entitled *The Way and Its Power*. "The way" referred to the natural order of things. Water was a favorite image for this philosopher: it is indispensable to all forms of life, yet it "humbly" flows to the lowest available spot. The wise man should be like water. Laozi wrote: "The man who withdraws from the world finds it…by giving up power, he becomes powerful…by not desiring riches, he becomes rich." Imagine a fisherman quietly waiting, watching the shimmering surface of the water, until — suddenly — the fish bites!

The Chinese word for "the way" is *dao*, and followers of Laozi became known as *Daoists*. They learned to achieve a state of inner calm through meditation and deep breathing exercises. Zhuangzi was a scholarly man who lived two centuries after Laozi. He wrote the second great book of Daoism (known as *The Zhuangzi)*. It explains the basic beliefs of the philosophy through a series of humorous anecdotes and stories.

Confucianism and Daoism seem to be very opposite, and yet, like *yin* and *yang*, they are complementary. Each serves a different need. Confucianism is practical, while Laozi's approach appeals more to the emotions. In centuries to come, both philosophies would have a profound effect upon Chinese civilization.

The Qin (221 – 206 BCE)

While Confucius and Laozi were proposing solutions for peace, the many small states in China continued to fight among

---

The Analects and *The Way and Its Power* continue to be widely read in modern China — and in other parts of the world.

themselves until one became dominant. By the 3rd century (221 BCE), the fearsome warriors of the Qin (Chin) had defeated all rivals and established their own dynasty. The Qin were the first to unify all of Inner China into an empire under a strong central government. They built a capital at Xianyang (not far from the ancient Shang capital, Anyang.) Their first ruler is known as Qin Shi Huangdi (Chin Shuh Hoo ahng dee, literally, "First Emperor of the Qin").

The Qin were not interested in the theories of Confucius or Laozi. They adhered to a different philosophy, known as Legalism, that defined people as weak and greedy. For a Legalist, the only way to keep the peace was by enforcing strict laws. Shi Huangdi tolerated no arguments or protest. His way was the only way.

The emperor ran the government with the aid of three top advisers, each of whom had his own staff. (Remember this. From this time onward, most Chinese governments would be headed by three ministries.) Shi Huangdi divided the empire into 36 districts. Every district had a civil and military governor, who were overseen by an imperial inspector. The districts were subdivided into counties, which were run by local officials appointed by and responsible to the central government.

Shi Huangdi oversaw several reforms to unify his empire. He standardized the Chinese system of writing, basing it upon a core vocabulary of about 3000 commonly used characters. He standardized the system of weights and measures and adopted a single coinage. The new copper coins had a square hole in the center so they could be strung together. Why square? Because that was the shape of the world, aligned by the four cardinal directions.

The emperor created a system of compulsory labor, in which peasants had to work for a month at a time on public projects. Among these was a project to build a network of imperial highways totalling over 4,000 miles. The axles of all carts and carriages were required to be the same width (6 feet) to facilitate travel over the roads. Another project involved cutting channels and canals in southern China to allow water transport for 1,200 miles from the Yangzi to Guangzhou. For purposes of defense, the emperor had several walls that had been built by rulers of earlier kingdoms connected and reinforced, forming an unbroken barrier along his northern border. This was the origin of the famous Great Wall.

Shi Huangdi traced his ancestry back

to the Yellow Emperor, a mythical ruler who had chased away evil creatures from the Yellow River valley and taught the people about writing, medicine, and other useful things. Yellow, the color of the loess soil, has been associated with China and its rulers from earliest times. Beginning with the Qin, it was the imperial color: only the emperor could wear yellow silk robes. At the same time, the dragon was adopted as the imperial symbol. Unlike the man-eating Western variety, the Chinese dragon was a benevolent creature that brought the rain to the farmer's crops. He was envisioned as a composite beast, having the body of a serpent, the scales of a carp, the ears of a camel, the whiskers of a cat, the claws of an eagle, and the eyes of a demon. The image of the dragon would appear on the emper-

or's yellow robe, on his throne, on the walls and ceilings of his palace, and in all sorts of other places connected with imperial rule. According to legend, the soul of a dead emperor ascended into the heavens on the back of a winged dragon.

Shi Huangdi had no liking for scholars, artisans, or tradesmen. In his view, the only important people were the peasants, who provided the crops (and the silk) that made up the wealth of the state, and the soldiers, who guarded the imperial borders. He went so far as to order all books (except those discussing "practical" matters, like medicine, agriculture, and divination) to be burned. When 460 scholars protested his actions, he had them buried alive! (Fortunately, a copy of every major work had been placed in the imperial library, and these were not touched.)

The first emperor believed his dynasty would continue for over a thousand generations. As it turned out, it would last less than 20 years. However, his principles of centralized government would endure, with some alterations, throughout the history of imperial China. And he gained immortality of a sort when archaeologists discovered a huge army of clay soldiers buried in pits near his tomb. His terracotta army has become one of the major tourist attractions in modern China.

The Han (206 BCE – 220 CE)

The harsh doctrines of the Legalists were a major cause of a rebellion that brought about the downfall of the Qin. Liu Bang was a man of humble origins who led the rebels and established a new dynasty, the Han. The capital was Chang'an (modern Xi'an).

The new government was modeled upon that of the Qin, without the nastier aspects of Legalism. The Han emperors adopted many of the ideas proposed by Confucius and tried to rule with reason and benevolence. Emperor Wudi established

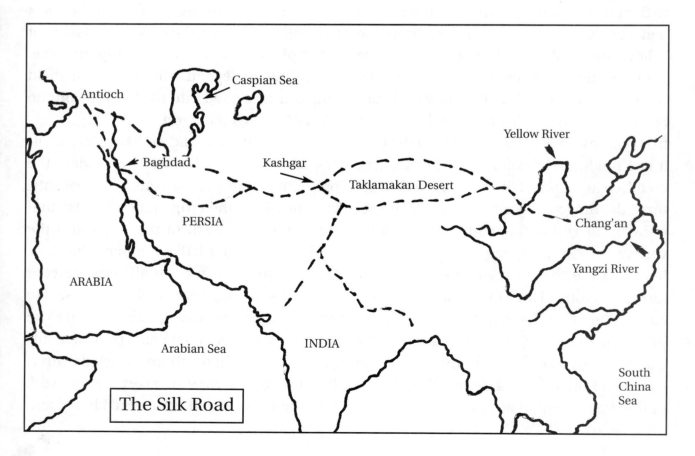

The Silk Road

the Imperial Academy for the study of Five Confucian Classics as well as *The Analects* and the writings of Mencius (a Confucian philosopher). A civil service examination system was created to select candidates for government office on the basis of their knowledge of the Confucian writings.

We know a great deal about the Han dynasty, as well as those who ruled before, because of the efforts of a historian named Sima Qian. He wrote the first major history of China. This was a vast undertaking —his book contained 130 chapters, each chapter filling one silken scroll. (Silk had replaced bamboo as the official writing material.) There were over half a million characters! The book begins in mythical times: the Chinese had been telling stories about god-like leaders, like the Yellow Emperor, for so long that they tended to include them in their lists of rulers. Using ancient records and a good deal of ingenuity, Sima Qian spun a colorful tale about each the dynasties up to and including his own. (His book has been described as a one-man account of the history of the entire known world!) Following his standard, official historians from every succeeding dynasty would document all major events and decisions, in an effort to provide their rulers with precedents to guide or justify their own policies. China has a longer written record of its history than any other people in the world.

The Han armies expanded China's borders until the empire nearly doubled in size. This was accompanied by the opening up of a huge trade network between China and the West known as the Silk Road. This thoroughfare led to the exchange not only of products like silk and ivory but of ideas, religious beliefs, and new technologies.

The tombs of Han rulers and nobility contained many clay figures of courtiers, musicians, and servants. These provide clues about life among the the wealthy elite, while models of dwellings and watchtowers offer a glimpse of what the cities might have looked like. Also placed in the tombs were the earliest surviving documents written on strips of bamboo, still tied together with silken cords. Two spectacular graves from the early Han period housed the bodies of a prince and his wife, which were totally encased in suits of jade. (Jade, remember, symbolized immortality.)

Early in the first century CE, a high minister named Wang Mang seized the throne and created his own, rather short-lived dynasty (the Xin). Wang had many good ideas for reforming the economy, but he couldn't win enough support to rule for long. Civil war broke out, Chang'an was burned, and he was driven out of power. In 25 CE, the Han dynasty was restored, with a new capital to the east in Luoyang. Trade was restored and the empire expanded once more until it nearly touched that of the Romans.

About this time, Daoism became a popular religion, absorbing many ancient superstitions and folk beliefs that had little to do with Laozi's original philosophy. Laozi was even made a god, who reigned among such other deities as the Jade Emperor and the Queen Mother of the West. Daoism was closely associated with alchemy — the search for an elixir that would make a person immortal. Unfortunately, alchemists often used toxic ingredients like arsenic and mercury, so their potions sometimes had the opposite effect of the one intended!

On a more scientific plane, Cai Lin, a member of the Han imperial court, created a remarkable new product — paper. His invention led to a dramatic increase in book production (paper was much cheaper than silk), and this, in turn, led to a great increase in literacy. Daoist priests, meanwhile, invented the compass. It was used, not for navigation, but to determine the direction of south when designing buildings.

In the later years, the Han were ruled by a succession of weak emperors. Rebellions broke out and the country was thrown into turmoil. Finally, a general named Cao Cao forced the abdication of the last Han ruler and claimed the Mandate of Heaven for himself.

An Age of Division

Although we think of Chinese history in terms of powerful dynasties, four hundred years separated the rich and enlightened age of the Han and the next major dynasty, the Tang. During these centuries, China was torn apart in a number of different ways.

At first, the country was divided into three kingdoms. The most memorable legacy of this period is a series of legends about its colorful characters. These were eventually written down in the 14th century in the epic novel, *The Romance of the Three Kingdoms*. After the short-lived dynasty of the Western Jin, the country was divided in half — the north was controlled by a series of non-Chinese rulers, while the south remained in the hands of successive Chinese dynasties.

The Sui (581 - 618)

In 581, the Sui dynasty reunited China, and the capital was once again at Chang'an. Although there were only two

The Han developed a form of script in which characters were formed by combining eight basic features. The formal versions of these characters have kept the same structure for more than 2,000 years. Calligraphy, the writing of Chinese characters with a brush and ink, became a fine art when paper was invented. Writers now spent countless hours perfecting the strokes of their characters.

Sui emperors, they laid the groundwork for the glorious Tang dynasty that would follow. The Sui recentralized and strengthened the government, developed the civil exam system begun by the Han, and established a new code of law.

During this period, a system of canals was built to connect the Yangzi with the Yellow River. Known as the Grand Canal, it linked up with the canal built by the Qin between the Yangzi and Guangzhou. This new network of waterways led to the expansion of trade between the north and south, and it kept the capital city well supplied with rice. The Sui also oversaw a number of other major projects, including the reinforcement of the Great Wall, the building of new roads, and the construction a number of grand palaces. But the government's incessant demand for laborers and taxes to pay for its work projects and military campaigns ultimately drove the people to revolt. The Sui dynasty tumbled in 618, and the Mandate of Heaven was claimed by the founder of the Tang dynasty.

Buddhism Comes to China

Before moving on, let's take a moment to learn about a new religion — Buddhism — which had made its way from India into China via the Silk Road. Buddhists believed that life was filled with suffering, and that this suffering was caused by human greed. People were born and reborn in this world, the quality of a person's present life being determined by his *karma* (the accumulation of good or bad deeds performed in his past lives). Selfish desires and the love of material comfort kept a person enmeshed in this chain of rebirth. But, according to the Buddhists, he could break free from the cycle by ridding himself of selfish desires. Through prayer, meditation, and living a truly virtuous life, he could achieve a state

---

The Chinese myth of origin was finally written down around in around the 3rd century. It told how the first being, Pangu, was born out of a giant egg of chaos. As he burst from the shell, all the heavy elements sank to the ground, forming the earth. They represented the primal force of *yin*. The lighter elements drifted upwards and formed the heavens. They represented the force of *yang*. Pangu grew and grew, holding up the heavens high above the earth. When he died, his body became the sun, moon, stars, mountains, valleys, rivers, plants and animals. The fleas from his body became the first human beings.

The earth was then ruled by a race of super-human kings, who taught the people everything they needed to know — how to hunt, fish, farm, make tools and weapons, irrigate fields and hold back floodwaters, keep a calendar, and prepare medicine. As the stories about these mythical figures merged with those of China's historical rulers, the history of China was extended back several millennia before recorded time.

Buddha

known as *Nirvana*, or enlightenment.

The founder of this belief was an Indian prince, Sihardta Gautama, who discovered the key to enlightenment by meditating beneath a tree. He came to be known as the "enlightened one," which is translated in Sanskrit as *Buddha*. Statues of him, serene in his meditative pose, appeared in every Buddhist home and temple.

During the years that China was divided in two, the northern rulers adopted Buddhism as their official religion. They sponsored several projects to carve huge Buddhist figures out of the faces of cliffs along the Silk Road. Sculptures varying in height from a few inches to thirty-five feet were carved in niches in the canyon walls above the Yi River near Luoyang. Wendi, first emperor of the Sui, was an ardent Buddhist. He devoted a great deal of energy to building Buddhist temples and filling them with statues and wall paintings.

Over the years, elements of Buddhism, Daoism, and Confucianism would mingle together, influencing the lives of most Chinese. They are known as the "three teachings." They usually coexisted peacefully, and paintings often depicted smiling figures of Confucius, Buddha, and Laozi trading ideas with one another.

The Tang (618-907)

The Tang dynasty was founded by Li Yuan, who ruled as Gaozu. He established a government similar to that of the Han. The Tang gave final form to the government created by Shi Huangdi. Because it would serve as the model for most future emperors, we should look closely at its basic structure.

The top level consisted of three ministries. The Secretariat and the Chancellery dealt with matters of high policy and advised the emperor. The third ministry, the Department of State Affairs, oversaw

Notice that there were nine ministries in the central government. Nine was considered an imperial number, since it is the highest single digit and is uneven (*yang*). Also, the Chinese word for nine sounds like the word for everlasting.

the second tier of the government. This second tier consisted of six ministries: the Civil Office (it dealt with all matters concerned with staffing of civil service), Rites (religious and ceremonial matters and with reception of foreign visitors), Revenue (taxes), Justice; War; Public Works (roads, irrigation, and the manufacture of work equipment). An additional organization known as the Censorate oversaw government operations as a whole and acted as a watchdog. (It was a Chinese version of our CIA.) A network of government offices functioned throughout the empire under the supervision of the upper levels of the bureaucracy.

Block printing was invented around the 8th century. This made the written word available to greater numbers than ever before. Even the sons of humble craftsmen learned to read, and the mass printing of the Confucian classics was a boon for the education of China's scholars. The Tang formalized the system of civil service examinations, and a growing number of scholars became government officials. The nobility, who had monopolized government appointments in earlier times, saw their power wane as academic merit, rather than wealth and family connections, became the means to political success. Those in power were now expected to be masters of Confucian philosophy and Chinese history as well as political strategists. The ideal

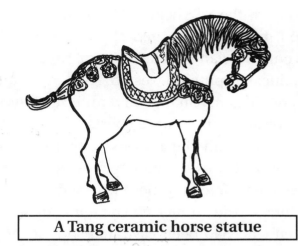

A Tang ceramic horse statue

courtier was also skillful in the fine arts of poetry, painting, and calligraphy.

The Tang dynasty was a golden age of poetry. Li Bo (Bai) and Du Fu, produced memorable verses filled with images of moonlight, beautiful mountain settings, the pleasure of friendship, and the sorrow of parting. And while artists like Wang Wei painted haunting landscapes, craftsmen molded realistic clay figures of courtiers, ladies, gods and demons. Among the most popular ceramic statues were prancing horses and camels laden with bolts of silk.

Under the Tang, China became a world power. The empire's borders expanded to the northeast and the west until it included more territory ever before. Diplomatic relations were established with nations as far away as Byzantium. Chinese luxury products — silk, porcelain, and lacquerware — were carried to many other parts of the world. Chang'an, the starting point of the Silk Road, became the largest and most sophisticated city in the world. When overland trade was disrupted by political disputes in western Asia, maritime trade began, Guangzhou and Yangzhou becoming important sea ports.

As with the Han dynasty, the Tang grew weaker as the quality of its emperors declined. Gradually, power passed into the hands of the eunuchs. (The eunuchs were men who had been castrated so that they could run the palace and live among the emperor's wives and concubines without the risk of fathering children.) Many eunuchs formed close relationships with the imperial family and used their influence for personal gain. By 780, the eunuchs held high positions in every level of the central government. Meanwhile, the people were burdened by heavy taxes and troubled by the lack of government leadership. Conditions were worsened by such natural disasters as floods, droughts, and epidemics. Clearly, Heaven was not pleased with China's rulers.

In 907, a military commander usurped the throne and declared the founding of a new dynasty (the short-lived Liang).

Five Dynasties and Ten Kingdoms

For the next half century, China was again in disarray, divided up into many independent states whose borders changed with amazing speed. With political and military power up for grabs, any strongman able to organize a defense against the rebels and bandits could become a local warlord and declare himself king. Five dynasties rose and fell in the north, none able to permanently secure its grip on the throne.

Meanwhile, the south was divided into the Ten Lesser Kingdoms. No self-proclaimed king ever consolidated much more land than that of a modern province. And yet, in contrast to the chaos of the north, life in this region was relatively peaceful. The balmy environment of the Yangzi River valley attracted poets, painters, and scholars. Crafts industries such as silk and pottery flourished, and trade prospered. The heart of Chinese culture appeared to have shifted to the warmer clime.

New Beginnings

When the ruler of the last of the northern dynasties (the Northern Zhou) died in 959, his wife became the regent for their seven-year-old son. But on New Year's Day (January 31) in 960, as the court gathered to offer good wishes to the boy, reports arrived of an invasion by the Khitan, a non-Chinese people from western Manchuria.

Zhao Kuangyin (Jow Kwahng-yin), a high-ranking military officer, was ordered by the empress dowager (wife of the dead emperor) to lead a force northward to repel the invasion. As the army moved out of the city, people gathered in the streets to cheer them on. They soon began clamoring for Zhao to become their ruler, rather than a child of unknown character. As the chants grew louder, even the army officers were drawn into the demand for change.

According to legend, Zhao was aroused from his sleep a few nights later by a group of his officers, who had entered his tent with swords drawn. They threw the emperor's yellow robe over his shoulders and announced that he had been chosen to rule China. Deciding he had little choice in the matter, Zhao accepted his new role, but on his own terms. He insisted that the officers swear an oath of obedience and promise that no harm would come to the current ruler or his mother — or any other royal relative, government official, or citizen. Then he led the army to Kaifeng, the capital city of the fast disintegrating dynasty. China was entering an exciting new age.

Review Questions:

1. What is Inner China?
2. What is loess?
3. Compare the climates of the northern and southern regions of Inner China.
4. What enabled the first groups of people to settle in one place?
5. What are the oracle bones?
6. Why did the Shang cauldrons have feet?
7. What was the Mandate of Heaven?
8. Apart from bones and bronze vessels, what did the early Chinese write upon?
9. What are *yin* and *yang*?
10. What were the three great books produced by the Western Zhou?
11. What was the major goal of Confucius?
12. How, according to Laozi, could people find peace and happiness?
13. Who was Shi Huangdi?
14. Why was the dragon considered a benevolent creature?
15. What did Sima Qian write about?
16. What was the civil examination system?
17. What important route connected China with the Western world?
18. What was the Grand Canal?
19. What are the basic beliefs of Buddhism?
20. Describe the top level of Tang government.
21. Who were Li Bo and Du Fu?
22. Who was Zhao Kuangyin?

Projects:

1. Make a timeline of Chinese history from Neolithic times through the Tang dynasty.

2. Carefully study a physical map of China in an atlas. Then make a relief map of the country using clay or paper mache, poster board, and paint.

3. Find out more about the symbols that appeared on the oracle bones and how they evoled into modern Chinese characters. Make a chart to illustrate how several symbols evolved from ancient to modern times.

4. Make a Venn Diagram to indicate the similarities and differences of early Confucianism and Daoism during the Eastern Zhou.

5. Zhang Qian led an expedition to India during the Han Dynasty. He is credited with bringing China into active trade relations with the west along the Silk Road. Find out more about Zhang Qian and write a short report.

6. Read a selection of translated poems by Li Bo (Li Bai) and Du Fu. Learn about the lives of these men and their visions of what poetry should be. Share your findings with your classmates.

7. Although China has long been a patriarchical society, a number of extraordinary women have appeared in the nation's history. Among these are Hua Mulan, who fought in her father's place in the army for 12 years during the Sui Dynasty, and Empress Wu, who took over the reins of power and ran the government of the Tang for many years. Choose one of these fascinating women and write a report about her.

8. Consult a copy of *The Analects*. Select ten of the philosophical statements. Think about how they might apply to modern society. Share them with your classmates.

9. Read selections of Laozi's *The Way and Its Power*. Then read *The Tao of Pooh* by Benjamin Hoff (Penguin Books, 1982) or *The Te of Piglet* (Penguin Books, 1992). Make a presentation, explaining how the children's classic illustrates certain principles of Daoism.

10. Emperor Qin Shi Huangdi was described by early historians as a ferocious warrior who "destroyed his enemies like a silkworm devours a mulberry leaf." Find out more about this controversial man. Then make a Venn diagram to indicate his positive and negative qualities as China's ruler.

11. Among the earliest product to make their way to China long the Silk Road were grape vines and cucumbers. Find out more about this famous trade network. Make a poster showing the major route from Chang'an to Antioch and indicating (draw pictures or use cutouts) the main projects carried East and West.

12. Read selections from *Confucius: Philosopher and Teacher* by Josh Wilker. Report on them to your classmates.

Chapter 2
The Northern Song
(960 - 1126)
The Rise of the Scholar-Officials

It was a cold February day when Zhao Kuangyin cautiously led his troops into Kaifeng, capital city of the crumbling Northern Zhou dynasty. He was still wearing the yellow robe that had been thrown over his shoulders when the coup began. To his surprise, he encountered little resistance, and his army was able to gain control of the city without the shedding of blood.

Now undisputed master of the day, Zhao entered the halls of the palace compound. How strange it must have felt to return to these familiar rooms in his new role. His officers soon gathered together the civil and military officials of the defeated dynasty to witness the ritual of the boy emperor abdicating his throne. Zhao was then installed as first emperor of the Song (Soong) dynasty. (It was named for a region in his home province.) He is known to historians as Taizu ("Supreme Progenitor"), an appropriate title for the founder of a new dynasty. We'll refer to him in that way from here on.

Taizu saw to it that the deposed imperial family was treated well. He awarded them noble titles and provided them with a residential palace in Kaifeng. Such a peaceful transition of power was unusual. The overthrow of a dynasty was generally accompanied by rioting and bloody civil war until someone finally grabbed the reins of power. The civilized approach of the Song founder marked an important shift in government policy from military force to diplomacy.

The Song dynasty would last for more than three hundred years (960-1276). Historians divide it into two parts. The earlier period is known as the Northern Song, because the capital, Kaifeng, was in the north. The Southern Song began when the imperial court was forced to relocate further south in Hangzhou. In this chapter you'll be learning about the Northern Song.

Highlights of This Chapter

Taizu Takes Charge
The Song government
The Emperor As Patron of the Arts
Gunpowder
Printing Books
The Growth of the Civil Exam System
Wang Anshi's New Laws
Su Dongpo
Sima Guang
Huizong, Emperor and Artist
Chinese Painting
The Storming of Kaifeng

Taizu Eliminates His Rivals

Before Taizu could begin his reign, he had to deal with those who had put him in power. He was well aware that he had been strong-armed into his present position by men who had been dissatisfied with their emperor. How could he be sure that they wouldn't turn against *him* some time in the future? The historical records were filled with accounts of ambitious generals seizing power. Taizu could not confidently perform his duties when he was plagued by such menacing thoughts.

The emperor solved this problem by inviting his top generals to a banquet at the palace. During the meal, he encouraged them to boast about their acts of valor on the battlefield. He praised their courage and offered a few anecdotes of his own. Later, after the men had enjoyed a splendid meal topped off by generous amounts of rice wine, Taizu arose to make a toast. He congratulated the officers for having honorably reached the end of their fighting days and announced that they would now be rewarded with large pensions so they could live very comfortably for the rest of their lives.

It was a brilliant move. The officers, glowing with pride and agreeing among themselves that they indeed deserved a reward, accepted Taizu's offer. With no hard feelings, the emperor had deftly removed his chief rivals and avoided the possibility of another military coup. But to be on the safe side, he insisted that the men reside in the region of Kaifeng — where he could keep an eye on them.

The New Army

Taizu then selected replacement generals among his most loyal supporters and began recruiting young men to fill the ranks of his new professional army. From now on, the military would be highly centralized, with divisions at the imperial and provincial levels. He had the best units in the regional armies transferred to the "palace army," which was under his personal command. To prevent the rise of regional strongmen, the top officers in the lower level armies were to be rotated every three years.

This policy of keeping the best troops under his own command at the capital strengthened Taizu's power and authority. But can you see where it also made his

---

Have you been wondering about the Khitan invasion that caused Zhao Kuangyin to be sent to the northern front? According to the official records kept by the Khitan themselves, the attack never took place! This has led many historians to believe that the events of New Year's day were part of a setup to remove Zhao Kuangyin from Kaifeng so he could take over the army and overthrow the ruling dynasty.

border regions vulnerable if they were attacked?

Rebuilding the Empire

With the army reorganized, Taizu set out to unify his empire and extend his control over the small independent states in central and southern China. But he was no warmonger. He instructed his generals to avoid bloodshed whenever possible and to outlaw looting and any other abuse of the civilian population. During the campaign, he was open to negotiation whenever possible, patiently allowing holdout leaders plenty of time to surrender and guaranteeing that no harm would come to those who acknowledged his authority.

By combining military might with diplomacy, Taizu eventually brought the small states back into the empire. By the end of his reign, only two remained independent.

The Song Government

Taizu modeled his new government upon that of the Tang. A Grand Council of high ministers oversaw the three main ministries — the Chancellery, the Secretariat, and the Department of State Affairs. The Council decided upon new policies after open and thoughtful debates. As emperor, Taizu had the casting vote, but he usually deferred to the majority view. This was a welcome improvement over earlier times, when ministers who disagreed with an emperor ran the risk of exile – or even execution! As before, the Department of State oversaw the six ministries that managed the courts, taxes and tribute, public works, ceremonies, the recruitment of officials, and the military. Taizu restored the annual civil service examinations to select officials to fill these important posts.

Below the top ministries was a vast network of offices and branches at the provincial and town levels. Inner China was divided into 24 circuits, each with a capital city. The circuits were further divided into prefectures, of which there were 300. Every member of the vast Song bureaucracy, from the humblest clerk in the smallest town to the most influential policy-maker at the top, was directly linked to the office of the emperor. A Board of Censors kept an eye on every level of the bureaucracy and reported any abuses that were observed.

Kaifeng

Taizu's capital, Kaifeng, was situated near the junction of the Yellow River and the Grand Canal. This strategic location provided the city with a plentiful supply of food and enabled it to become a prosperous center of trade.

Like most Chinese capitals, Kaifeng was square in shape and was surrounded by a thick earthen wall with massive gates on each of its four sides. Within the protective wall, the city streets formed a grid of lines going from north to south and from east to west, and, course, all major buildings faced south. The houses of the officials were surrounded by high walls and had inner and outer courtyards — the higher the official's rank, the more courtyards he had. The entrance to such a house was in the southeast corner and faced directly onto an interior wall. This was to prevent the entrance of evil spirits, which could not turn corners! Craftsmen, merchants, and the city's labor force dwelled in humbler abodes, but people from all walks of life mingled in the bustling marketplaces.

The heart of the city was the imperial palace, where the emperor lived with his family and concubines and presided over all important government functions. (A concubine was something like a secondary wife. Some emperors had hundreds of them.) Over the years, the palace grew into a sprawling complex. Surrounded by its own wall, it became a city within the city, with gardens, paths and covered walkways, pavilions, and artificial ponds set among the official buildings and the imperial residence.

Taizong Becomes Emperor

Taizu chose his younger brother as his successor rather than his own young son. Why this break with tradition? He well remembered how he had taken the throne from an underage monarch, and his brother had proven his leadership skills as commander of the Palace Corps.

When Taizu died in 976, his brother was well prepared to continue his policies. Known as Taizong, he needed only four years to complete the unification of the empire, winning back the two "holdout" kingdoms through skillful negotiations.

Dealing With the Khitan

Just beyond China's northern border lived the Khitan, the enemy that was supposedly launching an invasion just before Taizu became emperor. The Khitan had once been nomadic tribesmen, but in recent years they had gotten organized and become quite civilized. In 947 they founded a "Chinese style" dynasty (the Liao), whose high officials were highly literate and dressed in embroidered silken robes. The Khitan currently controlled a large region that included Manchuria and Mongolia.

Taizu had an inscription written on a large stone, which was kept in the palace. It bore the following instructions to those who would succeed him as emperor: the descendants of the imperial family of the Latter Zhou dynasty, which had been overthrown by the Song, were to be protected; officials and scholars were not to be executed; farming taxes were not to be increased; and civil servants were not to indulge in any sword-fighting.

Many Khitan farmers crossed the Great Wall and settled in northern China.

Taizu had avoided military confrontations with the Liao state in order to consolidate his power in China. Taizong, however, was determined to drive the "barbarians" beyond the Great Wall. (Anyone who was not Chinese was considered a barbarian.) In 979, he set off with a large army and headed north. But he underestimated the strength of his enemy and narrowly escaped capture, fleeing at night with a handful of officers. His soldiers, deserted by their leader, were easily defeated. After a second disastrous campaign, all thoughts of winning back the north were abandoned — at least for the time being.

The Emperor's New Image

Do you remember how the model Tang courtier was skillful in the arts as well as knowledgeable about affairs of state? This view was adopted by the Northern Song. Taizong himself was renowned for his abilities as scholar, poet, and calligrapher. He enjoyed quoting the words of Confucius, and he commissioned the publication of many copies of the Five Classics to help scholars prepare for the civil service examinations. He also built up an impressive collection of art.

Taizong set the standard for emperors to come. From now on, the Son of Heaven was expected to play the multi-faceted role of high priest, judge, head of government, military leader, sage, poet, and patron of the arts. That was a tall order!

Bargaining With the Enemy

Not long after Taizong died, the Khitan organized a full-scale invasion of China. The imperial court was forced to flee to the city of Nanjing and was later chased further west to Chengdu (in Sichuan). The new emperor, Zhenzong, negotiated a peace settlement in 1004. Many Chinese found its terms humiliating. Not only did Zhenzong recognize the Liao emperor as "elder brother," but he also agreed to pay a huge annual tribute of 200,000 rolls of silk and 100,000 ounces of silver. The treaty marked a new, accomodating attitude among China's foreign ministers. From now

Taizong was also an avid chess player. Chinese chess (*weiqi*) – known in the West by the Japanese name *go*, dates back at least as far as the Tang dynasty. It is played on a board marked with squares. There are two players, one using 180 white markers or "stones" and the other using 181 black markers. The black player goes first and places a number of stones on certain points on the board before the play begins. *Weiqi* means "surrounding stones" because the object is to place enough stones on the board to capture more territory by controlling more squares than the opponent. It sounds easy, but it really involves complicated strategies.

China in 1050

rolls of silk and 200,000 ounces of silver. The policy of buying off the enemy was becoming very expensive.

The Use of Gunpowder

Despite the treaties, the Song ministers continued to worry about defending their borders, and the size of the army increased — more than tripling between 975 and 1045 to about 1,250,000 men. The government manufactured arrowheads by the tens of millions per year, armor by the tens of thousands. But by far more useful than arrowheads and armor was a new weapon that would permanently alter warfare throughout the world — gunpowder.

The formula for gunpowder was discovered during the 9th century, when Daoist priests, seeking to produce a magical elixir, mixed together charcoal, saltpeter (potassium nitrate), and sulphur. Imagine their surprise when the concoction exploded! They later wrote down the ingredients they had used, adding the warning that the mixture might produce singed beards!

The new concoction was heralded for its explosive properties. Before long, it was being produced to make firecrackers for New Year's festivities. Batches of gunpowder were stuffed into bamboo tubes, which were then thrown into a fire. When the powder ignited, it produced explosions that shot sparks into the night sky. The display could be made more colorful by

on, the Song would seek ways to buy off their enemies and avoid warfare whenever possible.

The Tanguts ruled a second "barbarian" state in the northwest, known as Xi Xia. Like their allies, the Khitan, they had a Chinese style government. Conflicts with the Xi Xia led to a treaty in 1044 under Emperor Renzong. According to its terms, the Tangut ruler acknowledged China's border, and the Song agreed to pay him an annual tribute of 130,000 rolls of silk, 50,000 ounces of silver, and 20,000 pounds of tea to stay put. Not to be outdone, the Khitan then raised their own demands to 300,000 adding extra ingredients: indigo (to make blue), white lead carbonate (for white), lead tetroxide or cinnabar (for red), and certain sulfides (to make yellow). And the noise made by the explosions was loud enough to drive away even the worst of the evil spirits!

By the 10th century, gunpowder was being used with a more deadly design. Chinese soldiers kept supplies of "flame throwers" (tubes of bamboo stuffed with gunpowder) to defend the ramparts of their cities or to send terror into the hearts of the men behind an enemy line. The flame throwers were ignited and hurled toward the target. Archers sometimes affixed gunpowder paste to their arrows and lit it before launching them. The "flying fire" exploded upon impact. By the the 11th century, the Song army had produced a "thunder clap bomb." The high percentage of saltpeter in the gunpowder caused this bamboo missile to make an incredibly loud noise. In the same century, Emperor Renzong commissioned a forty-chapter manual on military matters. It contains the first official instructions for making gunpowder.

A Thriving Economy

Once the military policy became one of defense, the government could focus more attention on domestic matters. The remainder of the period of the Northern Song would be generally peaceful and prosperous.

Then as now, most of the Chinese were farmers, and a number of programs were enacted to improve agriculture. Song engineers supervised several water-control projects in southern China, draining marshes and building new dikes to increase the number of fields where rice could be grown. A new kind of quick-ripening rice was later imported from Annam (Vietnam), making it possible to grow two crops of rice

The New Year was the most important holiday in the Chinese calendar (and still is today). It took place in late January or early February to celebrate the arrival of spring. According to the storytellers, the festival began in very ancient times when a wild creature (the *nian*) had the nasty habit of eating many of the people in a small village village at the end of every winter. One year, the villagers scared the beast away by making a great deal of noise with gongs and drums. Ever since, at the beginning of the New Year, people in every town and city beat drums, sounded clappers, and rang bells to drive out evil spirits. Firecrackers proved to be the ultimate noise-makers. The highlight of the parade was the dragon dance, when a line of men danced through the streets while covered by a long, colorful cloth dragon. The people threw firecrackers at their feet to drive off the evil spirits and welcome the benevolent powers of dragon.

each year instead of one. Certain farmers specialized in the production of sugar cane, tea, oranges, bamboo, cotton, or mulberry leaves (to feed all those hungry silkworms).

Meanwhile, potters, silkweavers, jade carvers, and other artisans were busy in their workshops. And as China's output increased, so, too, did the class of merchants, who transported the products along the country's roads and waterways. Do you remember how the merchants were despised in earlier times? They were becoming an accepted (and necessary) element of society.

As the Song economy flourished, the population grew. By 1020, it was approaching 100 million people. Kaifeng alone was the home of more than a million. (This is about how many people were living in England at the time.) High employment rates and larger numbers of people meant that the government received more taxes, and its coffers were soon overflowing. China was becoming the wealthiest, most populous, and most advanced nation in the world. The emperor had good reason to boast about the Middle Kingdom.

Printed Books

Kaifeng was also the center of a thriving book-printing industry. Woodblock printing had been invented during the Tang dynasty. The process involved cutting characters (in reverse) into blocks of wood, coating the blocks with ink, and then pressing sheets of paper against them. Printing rapidly replaced the old method of tediously writing each page of a book with brush and ink. At first, the pages of a volume were pasted together to form a continuous scroll, which was read from right to left as it was gradually unrolled. The Northern Song produced the first "real" books, with pages sewn into a binding.

Most of the books were originally intended for the schools that had been established in each of China's 300 prefectures. (These were history's first public schools.) As more people learned to read, the number of books increased and the subject matter became more diverse. Now, besides the learned volumes on history, philosophy, and poetry, there were handbooks on agriculture, pharmacy, and even cooking. The growing passion for informa-

---

In about 1040 a craftsman named Bi Sheng made the world's first movable type using pieces clay characters fixed with wax in an iron-framed tray. (This was about 500 years before moveable type was known in the West.) But this technique did not become common in China. Since there are so many characters in the Chinese language, printers would have had to make about 40,000 separate movable blocks to represent them all! So most Chinese printers continued to work with blocks carved with an entire page of text.

tion led to the production of vast books of general knowledge. Taizong was the first emperor to commission an encyclopedia.

Wealthy families amassed thousands of books for their private libraries, while emperors added to the imperial collections. Emperor Renzong's library, carefully catalogued between 1034 and 1036, contained 80,000 volumes.

Becoming a Scholar

The booming book-printing industry and the expanded educational system made it possible for more young men to train for government service. This was a long process that began at the age of four, when, under the guidance of a parent or tutor, a little boy learned how to trace the strokes of a few large characters on paper. (Most characters consist of eleven strokes, which must be made in a particular order.)

The Chinese language consists of thousands of characters. (Today, an educated person knows at least 6,000 characters.) Each character represents a word, although its meaning varies, depending upon its use in a given sentence. There is no punctuation in the written language, nor is there specific tense, article, number, or person. (The word *ta* means he, she, or it; *ma* is horse or horses; and *zou* means go, will go, or went.)

By the time he was seven, the little student could read and write over a hun-

dred characters and was ready to begin school. Once he did, his first task was to master the Thousand Character Classic. This was a Confucian moralistic essay, made up of exactly one thousand characters. The characters — all different —were written four to a line in rhyming couplets. The student had to memorize the entire work by rote (mindless repetition), without the benefit of any explanation of its meaning. Once he thought he had it committed to memory, he recited it, standing with his back to the teaching master. The master held a whip, and any slip in recitation earned the student a whack on his backside!

From the Thousand Character Classic, the young student moved on to the daunting task of learning all the great works associated with Confucius — *The Analects* (collected teachings of the old master) and *The Book of Mencius* (Mencius was a follower of Confucius) as well as the Five Confucian Classics (*The Book of Changes, The Book of*

spring

summer

autumn

winter

Documents, The Book of Rites, the Book of Songs, and *The Spring and Autumn Annals*). Again, he was expected to memorize huge passages without considering the meaning of the texts. This process lasted a very long time.

Once he could demonstrate a certain mastery of the classics, he could begin the study of the commentaries written about them by noted scholars over the past centuries. (At last he was able to think about what he had read.) He also studied the histories of the preceding dynasties (remember all those official records?) and the lyrics of such great poets as Li Bo (Bai) and Du Fu. A final stage in his education involved composing his own poems and essays. He was expected to fill these with allusions to and quotations from the masterpieces he had studied for so many years — *and* they had to be written with elegant calligraphy.

Such was the education of a scholar during the Northern Song dynasty. The procedure changed very little during the next millennium — if anything, it became even more rigid. By concentrating solely on the traditional literature of China, the student had little exposure to such disciplines as mathematics and science. As a result of this approach to learning, China's ruling elite would be extremely conservative and limited in perspective. The educational system certainly extended the legacy of the great thinkers of China's ancient past, but it also prevented the country from exploring new avenues.

The Civil Service Exam System

The civil service exams were given at three levels. The first level exams, which tested a general knowledge of the Confucian works, were given in the capital of each prefect. They were highly competitive — less than 10 percent succeeded in passing. These lucky few became eligible to take a more difficult imperial exam in Kaifeng.

Those who passed the imperial exam were called *juren* ("elevated men"). This was simply a title of honor; it did not lead to a government position. Most of these men remained in the capital to sit for the highest level exams, which tested a candidate's knowledge of history and government as well as his moral ethics and poetic talents. He might be asked to write an essay discussing current political issues by relating them to selected passages from the classics, or to expound upon a definition given by Confucius. He might be instructed to compose verse that evoked such sensations as

Women were excluded from the civil service exams, as were artisans, merchants, and clerks (activities considered unfit for scholars) as well as priests and monks.

the brightness of the moonlight or the stillness of a mountain lake. Again, only 10 percent passed the exam. There was no shame attached to failure, and candidates were encouraged to try again — and again.The average age was 35, but some kept at it well into their sixties. There were even instances of grandfathers and grandsons taking exams together at the same time!

Those who succeeded in the highest exam were given the degree of *jinshi* ("advanced scholar"). The *jinshi* were ranked in order of excellence. The man who ranked first became famous throughout the empire. The other successful candidates were divided into two groups —those who "passed with distinction" and those who "formally qualified." But every man on the list was a big winner. He gained tremendous prestige for his family and access to a distinguished career in the highest levels of the government bureaucracy.

Beginning in 1065, the examinations were given at the prefect and imperial levels every three years. A given set of exams was conducted over a period of nine or ten days in a large public hall. The candidates had to present themselves at dawn of the first day, bringing with them enough food (cold rice and cakes) to get them through the long ordeal. They were searched upon entering the examination hall to find any memory aids or copies of previously successful answers that might be hidden in their clothing. Then they were assigned numbers, which they wrote on their examination papers. To remove the possibility of a judge recognizing a candidate by his handwriting (and losing his objectivity), a Bureau of Examination Copyists made uniform copies of the candidates' papers for two examiners to read. If the two examiners disagreed in their grading, they had to reach a compromise before handing on the test paper to the chief examiner. Any candidates found guilty of cheating, despite the

Kui Xing was said to have been the most brilliant scholar of his day, but he was physically repulsive. When he took the civil service examinations, he got the highest marks. Custom demanded that, as top scholar, he should receive a golden rose from the hand of the emperor. But the ruler took one look at Kui Xing's ugly face and refused to present the rose. The young man was so upset he went to the coast and flung himself into the sea. But that is not the end of his story. A strange beast – half fish, half turtle – rose from beneath the waves and carried him to the surface of the water. The revived scholar then flew up to Heaven, where he resided among the stars in the Great Bear constellation as the god of examinations. Ever since that time, exam candidates kept a statue in his image (a figure holding a writing brush and an official seal) in their homes, and across China millions of anxious prayers were sent to him by those waiting to hear their final results.

The carp, a fish native to China known for its tenacity to swim upstream against the current to spawn, became the symbol of the successful examination candidate. According to legend, a carp that succeeded in swimming upstream in the Yellow River and leaping over a stone barrier called the Dragon Gate would be transformed into a mighty dragon. A picture of a leaping carp came to symbolize good wishes for success, and celebrations of a man's achievement in the civil service exams would feature large, colorful banners of this feisty, persevering fish.

measures taken to prevent it, and any judges caught taking a bribe, were subject to extreme punishment and public humiliation — possibly execution!

Although training for the examinations was open to nearly all men, those coming from families with a good income had a distinct advantage over the typical peasant; paying for supplies and living expenses was costly, and most farming families could not afford to give up the labor of their sons. However, even a boy of humble means stood a chance of becoming the scholar, if he had the ability and could find the financial backing. It was the ambition of many families to have a son who could pass an exam, and parents of eligible girls would often study the published list of successful candidates and compete with one another for the top finishers by offering them large dowries!

Many historians consider the Song dynasty a turning point in the long history of Chinese government because during this period power permanently shifted from the hereditary nobility to those who had distinguished themselves in the exams. High political office was now closely linked with intellectual excellence. The government bureaucracy would soon be run by a professional service recruited almost completely through the examinations. The scholar officials, known as the "literati," formed a sort of brotherhood, drawn together by a knowledge of the classics and shared Confucian values. This provided great stability for the government, even in times of social chaos, and it was a major factor in the endurance of imperial China. Unfortunately, it would also lead to its fall, as you will see.

Wang Anshi

Wang Anshi was one of the most brilliant scholar-officials of his time. He passed the lower level civil service exam on his first attempt, then did the same thing in the imperial exams in Kaifeng. At the age of 21, he received the prestigious degree of *jinshi.*

For several years, Wang Anshi was governor of a bustling city on the Yangzi River. He proved to be an able administrator, who cared about the people of his district. He sponsored programs to improve the local irrigation and drainage system to end the frequent local flooding, and he set up a fund to loan grain to stricken farmers during years of drought. The success of his reforms would inspire him in his government work in later years.

The New Laws

In 1069, Emperor Shenzong summoned Wang Anshi to Kaifeng and made him chief minister of his Grand Council. At that time, the treasury was being drained by the tribute payments to the Khitan and Tanguts as well as the expense of maintaining armies to defend the northern borders. The government had looked for new sources of income, and this, of course, meant more taxes. Although the wealthy could well afford the tax increases, life became rather difficult for those who made up the majority of the population — the peasants. Families who were unable to pay were forced off their land, and even those who could pay were required to serve a certain amount of time on public work projects, such as the building of roads and the maintenance of canals and irrigation ditches. There are records of peasants who chose to commit suicide rather than leave their fields to work on these projects.

Wang Anshi was already familiar with the hard life of the peasants, and he felt that the government should take more responsibility for their welfare, lest they be "ground into the dust by the rich." Hadn't Confucius said that a ruler should be concerned about the lives of his subjects? Wang envisioned a society in which there was more equality. He put forward a program of reforms known as the New Laws.

These practical reforms promoted government efficiency and benefited a great many people. For example, one provision called for taxing families according to their wealth, and using the proceeds to hire men for the public work projects. (This is a key concept in our own modern tax program, but it was unknown in those early times.) The New Laws included a national aid program, known as Green Sprouts, in which the government served as a lender to needy farmers. The farmers could use the funds to buy seed in the spring and repay the loans with a low rate of interest after the fall harvest. In case of a bad harvest, payments would be deferred until the next year.

The New Laws also established local militia units, which were to be led by the wealthy gentry. The militia would serve as a local police force and as a source of reserves for the army in time of war. The units were to be made up of local families, grouped together in tens. Each group would provide ten soldiers to serve a one-month term of duty every year. The group would be responsible for the good behavior of all its members. If one person broke the law, the others would have to deliver him for punishment. If they did not, everyone in the group would be punished.

Wang Anshi sliced expenses in the state budget by 40 percent, and he demanded that all funds be accounted for. (All too often, these funds ended up in the pockets of corrupt officials.) He increased the number of government schools so that more candidates could prepare for the exams. And he took the unprecedented step of questioning the merit of basing the civil service exams upon a mastery of traditional literature and philosophy. Didn't an official need more practical training to do his job effectively?

He even looked into maritime matters, designing policies to strengthen the navy and encourage the growth of overseas trade. Believing that unreasonable profits were falling into the hands of greedy merchants and traders (as indeed they were), he proposed that the government take over the regulation of trade. This would include collecting duties from foreign merchants and putting the funds directly into the state treasury.

Wang Anshi's rules concerning the local militia units bring to mind Legalism, the philosophy embraced by Shi Huangdi and the Qin dynasty. Although Confucianism was dominant in Chinese culture throughout the imperial period, elements of the harsh code of Legalism remained just below the surface in the government and continued to influence the political and social lives of the people.

Opposition to the New Laws

Most people today agree that the New Laws made a great deal of sense. However, the Chinese were very conservative and resistant to change. The reforms drew sharp opposition from several sectors of society. Wang Anshi's vision of a more equitable society threatened the lofty status of the privileged gentry class, who supplied a majority of the candidates for the civil service exams. Some gentry protested the requirement of serving in the militia, which they found inconvenient and undignified, while others resisted any effort to tax the wealthy for the good of the poor. The scholar-officials opposed what they saw as the reformer's attempts to meddle in the quality of their lives. They argued that the reformer's arguments ran counter to the Confucian ideal of a hierarchical society, with officials at the top (just below the emperor). The merchants and moneylenders, of course, were not pleased about the government getting more involved in trade and cutting off some of their profits.

However, there were a number of more open-minded men who backed the reforms, so the imperial court was thrown into disarray as the officials divided up into the competing factions of pro-reform and anti-reform. Wang Anshi had become the most controversial man of his times. His foes tried to strengthen their position by criticizing the reformer's "unconventional ways." This was easy to do. Unlike most scholars, who prided themselves on their personal appearance, Wang Anshi seldom bathed or changed his robe. And he ate anything that was placed before him, hardly noticing what it was. His friends forgave his unkempt appearance and casual eating habits, assuming that he was preoccupied with great thoughts. His enemies, however, considered them a sign of bad character. They claimed that a man who did not act like other men must be "a great hypocrite and a scheming intriguer." Of course, the fact that Wang described his opponents as immoral "scum" didn't help his cause among them!

Su Dongpo

One of Wang Anshi's most outspoken critics was Su Shi (later known as Su Dongpo). Like many of his peers, he considered Wang's reforms anti-Confucian. He compared Wang's followers to crows feeding on rotten meat and their conversation to the croaking of frogs and the buzzing of cicadas. Su Shi was known for expressing his views, whether they were popular or not. In his own defense, he once remarked, "When I find something is wrong, it is like finding a fly in my food. I just have to spit it out!"

Su Shi was the very model of a Song scholar-official — he was a "superior gentleman," admired for his intellectual and creative abilities, his administrative skill, and his moral standards. He was one of China's greatest poets, a skillful essayist, a talented painter, a perceptive art theorist, and a gifted calligrapher. He was also a social butterfly, who loved to be surrounded by friends and often hosted dinner parties. (His recipe for pork is still prepared by modern chefs.) Sometimes, his dinner guests participated in cooperative painting games. One man would begin a picture, the next would add to it, and so on until the painting was complete. Su Shi considered wine a source of creative inspiration, and he would often consume several cups of it, fall asleep, and later get up to write or paint.

Over 800 of Su Shi's letters and 2,700 of his poems have survived to our times. Among his most famous works are two prose poems about his visits to Red Cliff, a scenic spot along the Yangzi River. In one of these, he describes a moonlit expedition in a boat with a group of friends, observing at one point how the moon has appeared from behind a cloud: "a dewy whiteness spanned the river, merging the light on the water into the sky." As the boat slowly drifts in the river's current, he and his friends feel as though they are "leaning on the void with the winds for a chariot." He also wrote many satirical poems, belittling Wang Anshi and his followers and describing the pain and suffering caused by their "mis-guided" acts.

Su Shi was banished from court several times because of his outspoken opposition to the reforms. During one period of exile in Hubei, he wrote a playful yet biting poem celebrating the first bath of his month-old son. In it, he chides his political colleagues, musing, "All I want is a son who is doltish and dumb. No setbacks or hardships will obstruct his path to the highest court posts." Another time, when he was arrested for slandering the emperor and his officials, he fully expected execution. Instead, he was banished to a remote district, where he was forbidden to write about the government. As it turned out, he lived quite happily on a small estate of 10 acres on the eastern slope of a mountain near the Yangzi. He wrote poetry and essays about the local village life and on more scholarly subjects (but never government). Because he now referred to himself as the Recluse of the Eastern Slope, and has come to be known as Su Dongpo ("Su of the Eastern Slope").

Su Shi spent his final years in exile on Hainan, a remote and mosquito-infested island off the southern coast of China. He turned for solace to the beliefs of Buddhism and Daoism, wondering during his final days about what might lie beyond the grave. He died on his way back from this last exile.

Other Worthy Opponents

Sima Guang was the official who led the opposition against Wang Anshi. He later resigned his position to protest the New Laws and found plenty to do in his free time. Do you remember *The Historical Records* of Han scholar Sima Qian? Sima Guang followed this precedent by writing a narrative history of China covering over 1,300 years (from the late Zhou dynasty to the founding of the Song). Entitled *The Comprehensive Mirror for Aid In Government*, it contained 354 chapters. He gathered his data from the official histories written by preceding dynasties, to which he added his own commentary. His work has remained one of the most authoritative and widely studied histories of China.

Ouyang Xiu, another of Wang Anshi's opponents, is also known for his work as a historian and poet. He was fascinated by the ancient inscriptions that appeared on stones and artifacts in many places in China. He made rubbings of over 1000 of them and compiled these in an analytical catalogue, known as *The Collection of Ancient Inscriptions*. It is considered a pioneering work in archaeology. He also worked with a colleague for 17 years on the officially commissioned history of the Tang dynasty. (It became a tradition for the government of one dynasty to write an official history of the dynasty it succeeded.) Just after completing this work, he became involved in the political struggle against the reformers and was banished to Yiling. That's when he wrote another major work, *The New History of the Five Dynasties.*

Sima Guang also wrote a widely read book on the proper etiquette for weddings, funerals, and other ceremonies. It provides a colorful view of life during Song times. Here is a sample, which describes some of the duties required on the day before the ceremony honoring a family's ancestors.

First, the man of the household organizes all male members of the family to dust and sweep the place where the ceremony will be held, to wash and clean the utensils and containers, and to arrange the furniture. Places for departed ancestors are so arranged that each husband and wife are side by side, arranged according to proper ranking from west to east, and all facing south. The mistress of the house supervises the women in cleaning cooking utensils and preparing the food. The food must include five kinds of vegetables and five kinds of fruits, and not more than fifteen dishes of the following sorts: red stew, roast meat, fried meat, ribs, boiled white meat, dried meat, ground meat, special meats other than pork or lamb, foods made of flour. If a family is poor, or if certain items cannot be obtained, then they must include several items from each category — vegetable, fruit, meat, flour-foods and rice-foods.

Ouyang took the pen name of Liuyi, which means "six ones" — it referred to one library, one archaeological collection, one musical instrument, one set of Chinese chess, one container of wine, and one old man (himself!), who enjoyed the other five.

The Fate of the Reforms

Although Wang Anshi had the full support of Emperor Shenzong (this explains the frequent exiles of his major opponents), his measures were only partially adopted. They were eventually defeated, not by human activities, but by a series of natural disasters — an earthquake, a plague of locusts, and a drought. His opponents claimed that these calamities reflected Heaven's disapproval of the New Laws. One high-ranking official actually wrote to the emperor from the provinces, blaming Wang Anshi for the drought and suggesting that he be asked to resign so that it would rain again. The next morning, after Shenzong suspended several of the New Laws, there was a cloudburst! Was this a sign from Heaven? Some interpreted it that way. A short time later, Wang Anshi reluctantly resigned.

Shenzong remained loyal to his minister, and after heavy rains ended the drought and the crisis was over, he ordered him back to Kaifeng. He even revived the New Laws. But Wang's health was failing, and he soon returned to his home in the provinces to spend his remaining time reading and writing.

When Shenzong died in 1085, the empress dowager served as regent to his young heir, Zhezong. Sima Guang was brought back into the government, and he moved quickly to remove every trace of the New Laws. Wang Anshi lived just long enough to see his program dismantled. Many of his proposals were instituted by later officials, and today he is revered as one of China's greatest political and economic reformers.

Science and Superstition

The early Chinese were very superstitious. The court astrologers were always consulted when the decision was being made about who should be the emperor's heir. In 1090, a mathematically-minded scholar named Su Song designed and constructed a huge, 39-foot high clock tower in Kaifeng. It was intended to provide data for the astrologers to prepare horoscopes of the emperor's sons to determine who would be best qualified to succeed him. Of course, it also told the time.

Su Song's creation was the world's first truly mechanical clock. A giant waterwheel powered the gears, which, in turn, rotated five platforms of puppets. The puppet figures announced the quarter hour by beating a drum and marked a period of two hours by ringing a bell. (The Chinese divided the day into 12 2-hour segments.) The clock's gears also turned an armillary sphere, which was positioned under a movable roof and was synchronized to follow the motions of the planets.

Su Song's invention is described in a book he compiled in 1086. The elaborate illustrations give a good idea of how it functioned. The clock operated from 1092 until 1126, when Kaifeng fell to an invading army. It was then dismantled and taken away to parts unknown.

The design of the water clock is a good indication of the technical skills of the Song. While most literati were debating issues of philosophy and good government or writing beautiful characters, other thoughtful men were fiddling with gadgets and designing new devices and machines. Engineers boosted trade by building locks on canals to safely raise and lower boats from one level to another. Other creative geniuses revolutionized the silk industry with the design of the spinning wheel.

A major innovation was the abacus. Chinese characters are not suitable for standard mathematical calculations, so from very early times counting rods were used to determine sums. These were the basis of the abacus, a device that used beads rather than rods to add, subtract, multiply, divide, and solve other math problems. The abacus consisted of a wooden frame and several columns of beads, which were separated by a crossbar. Moving from right to left, the columns represented units (ones), tens, hundreds, and so on. The beads above the crossbar each represented five, and those below the bar, one. Problems were worked by moving the beads toward and away from the crossbar. The abacus is still used in schools and businesses throughout China.

Huizong Savors the Arts

Huizong, the last of the Northern Song emperors, came to the throne in 1101 at the age of 17. He was a gentle soul, who loved beautiful things. Although he was poorly equipped to deal with the challenges of political life, he contributed greatly to the arts. And like a model courtier, he was a talented painter, poet, and calligrapher.

Huizong founded the School of Painting at the palace, where he personally instructed groups of artists. He often handed out subjects to be painted and set examinations, as though the painters were candidates for official posts. The theme was

During the Northern Song period, the iron industry produced huge quantities of tools of war and peace— swords, bows, arrows, spades, hoes, and plowshares. Iron was also used for chains for suspension bridges (another Chinese invention) and for huge Buddhist statues.

usually a line or two from a poem, and a painting was judged according to how subtly the artist responded to the imagery described. The more ingenious and allusive his interpretation, the better. One time, the emperor assigned the verse: "The horses' hooves were fragrant on returning from trampling flowers." The winning painting depicted butterflies, attracted by the flowery fragrance and fluttering behind the galloping steeds. When the theme was "a tavern in a bamboo grove by a bridge," the winner did not paint the tavern at all but simply suggested it by a signboard set amid the stalks of bamboo!

Chinese Painting

The Song dynasty is considered a high point in the development of Chinese painting, and the remainder of this chapter will focus upon some of the major works of the Northern Song. But first, let's take a few moments to look at the history and the major characteristics of Chinese art.

The oldest surviving paintings were done on the walls of halls, palaces, and tombs, but we know that painters began working on silk cloth quite early. When paper became available during the Han dynasty, many artists took advantage of its highly absorbent surface. Paper was also relatively inexpensive. However, silk remained the preferred material for works commissioned by kings, emperors, and members of the wealthy elite.

A painter's brush was similar to the one he used for writing. The handle was made of bamboo, and the tip consisted of carefully fashioned tufts of animal hair. The painter worked with ink or water-based paints (called washes) in subtle tints, mostly greys, tans, and blues. He produced light and dark effects by varying the brushwork (making thin or broader strokes) or by diluting the ink or paint.

A traditional Chinese painting consists of simple lines and shapes. It is two dimensional, distance being suggested by the size of an object or its placement. (Close objects appear at the bottom, distant ones at the top.) A scene in a painting is usually based upon something the artist has remembered seeing and evokes a certain state of mind. This is very different than a typical Western painting , which realistically describes a particular place. A Chinese painting is generally not fixed in time, although it is nearly always daylight, so there is no need for shadowing. Nor are there lines of perspective, converging at a single "vanishing point" as they do in most Western art. The perspective varies as the viewer's eyes move around the picture. And nearly every picture exudes a sense of calm. Violence or disharmony are seldom represented in a Chinese work of art.

The Chinese painter must have a steady hand, since any mark on the silk or paper cannot be altered. He conceives of an image in his head and then creates it stroke by stroke, confidently moving his brush without wavering or stopping until the figure is complete. He has to be technically proficient and imaginative at the same time, and his work reflects this curious blending of precision and whimsy.

Chinese painting is divided into four categories: figure painting, landscape painting, bird-and-flower painting, and ink painting. Let's take a closer look at each genre.

Figure Painting

Figure paintings originated in ancient times with portraits of Confucian scholars and other esteemed people. This led to paintings showing proper moral behavior, which were used as illustrations for Confucian texts. During the Han dynasty, when Confucianism became the official state policy, favorite subjects for painting included scenes of a dutiful son honoring and caring for his parents (demonstrating the highest Confucian virtue, *filial piety*).

In those days before photography, professional court artists were often commissioned to paint portraits of emperors, concubines, courtiers, scholars and other important people. These works emphasized the beautifully embroidered silk robes worn by the subjects as well as their digni-

---

In the fifth century, a painter and art critic named Xie He formulated the *Six Canons* (*Principles*) *of Painting*. These outlined the main points to consider in judging a painting. They are still observed today and can be summarized as follows:

1) a painting should have vitality — it should bring to life the spirit or essence of its subject
   (does the painting "come alive?" has the artist caught with his brushstrokes the
   energy that runs through every aspect of nature?)
2) the artist should demonstrate technical skill with the brush (are the lines precise?)
3) the artist should be faithful to the object being portrayed (is it realistic?)
4) there should be appropriate use of color (do the colors create the proper tone or mood?)
5) the objects should be properly arranged (is there a sense of proportion?)
6) imitation of ancient paintings should be evident (does the painting exude a proper
   respect for tradition?)

According to Xie, the most important of these principles was the first. The Chinese believed that each aspect of nature — plant, rock, or creature — had its own vital force, known as *qi*. A painting would only come to life if the *qi* of the painter and the *qi* of what he painted were in accord. If the presence of this force was lacking in a painting, there was no reason to look at it any further.

fied demeanor. Figure painting reached its full development during the Tang dynasty, when court artists depicted the daily life of the elite — scholars gathered to study and compose poetry, court ladies dressing their hair or strolling through a garden, or foreign dignitaries bearing tribute to the emperor. Tang emperor Taisong had very realistic portraits of two of his greatest generals placed outside his bedroom door to protect him at night!

Religious figure paintings date from the mid-4th century, when Buddhist priests created wall paintings and sculptures of Buddha and his followers in caves and temples. The most famous of these are the Magao Caves at Dunhuang and the Longmen temples near Luoyang.

Landscape Painting

During the Han dynasty, trees, rocks, flowers, and bushes were often painted in the background of figure paintings. This was the beginning of landscape painting. After the fall of the Han, many Daoist scholars living in southern China withdrew from the chaos of everyday life and turned for comfort to nature. They took great delight in such simple images as an undulating river current, the gently waving branches of a tree in the wind, or the odd formations carved in a rock by the wind and rain. Many incorporated such observations into their paintings to express their sense of communion with the natural world. Their scenes were dominated by rugged mountains and flowing streams or waterfalls. (In fact, the Chinese word for landscape (*shanshui*) literally means "mountain and water." If human figures appeared at all, they were very small, since, for Daoists, man played only a small role in the world of nature.

Tang artists were the first to paint panoramic landscapes on horizontal handscrolls — long pieces of silk (or paper), which could be easily rolled up, much like the early books. The viewer placed the scroll on a table and slowly unrolled it, beginning at the right edge. He viewed one small scene at a time (about two feet of the painting), slowly rolling up the right side of the scroll as he unrolled the left. As his eyes moved across the painting, he had the sense of taking an imaginary journey through the series of tableaux created by the artist. He had only to find the tiny figure in the painting, noting where he had already been and continuing the journey he was about to take, wandering along twisting paths, past groves of trees and mountain streams, through villages, and over bridges, perhaps taking a side trip to visit a Buddhist temple — always pausing to enjoy each view before moving on. The shifting perspective of the painting offered a fresh vista at every turn in the path and provided a sense of movement as the viewer progressed from one place to the next.

Some scroll paintings were vertical rather than horizontal. These could be mounted on a hook on the wall. A vertical painting also consisted of a number of small scenes, but the viewer "traveled" up (into the distance) as well as from right to left. Vertical paintings were seldom hung for more than a few days at a time. Like a good book, they were enjoyed and then safely put away again until the next viewing. Many scrolls, horizontal and vertical, have survived to modern times because they were usually kept rolled up.

Bird-and-Flower Painting

The painting of flowers was introduced into China by Buddhist monks. During the Tang dynasty, the flower paintings were enhanced by delicately drawn birds. This led to a popular new genre among courtiers, known as bird-and-flower painting. It was a highly decorative style that drew upon the technical skill of the painter. This style was closely linked to calligraphy, since the parts of the birds (beaks, claws and feathers) and of the flowers (petals, leaves and stems) were painted with the same basic brushstrokes as those used for writing characters.

Certain plants and birds have always had symbolic meanings in China, and these were favorite subjects for the bird-and-flower paintings. Pine trees, for example, signify endurance, bamboo symbolizes dignity and resilience, plum blossoms denote youthful energy, and cranes represent longevity as well the ideal of soaring to higher realms of understanding. Certain birds and flowers are often depicted together — river reeds and wild geese, for example, or plum blossoms and nightingales. A pair of white-headed birds beside a peony conveys the wish for wealth and riches throughout a long life.

Ink Painting

Ink paintings are done with black ink and brush. They're known in the West by the Japanese term *sumi-e* ("ink pictures"). Using a minimum of rapid strokes, the artist tries to capture the "essence" of his subject. This style of painting arose during the Tang dynasty and flourished during the Song. Because of its great simplicity and spontaneity, it is often associated with Buddhism and Daoism. Among the favorite subjects of the ink painter are birds and plants, particularly bamboo.

Ink paintings often contain a large proportion of empty space. This represents the "emptiness" out of which all things are created, the potential for something to take form out of nothing. An empty object in a painting suggests the same thing. For example, a ceramic bowl is an empty vessel into which rice or soup can be poured.

The Three Perfections

The disciplines of poetry, painting, and calligraphy are known as the "three perfections." They are linked in many ways. The same instruments — brush and ink — can be used to write a poem, paint a picture, or create a character. Poetry resembles painting in its emphasis upon visual images. Su Shi wrote that the purpose of painting was not to depict the appearance of things but to express the painter's own feelings, as in poetry. Calligraphy is an art in itself, requiring a balance of thick and thin strokes — skillfully yet spontaneously executed, broadening or narrowing, becoming heavier or lighter on the page, just like the lines of a figure in a painting.

Beginning in Tang times, the "three perfections" were often combined in a single work — the haunting scenes of a painting being enhanced by the beautifully written lines of verse that describe it. As you know, the Tang were the first to require a model courtier to be skilled in the these three disciplines.

Northern Song Painting

Now that you know something about Chinese painting, let's turn to some of the major works of the Northern Song. Many of the artists of this period were professional painters of the imperial court. As we've seen, Huizong was a very visible presence in their midst, frequently conducting his "examinations" and constantly looking over their shoulders as they tried to paint.

Just as historians and philosophers looked to the past to seek clues to the present, artists traditionally studied and even copied the works of the masters who lived before them. (This was the 6th principle of painting. See the box on page 41.) Song artists were particularly drawn to the landscape paintings of previous dynasties. They copied them, but they added a sense of the awesome majesty and grandeur of nature. They also placed great emphasis upon a realistic depiction of a scene. To sharpen their skills, artists spent long hours outside, studying such subtleties as the way each species of tree grew, the distinctive charac-

---

There are four general styles of calligraphy. Each requires the writer to handle the brush in a certain way. There are seal scripts (derived from characters used by ancient scribes), standard brush scripts (complicated scripts used for official purposes that were standardized during the Han dynasty), running script (a simplified script used for writing informal letters), and grass script (a sort of shorthand script). It was once believed that people revealed their moral and spiritual value through their writing. The tools of calligraphy are called the "Four Treasures of the Study" – paper, a pointed writing brush, an inkstick and an inskstone. Ink is produced by grinding the inkstick on the inkstone while adding a small amount of water.

ter of certain rock formations, the changing appearance of a mountain setting at different times of the day or year, the evolving shapes of drifting clouds, or the spiraling movement of water currents. Beyond duplicating the details of each leaf or blade of grass, the artists hoped to suggest the presence of *qi*, the primal force that flows throughout nature and binds everything together.

Let's see how these ideals were put into effect by three of the greatest painters of the period. Before continuing, consult a book about Chinese art and find illustrations of the following paintings: *Buddhist Temple in the Mountains After Rain* by Li Cheng, *Travelers Among Mountains and Streams* by Fan Kuan, and *Fishing in a Mountain Stream* by Xu Daoning. These are among the greatest works that have survived from the Northern Song. They were painted on silk, and over the centuries the background color has turned to the shade of weak tea. Even so, we can still appreciate their artistry. If you cannot find illustrations of these paintings, try to envision them as they are described.

Li Cheng's *Buddhist Temple in the Mountains After Rain* is a vertical scroll landscape. The first thing you notice is the dark, hulking presence of the huge mountain in the background. Its steep slope it silhouetted against another mountain, which rises even higher behind it and to the right.

This second mountain is bathed in rays from the sun. To the left of the center mountain, a cascading waterfall has cut a gorge and plunges through the mist below, catching the light. A second water fall empties into the river that is flowing toward you in the foreground. So far, we have the mountains and water that appear in nearly every Chinese landscape painting. But have you noticed how the great mass of the central mountain is balanced by the action action of the tumbling water, how dark, shadowy forms contrast with light? Think about what you've learned about the dual, yet complementary, forces of *yin* and *yang*. Now move your eyes to the central part of the painting, just below the huge mountain. The Buddhist temple stands on a small hill, surrounded by gnarled trees and rough-looking boulders. Like the distant mountain and the waterfall, the temple is bathed in light, which allows you to see the many details of its roofs and balconies. On the riverbank in the foreground is an inn, built for pilgrims who visit the temple. It has a number of open-air rooms, where you can see the people eating, drinking, or simply gazing at the river. Two travelers are approaching from the right. They will soon cross the bridge and join the others at the inn.

Li Cheng has invited you to enter his imaginary world. Although there is no path to travel along, your gaze is free to wander at will, from the steep mountainsides in the distance to the quiet activity in the foreground. Amid the powerful forces of nature, doesn't the inn seem a tranquil, friendly place? Wouldn't you say that the human element blends well into the natural landscape, yet remains distinct?

Now let's consider *Travelers Among Mountains and Streams*. The artist, Fan Kuan, was a shy, sensitive man, who lived as a recluse in the Qiantang Mountains of Shanxi province. Fan studied nature so intently that he was known to spend an entire day gazing from various perspectives at a single configuration of rocks, or an entire evening observing the effects of moonlight upon the fallen snow.

This painting is huge — almost seven feet high. And yet, the sense of grandeur radiates from the subject matter itself. Like Li Cheng's painting, Fan's landscape has different stages or levels. A large, low-lying group of rocks fills the bottom, extreme foreground. They overlook a valley, where a group of travelers and their mules are entering from the right. The valley floor is realistically portrayed, down to the bark patterns of the individual trees. There are even a few dead branches lying here and there. On the far side of the valley are two groups of rocky hills. They are separated by a series of waterfalls and cascades, the water tumbling into a river that flows to the left beneath the rocks of the foreground.

The curving rooftops of a temple can be seen among the pine trees clustered in the hills to the right. They are silhouetted against the sun-brightened mist rising from the valley beyond.

Beyond the mist looms a massive bluff. It dominates the painting, taking up almost twice as much space as the foreground and middle ground combined. It makes the human figures look like ants! From a cleft in the bluff, a narrow waterfall plunges — a thin streak of white against the dark rock. The artist has used short broken brush strokes to suggest the rough texture of the rock's surface. Unlike the highly detailed trees in the foreground, those on the mountain tops are painted in vague clumps. This creates the feeling of distance, which is further accented by the mist rising from the valley floor.

Have you noticed similarities between the this painting and the one by Li Cheng? Both contain huge mountains, waterfalls, a river, rising mist, and a human presence. In both paintings, dark mountains, rocks, and trees are outlined by bright mist. In both, objects in the foreground are realistically detailed, while those in the distance have a blurred quality. Finally, the human figures in both are very small, dwarfed by the dimensions of their natural surroundings. But what differences have you noticed between them?

One of finest handscrolls to survive

from the period is Xu Daoning's *Fishing in a Mountain Stream*. This is a river landscape, seven feet in length. Unlike the vertical scrolls, this wide panorama encourages you to follow a long path. The journey begins from a thatched hut in the right foreground. You progress down the slope of the hill and come to a broad, open area. From here you can admire the distant vista of mist and mountain peaks. Then you cross a footbridge and follow the path leading along the river bank. It passes beneath a group of very tall mountains, which seem to rise straight up to the heavens. You cross another footbridge, and, after passing under the tallest of the mountain peaks, you gaze ahead at a deep valley. Now you have a choice. Should you decide to enter the valley, you can rest in the nearby pavilion.

Turn toward the water and watch the group of fishermen, who are throwing in their lines. Do you see the others patiently waiting as their boats drift in the slow-moving currents? Should you decide to continue along the path, it will take you past another group of mountains, and another valley. When you cross a last footbridge, you will meet travelers coming toward you. They will enjoy your experience — in reverse. This painting offers experiences somewhat different than the first two. And yet, there are some very essential similarities. Can you describe what they are?

Court artists of the Northern Song produced a number of exquisite bird-and-flower paintings. Huizong loved this genre, and his highly detailed, delicately colored paintings of birds perched on the branches of flowering trees are considered among the finest ever made. The emperor also invented an elegant style of calligraphy, which he called "slender gold" for its delicate brushwork and sparing use of ink. He wrote short original verses about his birds and flowers in the slender gold style. The delicate lines of his characters seem in perfect harmony with the graceful strokes of his paintings.

A View of Kaifeng

Spring Time On the River On the Eve of the Qing Ming Festival is a 17-foot handscroll painted in first quarter of 12th century by Zhang Zeduan. (See if you can find an

---

Mi Fei was an artist who lived toward the end of the Northern Song period. He invented a technique known as "splashed ink" that used small blobs of ink made with the side of the brush to build up the shapes of mountains and rocks, giving them extra texture. Because he produced contours without distinct outlines, his paintings had what has been called a "boneless" quality. Although none have survived, his work is known through written descriptions of it and through the paintings of his son (Mi Yuren) and others who followed his style.

illustration of at least a section of Zhang Zeduan's masterpiece.) This lively panorama, so unlike any of the works you've been reading about, is filled with the bustling commercial activity of the city. It is a visual time capsule, providing us with an invaluable portrait of daily life in Kaifeng at the height of its prosperity. It seems as though the artist has scanned the banks of the river with a camera, capturing through his lens the interactions of the local inhabitants and visitors from the countryside as they throng the streets and the Rainbow Bridge of the city.

The painting contains over 500 figures, each about an inch tall, in a wide variety of activities — taking tea in tea-houses, listening to a storyteller, watching a theatrical performance, relaxing in a luxurious two-story restaurant, haggling with a shopkeeper, standing on a street corner catching up on the latest gossip, and a multitude of other preoccupations. Unlike the landscapes that revel in the beauty of nature, this painting seems to focus upon the human pursuit of profit. So many images bear testament to the capital city's prosperity — the cargo barges, which dip their masts to pass under the arched bridge, the shops with their prominent display banners, the donkeys, camels, and oxen-drawn carts laden with goods, and the human porters, bent-over by the weight of their burdens.

The buildings, gates, boats, carts, and the bridge itself appear extremely realistic, due not only to the intricate detail but also to the artist's skillful use of shading and foreshortening. These are techniques that would not appear again in Chinese painting until the 20th century.

Extravagant Tastes

Emperor Huizong loved to surround himself with beautiful works of art. He amassed in the Imperial Gallery the finest collection of paintings ever made in the Far East. He commissioned a 20-volume catalogue, which listed over 6,396 paintings by 231 artists spanning the nine centuries from the end of the Han dynasty to his own time. Unfortunately, his eagerness to acquire all this art would ultimately damage China's legacy of ancient works, as you will see.

Huizong's most ambitious project was the huge pleasure park he had built in Kaifeng. It contained a man-made mountain more than 90 feet tall with twin peaks. Water cascaded down the mountain slope into a vast pool, where geese and ducks happily swam about. It was a living land-

The Qing Ming Festival was a time when families would gather to tend the graves of their ancestors.

scape painting. Huizong also had exotic animals and rare plants brought to the park from distant parts of the empire for his own pleasure entertainment.

Ominous Signs

While Huizong presided over his lavish court and pursued his interests in art, the foundations of the Northern Song were slowly crumbling. The emperor's expensive tastes had created a burden on the state treasury, already drained by military expenditures and the tribute payments to the Khitan and Tanguts. His ministers were forced to raise taxes and issue more paper money. But the increase in paper money led to inflation, and this sparked a serious rebellion in 1120.

Meanwhile, since Huizong had little interest in government, his top officials vied with each other for power. No one was quite certain who was in charge. And just when the dynasty was most vulnerable, big problems arose in the north. The Jurchen, hard-riding hunters and herdsmen from central Asia, had entered Manchuria in the last century. In 1114, they created their own Chinese-style dynasty, the Jin ("gold"). Before long, they began moving into Khitan territory. Now it looked like China was their next target.

The Storming of Kaifeng

After much quibbling about the menace to the north, Huizong and his advisors agreed upon a short-sighted plan that would bring disaster to the empire. They formed an alliance with the Jurchen. Why do such a thing? China was still paying a huge annual tribute of silver and silk to the Khitan. A Jurchen victory, the ministers reasoned, would end the tribute payments. It also might enable them to recover land in northern China previously seized by the Khitan. Huizong should have paid more attention to his history books, which warned of the risks of helping one potential enemy to defeat another.

When the Chinese army moved against the Khitan, they were easily repulsed. So the Jurchen went on to conquer their enemies on their own. With the Liao capital in their hands, the Jurchen horsemen turned on the demoralized Chinese and chased them back into China. In 1126, the Jurchen troops moved on Kaifeng and layed siege to the city.

Huizong quickly abdicated in favor of his eldest son, Qinzong. He took for himself the title "Master of Learning and the Way." (He was actually much happier in this role than he had ever been as emperor!) Qinzong tried to hold off the invaders by agreeing to pay a huge indemnity. Perhaps once again the Song could buy off their enemies. Many hoped that this was the case. The Jurchen retired briefly, but then returned the following year and stormed the city. This is when most of the art in Huizong's Imperial Gallery was destroyed, although the catalogue survived. Historians and art lovers wish that the emperor had not been such an avid collector.

While the capital city burned, the invaders rounded up the imperial retinue — Qinzong, Huizong, their empresses, dozens of relatives and concubines, and 3,000 imperial retainers and officials. They herded them together on a long and difficult trek to Manchuria, taking along an immense train of carts laden with loot from the Song palaces. The entourage left in May and did not reach their destination for over a year. Many died along the way, including the two empresses.

A New Emperor

Huizong's ninth son, Zhao Gou, escaped the fate of his family. He had been sent to the Jurchen camp on a mission of negotiation before Kaifeng was stormed. En route, his party was stopped by Chinese soldiers, who thought Zhao was being sacrificed to the enemy. They killed the official negotiator and persuaded the prince, then just 20, to lead a resistance against the invaders. (Does this remind you of Zhao Kuangyin?) When the Jurchen attacked Kaifeng, Zhao realized how closely he had escaped disaster. He began regrouping the field armies of the Song resistance.

On June 12, 1127, Zhao Gou was crowned emperor in Shangqui, a town nearly a hundred miles southeast of Kaifeng. He would rule as Gaozong. After mounting a hastily-made altar to receive the Mandate of Heaven, he announced that he was the legitimate heir to the throne, forced by circumstances to take the place of his father. Then he bowed his head and wept aloud, grieving for "the two emperors" far away in Manchuria.

Huizong and Quinzong languished for the rest of their lives in the cold forests of the north. Huizong gradually soon went blind, a cruel fate for someone who loved to look at beautiful things. He died in 1135 at the age of 53. Qinzong, white-haired at only 36, spent the remaining 29 years of his life in captivity.

Review Questions:

1. In what ways did Taizu's treatment of his former enemies differ from that of his predecessors?

2. How did Taizu reshape the army?

3. Describe the basic structure of Taizu's government.

4. In what ways was Kaifeng a typical Chinese city?

5. Who were the Khitan?

6. How did Taizong deal with the Khitan?

7. How was gunpowder invented?

8. How was gunpowder first used by the Chinese?

9. What effect did the printing of books have on the education system?

10. What was the *jinshi*?

11. What was the main purpose of the New Laws?

12. What groups opposed the New Laws, and why?

13. Choose three adjectives to describe Su Shi (Su Dongpu).

14. What moved the gears of the clock tower?

15. What were Huizong's major interests?

16. What did Xie He consider the most important of the Six Canons of Painting?

17. What are the four categories of Chinese painting?

18. What are the "three perfections?"

19. How would you characterize the landscape paintings of the Northern Song?

20. Why is the famous painting of Kaifeng described as a time capsule?

21. What fatal mistake did Huizong make in his dealings with the Jurchen?

22. Why wasn't Zhao Gou sent to Manchuria with his father and grandfather?

Projects:

1. Make a timeline of the Northern Song dynasty.

2. If a Western landscape is like a photograph, a Chinese painting is like a movie camera in a hot air balloon, moving across country. Write a short essay explaining what this statement refers to.

3. *Spring Time on the River* was painted at about the same as the Bayeux Tapestries were woven in Europe. Find out about these tapestries. Then write a essay comparing them to the Chinese painting.

4. The Chinese literati favored intellectual pursuits over military might. In fact, the scholar-officials looked down upon soldiers, considering them as muscle-bound oafs of little brain. This attitude would have a great influence upon the future of Chinese civilization. From what you know so far about Chinese history, try to predict in what ways this might be true.

5. Write a play about the the life of a student, from the time he learns to write his first characters until he makes it to the final civil service exam in Kaifeng. Feel free to improvise about character development and to add humor. Once you have a script, enlist the talents of some classmates to perform the play for the rest of the class.

6. Find a collection of English translations of the poetry of Su Dongpo. Read 10 or 12 of the poems. Analyze them and choose 5 to read to the class.

7. Consult several books on Chinese art about bird-and-flower paintings. Try to find examples of the works of Huizong. Learn more about this genre. Share your findings with your classmates. Be sure to show them examples from the art books.

8. Become a landscape painter! Consult *Chinese Landscape Painting for Beginners* by Audrey Quigley. Another useful resource is *The Way of the Brush: Painting Techniques of China and Japan* by Fritz Van Briessen.

Happenings in Other Parts of the World
(960 — 1126)

Otto I crowned Holy Roman Emperor — 962
Viking settlements in Greenland — 986
Toltecs flourish in Mexico — 1050
Pisa Cathedral built — 1063
Norman Conquest of England 1066
Domesday Book in England — 1086
Jerusalem captured by the Crusaders — 1096
Henry I crowned King of England — 1100
Almohad Dynasty founded in North Africa — 1121
Beginning of construction of Chartres Cathedral — 1194

Chapter 3

The Southern Song
(1127 — 1276)
Civilization Moves South

The young emperor, Gaozong, began his reign on very shaky legs. The Song government was in shambles, and he had to hustle together as many advisers as he could find to begin forming a new one. It wasn't long before he received word that the Jurchen horsemen were breathing down his neck. He had no choice but to flee with his fledgling court further south to Yangzhou, a city on the northern bank of the Yangzi River. And even there they weren't truly safe.

A casual observer might have concluded that the Song dynasty was doomed. But, as you will see, it would not only survive the great dislocation but flourish, building upon its past achievements while capitalizing upon the advantages of its new home.

Flight to Hangzhou

The city of Yangzhou offered Gaozong and his retinue a warm welcome and comfortable lodgings. They remained there until February of 1129, when the news arrived that enemy troops were fast approaching. The court flew into a panic.

Gaozong ordered a group of courtiers to flee south across the river with his infant son and proceed to the city of Hangzhou. Everyone else waited in Yangzhou, reassured by the nearby presence of the Song army. But when the defensive troops began fleeing the battlefield, Gaozong and a few attendants jumped on their horses and galloped to the river, passing thousands of others who were fleeing on foot. The young emperor was guided to a boat, and he rowed himself to the far shore. A few days later, he arrived in Hangzhou.

It was a gloomy gathering. The Song officials straggled in, exhausted from their

Highlights of This Chapter

The Jurchen invade the south
Li Qingzhao
The Peace Settlement
A Center of Trade
Porcelain, Silk and Lacquerware
The Jin Attack Again
Hangzhou
Neo-Confucianism
The Maritime Silk Road
An Age of Affluence
Landscape Painting

escape from Yangzhou and, in many cases, uncertain about the fate of their wives and families. The future looked dim, and a number of men questioned whether Gaozong had the skills to restore the dynasty. On one occasion, a coalition of disgruntled officials convinced the emperor's bodyguard to turn against him, forcing him to abdicate in favor of his three-year-old son. An urgent call for help went out from Gaozong's supporters to the generals based outside the city. They quickly responded and restored the emperor to the throne, but this episode shows how tentatively he held the reins of power.

Escape to the Sea

In mid-summer, two Jurchen armies crossed the Yangzi and began raiding the countryside. A few months later, they were on the outskirts of Hangzhou. Once again Gaozong and his court were forced to flee for their lives. This time, they headed to the port city of Zhejiang, where they boarded a fleet of ships and immediately set sail for the safety of the open sea.

Empress Meng was one of the more colorful characters in these turbulent times. Long before the sack of Kaifeng, when she was 16, she had been selected from among 100 candidates to be the bride and future empress to Huizong's predecessor, Zhezong. The emperor later transferred his affections from his wife to one of his concubines, the alluring Liu, who then conspired to bring charges of witchcraft against Meng. The empress was found guilty (palace retainers were forced to accuse her against their wills), deposed in favor of Liu, and then exiled to a Daoist sanctuary.

Years later, when the Jurchen overran Kaifeng, Meng was overlooked while others in the ruling family were rounded up and marched off as prisoners. The invaders installed one of their own men as Jin emperor in Kaifeng. He found out about Meng and asked her to serve as his regent, believing this would help to legitimize his regime. She agreed, but when she later discovered Gaozong had survived, she stepped down as regent and acknowledged *him* as China's rightful emperor.

When he heard of this, the grateful Gaozong had the former empress spirited out of Kaifeng and welcomed her to his court in Hangzhou. This is when the group of conspiring courtiers forced the emperor to abdicate in favor of his three-year-old son in 1129. The conspirators asked Meng to serve as regent to the child. She agreed, reluctantly, in order to protect the little prince. And when the military leaders quashed the conspiracy and restored Gaozong to power, Meng gladly gave up her regency, returning the boy to his father's care.

Meng remained at Gaozong's court in Hangzhou as an honored figure. By the time she died in 1134, the future of the Song dynasty was assured. The empress was revered afterwards as one of the true guardians of China.

The Jurchen soldiers continued to rampage through the south until the summer heat and heavy rains drove them back north. Once the coast was clear, the fleet returned and the emperor and his court disembarked. But they had to remain in Shaoxing for three years until Hangzhou, badly pillaged by the invaders, could be restored.

Yue Fei

During these unsettled times, many a hero appeared whose exploits so impressed his countrymen that he became a popular legend. One of these heroes was Yue Fei, a peasant who had become a resistance fighter. When the Song court fled from Hangzhou to the coast, Yue Fei led a detachment, made up mostly of peasant rebels and local bandits, to harass the Jurchen invaders and try to drive them back across the Yangzi. Yue's courage and leadership skills drew the attention of the Song generals, and in 1130 he was put in charge of the armies in the central Yangzi region.

Three years later, Yue Fei led a daring offensive against the Jin dynasty (the Jurchen state in the north), capturing several important military bases. He was fast becoming a national hero. Gaozong now made him commander of all of his troops in Central China. The ranks of the army swelled dramatically as young Chinese men fleeing from the north rushed to join the army to become part of the invincible force led by the fearless freedom fighter.

Li Qingzhou

While history was being made on the military front, one of China's greatest poets was waging her own battles. Her name was Li Qingzhou. She and her husband, Zhao Mingcheng, came from well-known families of the Northern Song. Li's mother was a poet and her father, a high-ranking official, was a good friend of Su Shi. Zhao's father was Chief Counselor early in the reign of Huizong. The young couple married when Zhao was 20 (and studying for his civil service exams) and Li was 17. They lived in Shandong province and shared their love of poetry. The newlyweds often had literary contests with each other and with their literary friends. (These were rather one-sided contests, since most of their friends agreed that Li's poems were far superior to any of the others!)

Zhao and Li also shared a deep interest in ancient artifacts, especially bronzes dating from the Shang and Zhou dynasties. While Zhao was still a student and they had little money, the couple would often pawn their belongings to acquire a piece for their collection. After Zhao became a government official, they were able to buy many more bronzes. Zhao made rubbings of the ancient inscriptions on many of the bronzes, then carefully deciphered them.

The couple later compiled *The Catalogue of Inscriptions on Bronze and Stone*, recording the texts of 2,000 inscriptions and including detailed notes about them. It is considered the best critical study and anthology of ancient Chinese characters ever written.

When the Jurchen troops invaded northern China in 1127, Li and Zhao were forced to flee. Their home was burned, and they lost most of their collection of books and ancient objects. Fortunately, their catalogue survived and was later retrieved by Li. Zhao was assigned to a new post, but he fell ill from malaria and died. His grieving wife traveled to Hangzhou, then settled with her brother's family in northern Zhejiang province. She lived until her seventies, writing poems and working on a revised edition of the book on ancient inscriptions.

Li Quinzhao is considered China's greatest female poet. During her lifetime, she produced six volumes of verse as well as seven volumes of essays. The poems were in written a delicate lyric form (known as *ci*), which consists of long and short lines with intricate interior rhymes and rhythms. Unlike most poems written about women at that time (these described the woes of a deserted wife or abandoned female lover and were written mostly by men), Li Qingzhao's verses were autobiographical. They are divided into three groups — those describing the happier days of her life when Zhao was alive, those depicting her despair following his death, and those expressing the unhappiness of growing old alone.

Despite her great talent, Li Quinzhao was not accepted by the male-dominated society of the literati, and she died in poverty. Only after her death were her poems recognized for their brilliance. About a fifth of her works have survived to modern times.

The Peace Settlement

In 1141, after years of battles and skirmishes between Jurchen soldiers and Song resistance fighters, both sides finally agreed to a peace treaty. Yue Fei was not pleased with this decision, since his goal was to drive the Jurchen back to Manchuria. Gaozong's top minister, Qin Gui, worried that Yue Fei's superpatriotism would endanger the peace, so he (falsely) accused him of treason. Yue was arrested and later poisoned in his prison cell — on the minister's orders. Sympathetic jailers

---

The Jurchen were not as brutish as you might imagine. The Jin government was actually modeled on that of China, and it even had a civil service exams system. The ruler wore Chinese-style imperial garb, and he was entertained at court by Song musicians. According to his instructions, the 49th generation descendant of Confucius was made a duke, and he personally attended the annual sacrifice to Confucius.

stole the hero's body and buried it in a secret place. (Twenty years later, Yue Fei's name would be restored to honor, and he would be reburied and revered as a martyr.)

According to the terms of the peace treaty, a frontier was drawn roughly along the line of the Huai River valley. (The Huai River flows eastward, midway between the Yellow River and the Yangzi.) The Jin dynasty was recognized as the ruling power in the north (with a capital at the site of modern Beijing), while the Song officially controlled the south. However, the Song had to pay the Jin an annual tribute of over 200,000 ounces of silver and 200,000 bolts of silk. Many members of the Song court cringed when they heard the terms, but at least they could stop worrying about the threat of invasion.

A Fertile Region

As you know, the lush and misty south was very different from the arid, wind-swept plains of northern China. The court did not feel at home there, and for a long time they referred to Hangzhou as their "temporary residence." And yet, the move to the Yangzi River valley turned out to be a very lucky break, since this was the richest and most productive part of China.

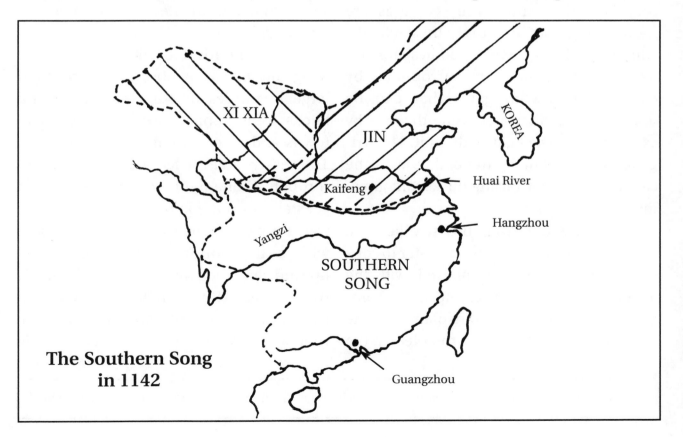

XI XIA

JIN

KOREA

Kaifeng

Huai River

Yangzi

Hangzhou

SOUTHERN
SONG

**The Southern Song
in 1142**

Guangzhou

The warm temperature and plentiful rainfall had enabled the southern farmers to provide rice for most of China for centuries. Rice is a nearly ideal food source. It tastes good, is highly digestible, and, when eaten along with products of the soybean (another southern product), it offers excellent nutrition. Rice is the only grain that can simply be boiled and eaten without dissolving into mush. When milled, it stores well and is easily transported. And rice plants produce more calories per acre than any other crop.

Growing rice is a labor intensive activity. Since early times, the process has remained the same. Rice seedlings are grown for about a month in seedbeds, while the fields (known as paddies) are prepared. The paddies are surrounded by earthen dikes with gates that can be opened to let in water from the nearby canal to flood the field or drain it. The irrigation ditches linking the paddie with the canal are ideal for raising ducks and growing water chestnuts.

Before planting, the paddies are flooded with an inch or two of water to soften the ground and then plowed, with the aid of a water buffalo. Everyone in the community helps with transplanting the seedlings. Rows of planters, their feet in the mud, bend at the waist and move slowly backwards through the field. After the rice is planted, there is the labor of weeding and maintaining water levels. When the plants are mature, the paddies are drained and the rice is harvested.

A Center of Trade

Hangzhou grew quickly, as more Chinese, rich and poor, fled there from the north. Artisans set up workshops, while enterprising businessmen formed companies for making paper and printing books. The city was ideally situated to become a major trading center, since it lay at the southern end of the network of waterways making up the Grand Canal.

The political border between the Song and Jin was no obstacle to trade, and large quantities of tea, rice, sugar, and books were shipped north as well as to towns and cities within the Song empire. The vessels that carried much of the cargo through China's inland waterways and coastal routes are known as junks. A junk was a broad-beamed wooden sailing boat with a flat bottom, sides that curved upward, and a squared off bow and stern. It was steered with a single stern-mounted rudder (another Chinese invention). The rudder could be raised or lowered, a big

In 1978 archaeologists discovered rice remains in the Hangzhou region dating from about 4000 BC.

advantage in the shallow waters of the canals and some of the rivers. A junk had several four-sided sails made from panels of woven hemp cloth. Each sail was stiffened by horizontal battens made of bamboo and could be easily raised and lowered, like a modern venetian blind. Smaller cargo boats (called sampans) had no sails but were propelled by a long-handled sculling oar maneuvered by standing oarsmen. Wide barges were pulled along the canals by ropes. Many families lived in boats that were moored along the canals, making their living by transporting goods from one place to another.

Merchants now formed a large core of the growing middle class. As they acquired greater wealth, many could afford to live like the gentry. They built elegant homes and furnished them with beautifully carved tables and chairs, screens decorated with silk paintings, intricate lacquerware, and handsome stone statues. At the same time, many landowners, who in earlier times would have remained on their country estates, now moved to the cities and conducted business there. China was becoming a capitalist society.

Porcelain

Southern China is especially rich in deposits of kaolin, the fine white clay that is the main ingredient of porcelain. When kaolin is mixed with ground up bits of feldspar and quartz, shaped into a vessel and fired in a kiln at a high temperature (2000 degrees F.), it undergoes a physical change (called vitrification). This process makes the surface of the vessel translucent and inpenetrable by water. If it is covered with a glaze and fired again, the surface acquires a glossy finish so hard that steel cannot scratch it.

Clay pottery, of course, has been made in China for thousands of years. As early as the 1st century CE, potters knew how to build kilns that could fire at extremely high temperatures, producing large quantities of porcelain. The new style of pottery was less expensive than bronzeware, stronger than earthenware (ordinary, unglazed pottery), and was easily made from local materials. Its popularity led to experimentation with liquid glazes, and new techniques were gradually developed for decorating the vases, plates, and other vessels. By the 8th century, Tang craftsmen were producing porcelain of such high quality that poets wrote verses about it.

During the Northern Song, the Ru kilns near Kaifeng produced elegant vases and vessels, which were glazed in subtle shades of light grayish-green with faint lines resembling the crackling of a broken eggshell. The crackled look was probably first produced by accident, when a glaze shrank more than normal as the vessel cooled after firing. Before long, potters were purposely shrinking the glaze to create the unusual crackling effect. This style was later called celadon by Westerners. Ding was a type of ivory-white porcelain that was exceptionally thin and translucent.

When Kaifeng fell to the Jurchen, most of the local potters fled south, taking with them the accumulated experience of centuries. Kilns were set up around Hangzhou and Jingdezhen, and new generations of southern potters produced elegant vases, bowls, and cups with perfectly balanced shapes and crystal-pure, grayish-green glazes, many with the distinctive crackling.

Silk and Lacquer

Many farms in the south specialized in growing mulberry leaves and raising silkworms. Silk weaving and embroidery actually became organized craft industries during the Song dynasty. Great quantities of the beautiful cloth were produced in imperial workshops in Hangzhou and in other shops throughout the southern countryside. Even today, a third of China's silk is produced in the region surrounding Hangzhou.

For centuries, silk cloth had ranked in value with silver and gold. Bolts of silk were often used for the payment of taxes, and, as you've learned, they could constitute a form of tribute. Of course, it was the importation of silk cloth to the West that later gave the Silk Road its name.

Lacquer is a plastic-like surface coating derived from the sap of the lac tree (*Rhus verniciflua*), which grows in southern China. You learned earlier how in ancient times lacquer was applied in layers to the surface of objects made from wood or bamboo to render them waterproof. By the Han dynasty, imperial lacquer factories had been set up in Sichuan. Workers produced a wide variety of items — from cooking spoons and bowls to coffins and even boat hulls. The liquid lacquer was usually blackened with soot or colored red with a mineral called cinnabar. The process of lacquering an object took a long time, since one layer had to be completely dry (which can take weeks) and then buffed and polished before the next layer was applied. The thick, lacquered surfaces of luxury objects were often delicately carved. Tang craftsmen were the first to inlay mother-of-pearl in the top lacquer layer of a box or tray before it dried.

Artisans of the Southern Song were very skilled at carving rich floral designs into lacquerware. They also invented a process that involved coating a wooden object, usually a bowl, tray or box, with as many as two hundred coats of lacquer in an array of colors. The lower layers were usually red and yellow, even white, while the outer ones tended to be brownish black.

Once all the lacquer had been applied, the craftsman began carving scroll patterns in V-shaped channels. As he worked, the colors of the various layers were slowly revealed, adding a very elegant dimension to the artwork.

The Jurchen Attack Again

Although the economy of the Southern Song was strong, the government officials at Hangzhou remained uneasy about the nearby presence of the Jurchen. So they kept the military on the alert and added to their arsenal of weapons. In 1150, Song soldiers discovered they could shoot an arrow without a bow. They simply strapped a gunpowder charge wrapped in oiled paper to its shaft near the arrowhead, ignited it, and watched it take off like a rocket. An iron weight fixed at the rear of the arrow provided balance, enabling it to fly 500 to 1000 feet without nose-diving. This innovation led to the development of wood and bamboo rocket launchers that could send a barrage of arrows toward an enemy's front line.

The Song also built up their fleet of ships, including many paddle-wheeled warships. Paddleboats had been used in China for centuries. They had a large stern wheel and as many as twelve additional wheels on each side. The wheels were operated by manpower, through the pedals or cranks of a treadmill. Paddleboats could sail effectively in any direction without any need for the wind, often reaching impressive speeds.

The decision to strengthen their defense proved to have been a wise one when the Jurchen made an unprovoked attack in 1161. The enemy soldiers tried to cross the Yangzi, covered by local boatmen who had been hastily (and forcefully) pressed into service. They were met by a a fleet of paddleboats, the wheels camouflaged so that the vessels appeared to move by magic. The Jurchens, terrified by the "magic" warships and bombarded by a full inventory of bombs, rockets, and fire-rafts, quickly retreated.

The Jin emperor had built up his own fleet of ships, and he sent these to deal with the Song sea patrols. Having been alerted to the impending danger, the Song military command ordered a fleet already at sea to intercept the Jin ships. The Song vessels, equipped with iron battering rams as well as rocket launchers, easily destroyed the enemy fleet off the southern coast of Shandong.

On December 15, the Jurchen generals, convinced that another attempt to cross the Yangzi would meet with failure, murdered their emperor at his camp near Yangzhou. So ended the Jin invasion. The Song navy had proved its mettle, and the government officials could breathe a long sigh of relief.

Hangzhou

Hangzhou soon surpassed Kaifeng in size, becoming the largest city in the world. It was also one of the most scenic. It was ringed by forested mountains on the north, west, and south, and the Qiantang River, which flowed along the city's eastern edge. And nestled between Hangzhou and the mountains was beautiful West Lake.

The city was protected by 30-foot-high walls of packed earth and entered through one of 13 arched and towered gates. Unlike a traditional Chinese city, which was laid out as a square (or rectangle) with a grid of streets meeting at precise angles, Hangzhou had an irregular shape. This was because it was built on a narrow strip of land that was sandwiched between the lake and the river. However, the main avenue (Imperial Way) ran through the center of the city from north to south. The imperial palace complex stood in the southern area of the city.

Visitors also arrived by boat, passing through one of the water gates that opened into the city's system of canals. The canals were spanned by stone bridges and shaded by plum, peach, pear, and apricot trees. Many of the canals were lined with bustling arcades and marketplaces, where one could buy anything — from salted fish and oranges to silk cloth and printed books. There was always a great deal of traffic on the water — taxis and other small craft darted around the long lines of barges that carried rice and other supplies into the city. (Hangzhou's population consumed over two tons of rice a day.)

Every day, a squadron of "pouring men" swept the streets and carted away the "night soil" (human waste) from the public lavatories. (The night soil was sold as manure to local farmers!) The local residents kept themselves clean in the many public bathhouses that were scattered throughout the city.

Because building land was scarce in the city, many of the houses had several stories. In most cases, the ground floor was

Along the northern bank of West Lake is the burial site of Yue Fei. Twenty years after his death , the patriotic warrior was "rehabilitated" in eyes of the court and people as a fallen hero. Today a temple stands next to his tomb. It encases a statue, 14 feet high and in full military gear. Above the statue are the four characters meaning "Return the Mountains and Rivers to Us," a reference to Yue Fei's resistance against the Jurchens. Before his tomb are four cast iron statues in a kneeling position. They represent prime minister Qin Gui, his wife, and two accomplices — the four people held responsible for Yue's murder will kneel in penitence for eternity. Today, modern Chinese tourists spit at the statues, and tourists are advised to bring an umbrella!

occupied by a shop or workroom, while several families shared the living space in the rooms above. Because fire was a serious danger, fire-fighters were posted in observation towers around the city. When a fire was spotted, they rushed to the site with their buckets and ropes. (This was probably history's first fire department.)

Just beyond the city walls lay the gleaming expanse of West Lake. This was originally a shallow bay, but its outlet to the Qiantang River silted up around the 7th century, making it a lake. At one time Su Shi, Wang Anshi's persistent opponent, had been a governor in Hangzhou. He drained and cleared the lake, turning it into a freshwater reservoir. He also had a causeway built so pleasure walkers could admire the still waters of the lake and the reflections of the pine-covered mountains rising just beyond. (Su Shi, remember, was also a poet.) Pagodas and pavilions rose here and there around the lake's circumference. Lotus flowers floated around the edges of the water, and willows gracefully dipped their branches along the gently sloping shores. Pleasure boats drifted across the water's sparkling surface. Some were floating restaurants, where a customer could enjoy a long, leisurely meal of rice, green beans, and roast duck or carp (from the very waters of the lake), washed down with the local rice wine.

As more workers crowded into the city, those who could afford moved to the hills surrounding the lake. This became the city's most prestigious address. The lavish homes of the wealthy were set around landscaped courtyards. Their sloping roofs of yellow or green tiles had up-curved edges. (Apart from the attractive look, the curved up edge of the roof of a Chinese dwelling, hall, or temple was intended to ward off evil spirits, which only move in a straight line.) The rooms of these homes were furnished sparsely with a few elegantly carved and inlaid tables, chairs, and couches. The beds had silk curtains that could be closed at

---

The Qiantang River flows along the eastern edge of Hangzhou toward the sea. Every year, just after the mid-autumn festival in September, crowds thronged to the estuary to watch the strange phenomenon of the river tide foaming against the sea walls. It began as a silver line across the horizon, approaching and growing with a noise of thunder until it could be seen as a line of foaming billows more than 12 feet high. This was the Angry Tide, or East Tide. Before it could subside, another line of high waves swept up from the south, collided with the East Tide and sent columns of water spouting high in the air. The waves were the result of high equinoctial tides being driven by strong winds through the funnel shape of the estuary. This strange phenomenon still happens today.

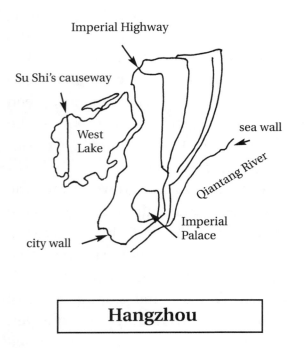

Hangzhou

lands in the north, looked for ways to strengthen the core of Chinese culture in their new setting. They founded academies of learning, promoted new printings of the Confucian classics, and debated how Confucian ideals should best be applied to the workings of government.

As you know, Confucius believed that good government was based upon the social hierarchy and strict codes of behavior practiced in traditional Chinese society. He assumed that people were of good intent and needed only to be taught how to lead virtuous lives. The king, or emperor, set an example of virtue for his subjects and ruled with the benevolent authority of the typical head of a family.

Over the centuries, elements of Daoism and Buddhism added a spiritual element to the Confucian code of ethics. Confucianists now began to speak in abstract terms and to concern themselves with cosmic forces, such as *yin* and *yang* and the universal energy force, *qi*. This eventually led to a reinterpretation of the philosophy, which is known as Neo-Confucianism.

night. Every room had a display of flowers, perhaps a group of peonies in a porcelain vase, or a single lotus blossom floating on the water in a shallow bowl — a microcosm of West Lake.

Neo-Confucianism

In the early years of the Southern Song, many scholars, disappointed with the failure of the government to regain the lost

---

The White Snake is a Chinese opera that has become popular in the United States. It is set at West Lake. Two snakes, one black and one white, turn into two beautiful maidens. They meet a handsome young man. One maiden (Suzhen) falls in love with him and marries him. The other (Xiao qing) serves as a housemaid. Later, a Buddhist priest discovers the secret of the bride's origins and captures her. She is buried in a magic bowl and a pagoda is built on top of her. Years later Xia Qing returns with an army of fighting crabs and shrimps to rescue Suzhen from her prison.

Zhu Xi (1130-1200) was the leading proponent of Neo-Confucianism during the Song dynasty. He combined the many interpretations of Confucian belief that had developed over the years and the new ideas proposed more recently into a unified whole. He wrote, compiled, or edited almost a hundred books, including many commentaries on the Confucian texts. He also helped establish academies in quiet mountain settings for teachers of Neo-Confucianism and their disciples to gather.

Zhu Xi believed that the human mind was linked to the primal forces of the universe. By developing his own intellectual potential (a process he called self-cultivation), a scholar should be able to understand the principles behind all living things. Zhu Xi used as the basis of his teaching two chapters from *The Book of Rites* (one of the Five Confucian Classics). He made these chapters into two separate new books, entitled *The Great Learning* and *The Doctrine of the Mean*. The first of these new books provides a model education for the individual, while the second describes such concepts as "the nature of the superior man." This superior man (*wen ren*) was a bookish fellow who devoted most of his time to "cultivating" his intellectual and artistic abilities. He became the ideal of the Neo-Confucian scholar official.

A century after the death of Zhu Xi, every candidate for the civil service exams had to master not only the Five Confucian Classics but also what came to be known as the Four Books of Confucianism (*The Analects*, *The Writings of Mencius*, *The Doctrine of the Mean*, and *The Great Learning*). Not only that — he had to know all of Zhu Xi's commentaries as well.

Overseas Trade

By the middle years of the Southern Song, an increasing number of ocean-going junks were carrying Chinese products to distant seaports. This was partly because the Silk Road, the major thoroughfare between East and West, was now blocked by unfriendly tribesmen. The sea routes made up what is known as the Maritime Silk Road. The cities of Guangzhou, Quanzhou, Xiamen, and Fuzhou became major shipping ports along China's southern coast.

As China took to the seas, her ships became the most advanced in the world. Watertight bulkheads with separate compartments in the hold enabled them to stay afloat even when they sprang a leak. They had as many as four decks, four or six masts, and a dozen sails, which were easily trimmed in the fierce storms that raged in the South China Sea. These large vessels could easily carry 500 men.

The ship's navigator used a compass to plot his course. The compass dated back to the Han dynasty, when it was discovered that lodestone (a type of iron ore) could be made to point south. Before long, someone found that a needle could be magnetized to do the same thing. By about 1000 CE, the Chinese had figured out the difference between the true north and magnetic north. The compass was used for centuries to align buildings. Its use as a navigation device was first mentioned in a book with a preface dated 1119.

The Chinese trading ships carried the products you would expect — tea, silk, lacquerware, porcelain, and books. They brought back rare woods, precious metals and gems, spices, and ivory. Sometimes, items as exotic as rhinoceros skins and crocodile teeth appeared in the markets of Hangzhou.

Foreign trade indirectly improved the lives of the Chinese peasants, because by collecting import duties from merchants the government was able to lessen the land tax. Another effect of the growth of trade was the increased use of paper money. A paper currency was nothing new. The Tang had used "flying money" (paper certificates for government purchases) in order to reduce transport costs. (Bags of metal coins are very heavy.) The world's first true paper money was printed in Chengdu (Sichuan) in 1024. The quality of the notes, which were printed in color on special paper, was backed by the government. By the late Song period, paper money was being used throughout China as well as abroad. Checks (written promises to pay certain amounts) also became common.

An Age of Affluence

The population continued to expand until, by the 13th century, nearly two million people lived in Hangzhou alone. The total population of China was about 120 million, over half of whom lived in the south. As more people reaped the benefits of trade and commerce, the upper classes expanded dramatically, and the demand for luxury objects was greater than ever.

The wealthy proclaimed their status by wearing clothes that tastefully set them apart from those of lesser importance. High officials showed their rank by the color of the robe they wore. Purple was the most prestigious hue, followed by crimson. Most officials wore caps with "feet" — strips of cloth that hung from each side. The feet were stiffened with wire or bamboo to make them curve or stand out. Lower officials their cap feet curved and crossed below their chins, while higher officials wore theirs straight. Only the emperor had the feet on his cap sticking straight out, par-

But while overseas trade blossomed, the majority of China's commerce took place through the country's vast network of waterways, which stretched for something like 30,000 miles.

powder, and cheeks were tinged with rouge. (A woman's pale face was considered an indicator that she never had to labor under the hot sun.) Eyebrows were removed and then redrawn as thin, black arches. This doll-like appearance was a far cry from the "natural look" that is so popular modern times.

Footbinding

In China's male-dominated society, women had few rights. Although a son had great respect for his mother (owing her the rites of *filial piety*), a woman was generally expected to perform her household duties without complaining and to do as she was told. Wealthy men took pride in the fact that they could afford to have wives who did no manual work at all. This idea was taken to extremes during the Southern Song period when footbinding became a common practice. The practice began in the 11th century among dancing women at court, who believed that smaller feet made them look dainty. This highly impractical procedure later became the fashion among the families of the courtiers and officials themselves, and it would spread to the population at large in later dynasties.

Footbinding was a painful process. When a girl reached the age of around five, her mother would wrap her feet tightly in long bands of wet cloth, bending the toes under the sole of the foot and forcing the

allel to the ground. Above is a portrait of Emperor Renzong wearing his cap with pointing feet. To show how little acquainted they were with manual labor, many literati let the nails on their little fingers grow very long to show. In fact, special hollow caps made of ivory or bamboo (highly decorated, of course!) were often worn to protect the long nails.

Fashionable women distinguished themselves by their delicate robes, blouses, and capes made of silk, and they prided themselves on their hairstyles. Most wore their lustrous black hair in buns, which could be more than a foot tall. (A woman never cut her hair unless a relative or close friend died.) The elegant coiffures were studded with ivory pins and silver or golden combs shaped like flowers, birds, phoenixes, or butterflies.

Wealthy women painted their nails with pink balsam leaves crushed in alum. Their pale faces were made even paler by arch into a high curve. The cloths shrank as they dried. When the foot stopped hurting, the bandages were removed and tightened. These wrappings, maintained throughout childhood and adolescence, naturally prevented the feet from achieving their normal growth. Gradually, over the course of several years, the arch of each foot would break and the toes would be permanently curled under, liked a deformed claw. The resulting tiny, misshapen foot, was called a "lily foot." Over time, the ideal foot size became smaller and the binding more crippling. By the 13th century, a lily foot was scarcely five inches long. Ultimately, the goal became a length of about three inches! A woman with bound feet wore special tiny silk shoes, which were beautifully embroidered. Since only the back edge of her heel could support her weight, she could not walk properly. Her attempts to walk resulted in a swaying gait that was considered feminine and graceful.

Like the long fingernails of the literati, bound feet were considered a badge of wealth and status, proclaiming that a family could afford to keep women who were incapable of physical labor. As the practice spread to the middle classes, bound feet became an essential requirement for obtaining a good marriage. This inhumane practice persisted until the 20th century.

Marriage In High Society

Marriage in China was a strictly practical matter, an alliance in which the interests of the two families took precedence over the feelings of the bride and groom. Marriage talks were often initiated by matchmakers, women skilled in the art of assessing the merits and requirements of the two sides and arranging terms. In some cases, the bride might not even meet the groom until the day of the wedding, when she rode to her husband's home in a red litter with her face veiled. (She certainly couldn't walk down an aisle with her bound feet!)

Once married, a woman became part of her husband's family, bound by the same obligations of filial piety to his parents as he was. If a husband died, his widow was forbidden to remarry. It was not the Confucian way.

Every father wanted sons, because they enhanced the family by bringing wives and children into his home. (Of course, he also needed a son to take his place as head of the family when he died.) Daughters, on the other hand, were expensive to raise, since they had to be provided with dowries. In many cases, parents did not form close attachments to their daughters, since they knew that they would be living with them a relatively short time.

Landscape Painting

The emperors of the Southern Song continued Huizong's tradition of patronizing the arts. Gaozong revived his father's Academy of Painting, and he actively encouraged poets, artists, and scholars from the north to come to his court in Hangzhou.

The change of venue had a tremendous effect upon landscape painting. In contrast to the rugged and majestic panoramas so typical of the northern paintings, the southern artists created scenes that seemed softer, more lyrical and serene. Using paler ink and wet brushstrokes, they tried to evoke the ethereal beauty of the mist-filled marshy waterlands of the Yangzi River valley. The wilder aspects of nature were tamed as artists took a gentler approach toward their art. Their works offered an intimacy that was lacking in the earlier works. Human beings were no longer tiny, nearly insignificant figures dwarfed by majestic mountains. Still very much in tune with their natural surroundings, the figures took on a greater role. Sometimes, a figure represented the artist himself, as he stood or sat admiring the view around him. A southern artist often created a sense of space by placing the landscape on one side and opening up a vista of limitless distance on the other. The viewer was invited to imagine what lay beyond. A poem was often inscribed in the space, written in elegant calligraphy, of course.

Although many of the paintings of the Southern Song painting have been lost, those that have survived give us a clear idea of the new style. The greatest landscape artists of the times were Ma Yuan and Xia Gui . Let's take a look at some of their works. As before, it will be helpful for you to find copies of the major paintings to be discussed: Ma Yuan's *On a Mountain Path in Spring* and Xia Gui's *Landscape in an Autumn Storm* and *A Pure and Remote View of Rivers and Mountains*.

A scholar in silken robes and cap is the subject of *On a Mountain Path in Spring*. He has been walking with his servant along the bank of a stream and has just stopped to watch an oriole take flight. The bird's mate sits on a branch of a willow, which is blowing gently in the breeze. To the left, softened peaks of mountains are poking above the mist, while to the right the stream flows into the distance. The scholar holds his hands close to his chest as if marveling at the beauty before him. The upper corner right corners has been left empty. It contains a verse describing the scene: "Brushed by his sleeves, wild flowers dance in the wind; fleeing from him, the hidden birds cut short their songs." As you view this gentle scene, your gaze is drawn from the details of the willow tree, the small bushes, the servant, and the scholar into the openness through which the oriole is flying. It seems like an invitation to move from the material world to a spiritual one. Using only a few simple elements, the artist has created a mood. Even without the lines of verse, the painting is a poem.

Xia Gui's *Landscape in an Autumn Storm* is a more dramatic scene. The leaves are being ripped off a tree that is bending in a violent wind, and a man wearing a floppy rain hat struggles over a footbridge to a hut beneath the tree. You can almost hear the wind howl. The top two thirds of the picture contain only a part of a sloping crag, with a forlorn-looking tree upon it, and the hint of a mountain peak far beyond. The rest is open space — imagine in it what you will.

A Pure and Remote View of Rivers and Mountains is a paper handscroll by the same artist. The rugged surface of the rocks and cliff face were made with brusque movements of the brush, known as the "ax-cut" stroke. In places, it seems as though the artist had stabbed the painting with his brush. The rough surfaces contrast with a frail and ricketly bridge, over which a single traveler is crossing. Beyond, the mist rises above the water and fills the rest of the painting, a few mountain peaks rising in the distance.

Calm Before the Storm

As the Southern Song dynasty entered its final years, the economy was buzzing, artists and artisans were creating beautiful works, and the government was running smoothly in the capable hands of the literati. Hangzhou had become the lively center of Chinese culture. But while the people of the balmy south were enjoying peace a prosperity, ominous changes were occurring in other parts of Asia that would threaten the serenity of the Yangzi River valley.

Buddhist monasteries lay in the hills above West Lake. In this idyllic setting, a number of priests were inspired to paint, but their works were very different from those of their contemporaries. Muqi painted a variety of subjects, including monkeys, birds, and tigers. In each case, he drew his subject with broad strokes, concentrating details in one place and surrounding it with open space. His painting entitled *Six Persimmons* is an excellent example of his ability to lend great significance to the simplest thing. Often was is not seen is most important. Zan Ran's *Seeking Instruction in the Autumnal Mountains* has no human figure visible, only the faintly seen thatch of a rustic monastery nestled in at the foot of a hill.

Review Questions:

1. How would you describe Gaozong's state of mind during the early months of his reign?

2. Who was Yue Fei?

3. What was unusual about the poems of Li Qingzhao?

4. What settlement did the Southern Song make with the Jin in 1135?

5. Why was southern China (the region of the Yangzi) a richer region than northern China?

6. What were the advantages of Hangzhou's location?

7. What are the two or three basic steps in making porcelain?

8. What is lacquerware?

9. What enabled the Song to drive back the Jurchen invaders in 1150?

10. Describe the area of West Lake.

11. How did Neo-Confucianism differ from Confucianism?

12. How did overseas trade affect China's economy?

13. What was the purpose of footbinding?

14. How did the landscape paintings of the Southern Song differ from those of the Northern Song?

15. Who were the major painters of the Southern Song?

Projects:

1. Make a timeline of the Southern Song dynasty.

2. Read some of the poems of Li Qingzhao and share them with your classmates.

3. Some of the finest Chinese porcelain was made during the Song dynasty. Consult several books on Chinese art and find out more about specific styles, such as celadon. Write a report or make a poster, using xeroxed pictures from the art books (or those downloaded from the Internet) as illustrations of Song porcelain.

4. Consult several sources about Chinese junks. Write a report or make a model of one of the ships.

5. Throughout much of Chinese history, emperors were able to balance the multiple beliefs of the "Three Teachings." Southern Song Emperor Xiaozong (reigned 1162-89) once remarked that he valued "Buddhism for control of the mind, Daoism for control of the body, and Confucianism for control of the world." Explain what he meant by this statement. Give examples to support you explanation. Lead a discussion based upon his statement with your classmates.

6. Consult several art books and find other examples of Southern Song landscape paintings. Choose one. Study it closely. Try to describe its style and content in your own words. Find out more about the artist. When you feel you know the work and its creator well, make a presentation about them to the class.

7. Using clay, cardboard, and whatever other materials you can find, make a model of West Lake and its scenic shores. Or make a model of Hangzhou.

8. Learn more about Chinese festivals. Read *Mooncakes and Hungry Ghosts: Festivals of China* by Carol Stepanchuck and Charles Wong (San Francisco: China Books and Periodicals, 1991.)

8. Chinese pictures contain more meaning than might be evident at first viewing. Symbols abound, mood is suggested by darkness and light, and the very placement of objects and natural features indicates certain things. The principles of *feng shui* are as important in a landscape painting as in the design of a city. The presence of ominous forces lurking about or more felicitous spirits are indicated by the shape of clouds, the type and positioning of trees, the flow of a stream, the depiction of the grass, the contour of a rock, the orientation of a mountain, and even the posture of a figure. Find out more about *feng shui*, and apply some of its principles to the paintings you have studied so far.

Important Happenings Elsewhere In The World
(1127 — 1276)

Second Crusade — 1147-49
Khmer temple Angkor Wat built in Cambodia — c. 1150
Aztecs destroy Toltec Empire in Mexico — c. 1166
Jury system established in England — 1166
Bologna University granted charter by Frederick I — 1158
Magna Carta — 1215
Louis XI King of France — 1226-70
Mali Empire established in West Africa — c. 1235

Chapter 4
The Yuan Dynasty
(1271 - 1368)
The Mongolian Interlude

For to the north of China, beyond the Gobi Desert, lies Mongolia. It is part of the Asian steppes, a vast arid grassland that stretches all the way to Europe. Temperatures here range from 40 degrees below freezing in winter to over 100 degrees in summer, and in all seasons ferocious winds can blast down from Siberia with enough force to blow a rider off his horse.

The Chinese had been defending their borders against nomadic tribesmen from the north for centuries. Shi Huangdi had built the original Great Wall in the 3rd century BCE to protect his empire against such attacks, and the long barrier had been reinforced by his successors. But, as we have seen, non-Chinese forces managed not only to get through the wall but even to set up their own states within it.

In the 12th century, bands of tribesmen known as the Mongols made their home in the desolate region that bears their name today. They were destined to have a great impact upon China as well as other places as distant as eastern Europe.

Life on the Steppes

The Mongols forged a way of life in the unforgiving climate of the steppes by herding sheep and horses. They lived in family bands and moved with the seasons, seeking pastures for their animals in the open grasslands in the summer and returning to the protection of more protected valleys when winter approached. Their sheep provided them with wool and meat — mutton stew was the typical meal, and roasted sheep tails were considered a special delicacy. The horses were used for transport and warfare. Many bands also kept camels and oxen as pack animals.

Highlights of This Chapter

The Rise of Genghis Kahn
The Mongols Invade China
The Rise of Kublai Kahn
The Conquest of the Song
Yuan Society
Kublai's Capitals
Marco Polo
Protest Through Art
Chinese Drama
The Red Turbans

Mongol families lived in round tents called yurts. These were made of felt — thick blanket-like material made from boiled wool. The felt was stretched over a framework of wooden poles. (It was often coated with animal fat to make it waterproof.) A yurt was a sturdy shelter that could withstand very high winds. A fire burning in the central hearth kept it warm and cozy in winter, the smoke escaping through a hole in the center of the roof. Since there was little wood on the steppes, the fire was fueled with the dried dung of the animals. The family sat and slept on blankets and sheepskins around the hearth. When it was time to move on, the yurt was easily disassembled, although the large dwelling of a chieftain was often moved intact on a wagon drawn by oxen.

The Mongols had a deep respect for the natural elements that governed their lives. The father of each family bowed before the sun at dawn to thank the spirits for the blessings of a new day, and before each meal he rubbed meat over the mouths of small statues of nature gods, sharing his bounty with them. Shamans (religious leaders) claimed to have the power to summon spirits, to foretell the future, and to heal sickness. They led tribal rituals, during which the men often consumed an intoxicating beverage made from fermented mare's milk, known as *koumiss*.

Fearsome Warriors

At the age of three, a Mongol boy was taught to ride a gentle horse by his mother. He received his first bow and arrows soon afterwards, and by the age of ten he could shoot a moving target while guiding his mount with his legs. Every male in a clan between the ages of 14 and 60 was ready to jump upon his horse and fight whenever called upon. And there were plenty of opportunities, since rival bands frequently battled over rights to pastureland, and raids of Chinese farming settlements were not uncommon. Each man swore loyalty to his leader, and cowardice was simply not tolerated.

A Mongol warrior had between three and eight horses, which he took with him on battle campaigns. Although the horses were small of stature, they had tremendous stamina. Specially designed saddles and iron stirrups gave the horsemen stability, enabling them to fire their arrows with deadly accuracy — either forward or to the rear — while moving at a full gallop.

The Mongols specialized in surprise

The "Mongolian hot-pot" is a popular dish today derived from the mutton stew eaten by the tribesmen centuries ago. Modern diners sit around a circular vessel filled with boiling water and heated by a small charcoal burner. They dip pieces of mutton and vegetables in the water until they are cooked.

attack, often forming columns of riders to surround an enemy before moving in for the kill. They didn't take prisoners. Fighting was a way of life for the Mongols — it provided the means of acquiring riches, personal honor, and power.

The Rise of Genghis Kahn

Around the middle of the 12th century, groups of Mongols were fighting for dominance against a rival tribe, known as the Tatars. In 1161, the Tatars allied themselves with the Jurchen rulers of northern China and defeated the Mongols. But the lull in the fighting was only temporary, and hostilities between the two tribes soon resumed.

The following year, a boy was born to a Mongol chieftain who would become one of the great legends of history. His father named him Temujin, after a Tatar leader he had captured in battle. When Temujin was nine years old, he was taken by his father to eastern Mongolia to find a bride among his mother's people. He was soon betrothed to

Borte, the ten-year-old daughter of a local chieftain. Temujin was left there to be brought up in the yurt of his future father-in-law, according to the Mongol custom. As his father was traveling home, he was captured, poisoned, and left to die by a party of Tatars. He survived long enough to return to his camp and tell his men what had happened.

Temujin was immediately summoned home to succeed his father as chieftain. He was to be advised by his uncles

A fighting unit of Mongols on the move could cover nearly 60 miles a day. Sometimes this meant sleeping in the saddle. And if there was no water, a rider would slit open one of his horse's veins, drink the blood, and bandage the wound before pressing on. The Mongolian horses were an exceptionally hardy breed, and they were highly valued by the tribesmen. When a warrior died, his faithful steed was killed and buried with him.

until he came of age, but his claim to power was soon challenged by a strong faction of clansmen. Temujin was forced out, and he and his mother and siblings had to fend for themselves, subsisting on wild plants and mice. He vowed that he would avenge his family's loss of wealth and authority.

Eventually, the little family acquired a few sheep and horses and joined another band. As he grew older, Temujin impressed his new kinsmen with his cunning and courage. He later became a chieftain, and by the time he was thirty he had built up a large army. In 1202 he invaded the Tatar homeland and brought his old enemies to their knees, thus avenging the death of his father. He then continued on an aggressive campaign across Mongolia, destroying those who resisted him and luring others over to his side.

In the spring of 1205, the tribal princes assembled near the sources of the Onon River in northern Mongolia to swear loyalty to Temujin. They bestowed upon him the title of *Genghis Khan* (Jeeng gus Kawn, "Universal Ruler"). As he hoisted his standard of nine white horsetails, he accepted the honor in the name of the gods, proclaiming that they (the gods) had ordained that he should "rule all nations beneath the blue skies." Clearly, his ambitions had no limit.

The War Machine

Under the leadership of Genghis Khan, the Mongols became the greatest nomadic fighting force of all time. He divided his vast army into 95 units. Each unit (called a *quran*) was made up of 1,000 armed horsemen, who lived with their families on pasturelands that had been assigned to them. A *quran* was divided into squadrons of 100 men. A squadron was further divided into 10 squads of 10 men. Genghis insisted upon strict discipline among his troops and required daily drills so that they would be prepared to respond quickly to a variety of battle strategies.

The Imperial Guard was an elite corps of bodyguards, who served the khan directly. It was made up of the sons and brothers of his commanders. The guard became a sort of officers' training school, supplying a pool of highly trained young leaders familiar with the khan's methods of warfare and personally devoted to him.

A key to a successful military campaign is communication, and Genghis Khan had a master plan. He established a highly efficient messenger system, which

Every Mongol warrior wore a shirt fashioned from tightly woven silk as added protection against arrow wounds. An arrowhead would push the fabric into the wound ahead of it; a physician could later remove the arrow by gently pulling out the silk.

enabled commanders hundreds of miles apart to communicate with one another. His network of relay stations stretched across Mongolia, and would later be extended well beyond the borders of his homeland. Hard-riding messengers galloped from one relay station to the next, leaping upon a fresh mount at each one. (The horses wore bells to warn of their approach.) Riding his horses to the point of exhaustion, a messenger could cover over 200 miles in a day.

The Mongols Invade China

With Mongolia under his control, Genghis led his troops east to conquer Manchuria and Korea. Then he moved south, chasing the Jurchen soldiers through the Great Wall. After sweeping down China's western flank and subduing the Tanguts, he was ready to proceed into the heart of northern China. He wasted no time launching his assault, crushing armies and sacking over 90 cities as he marched east toward the Jin capital. In 1214, his warriors advanced to the gates of the city, but were bought off (temporarily) with the offer of a Jin princess (and a huge dowry) for the khan. (Genghis would eventually have 500 wives!) As the Mongols withdrew, the Jin court quickly fled to Kaifeng, where they would govern a much-reduced territory for about 20 years. The next year, the old Jin capital was attacked and taken by Genghis Khan. According to legend, it burned for over a month.

The Expanding Empire

With most of northern China in his pocket, Genghis led his warriors westward into Central Asia. They mowed down every army that rose against them. In 1221 they

When Temujin was rising to power, the Mongols had no written language. In the process of uniting the tribes of Mongolia, he came into conflict with the Uighurs, a nomadic tribe that had a written alphabet. After an army of Uighurs (Wee gurs) was defeated by Mongol warriors, one of their scribes was captured on the battlefield as he searched for his master. Temujin summoned him to his headquarters and gave him the task of transcribing the Mongolian language into the Uighur script. This was a daunting undertaking, but the scribe was able to devise a Mongol alphabet.

Thanks to his efforts, the Mongols were now able to record military messages, treaties, and decrees. They also published a code of laws (the *Yasa*), which was followed during the lifetime of Genghis Kahn and for a considerable period afterwards. The *Yasa* reaffirmed the kahn's absolute authority, spelled out harsh penalties for crimes such as murder and stealing, and required every man and woman to keep ready for battle. The earliest example of a Mongol chronicle that still exists is *The Secret History of the Mongols*, dating from 1228. It describes the exploits of Genghis Khan and his ancestors and is a priceless resource for modern historians.

conquered modern Turkestan, including the major trading cities of Bukhara and Samarkand. Some squadrons even moved into Russia. By the time Genghis died in 1227 (he fell from his horse in battle), the Mongols controlled a vast empire stretching from the Pacific Ocean to the Caspian Sea.

The Next Generation

After the death of Genghis Khan, the empire was divided into four parts. Each part was to be governed by one of the khan's sons or grandsons. His third son, Ogodei, was named ruler of Mongolia; since he controlled the homeland, most considered him the heir of Genghis Khan. (He would be known as the Great Khan.) Ogodei finished off the Jin in 1234 and took over the rest of northern China. There is a famous story about one of his commanders suggesting that the entire Jin population (Chinese and Jurchen) be eliminated and the land used as pasture for the herds of Mongol horses. Yelu Chucai, a former counselor of the Jin who had joined the Mongol side, argued that the local people should be left in possession of their lives and land. He pointed out that taxation was a more reliable long-term source of wealth than plunder. Ogodei saw the logic of his argument. Thanks to Yelu Chucai, the lives of many thousands of people of northern China were spared. The people of Chengdu, the major city in Sichuan, were not so lucky. Ogodei led his warriors on a rampage through that area, striking a deadly blow to city after city. Although Chengdu put up little resistance, he ordered the slaughter of over a million people who lived there.

Ogodei then joined his brothers in a western campaign. Having expanded the ranks of their armies with warriors recruited from other tribes, they set out on a ruthless march across Central Asia, attacking and plundering city after city. Those who resisted were herded outside the city walls and executed. After the grisly massacre, the buildings were thoroughly razed to the ground: the Mongols boasted that if a horseman galloped over the site of a city they had destroyed in the darkness of night, his horse would not stumble on a single brick. As word of the atrocities spread, most cities in their path immediately surrendered.

The terrible slaughter extended into Europe. Batu, a grandson of Genghis Kahn, led his warriors across Russia, capturing Moscow and Kiev. Then the army fanned out into Poland, Bohemia, and Hungary. The Mongols who invaded Europe came to be known as the Golden Horde – "golden" for all the riches they acquired and "horde" after the Mongolian word *ordo*, which means "elite cavalry force." They inspired such terror that mothers hushed their children with the warning, "Be quiet, or the

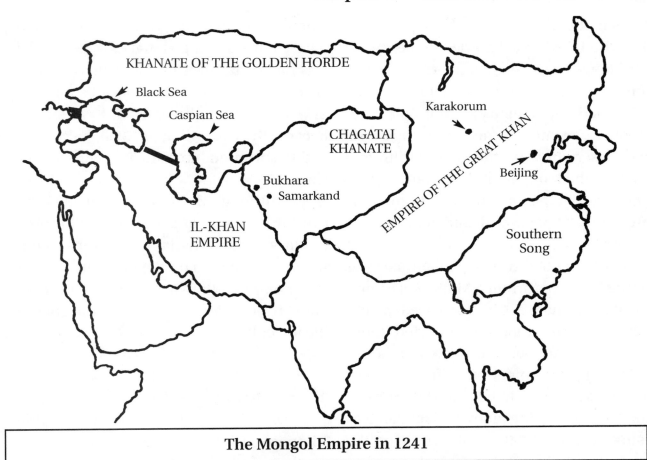

KHANATE OF THE GOLDEN HORDE

Black Sea

Caspian Sea

CHAGATAI
KHANATE

Karakorum

EMPIRE OF THE GREAT KHAN

Beijing

Bukhara
Samarkand

IL-KHAN
EMPIRE

Southern
Song

The Mongol Empire in 1241

Mongols will come and get you!" Late in 1241, an army of warriors was preparing to assault the walls of Vienna when news arrived that Ogodei had died. Europe was spared further devastation only because the Mongol leaders had to return to Karakorum, their capital in Mongolia, to elect a new Great Khan. Batu's descendants, however, would rule southern Russia for the next 200 years.

After these conquests, the Mongol empire was immense. It was divided into four parts: the Khanate of the Golden Horde, the Chagatai Khanate, the Il-Khan Empire, and the Empire of the Great Khan. (Find them on the map above.)

Ogodei's Successors

Ogodei was succeeded by a grandson, Guyug. Soon after his crowning in Karakorum, Guyug greeted 60-year-old Franciscan friar, John of Plano Carpini, an envoy of Pope Innocent IV. The friar presented the Pope's request that the Mongols stop their relentless campaigns and convert to Christianity. Guyug responded that his forces had every reason to annihilate peoples who failed to acknowledge the rule of the Mongols, since their authority came from the gods themselves. (Remember the claim made by Genghis Khan on his coronation?) Carpini returned to Europe with vivid descriptions of the great wealth and power of the Mongols and the warning that the savage horsemen intended "to overthrow the whole world and reduce it to slavery."

Guyug died two years later and was succeeded by his brother, Mongke. The new Great Khan had a Chinese-styled palace built in Karakorum. He imported thousands of craftsmen from distant lands, including a goldsmith from Paris. Meanwhile, armies led by another brother, Hulagu, overran the cities of Baghdad and Damascus. In 1259, while Hulagu was preparing to march on Jerusalem in an alliance with the Christian Crusaders, Mongke suddenly died.

The Rise of Kublai Kahn

Mongke was succeeded by his brother, Kublai (Koo bly). This new ruler was to be the greatest of the descendants of Genghis Khan. Kublai had been born the year his grandfather captured the Jin capital. He was raised and educated in China, where he developed a great respect for the local culture. During Mongke's reign, Kublai was made the governor of northern China. He depended upon the advice of a number of Confucian scholars, and when he became the Great Khan in 1260, he continued to surround himself with Chinese officials.

Although he was technically the overlord of the entire Mongol Empire, Kublai's actual domain was the region shown on the map on the previous page as the Empire of the Great Khan. The three other regions remained under the rule of the lesser khans.

The Yuan Dynasty

In 1271, Kublai assumed the title "Emperor of China," even though the Southern Song dynasty was still flourishing in the south. He named his new dynasty Yuan (Yoo ahn, meaning "Great Origin"). This name appeared in the Confucian classic, *The Book of Changes*, and Kublai hoped that by adopting it he would demonstrate his support for Chinese culture and strengthen his position among the Chinese people. He transferred his capital from Karakorum to a site near the ruins of the Jin capital and began building an impressive

The Mongolian name for the Yuan capital near present-day Beijing was Khanbalik, "City of the Khan."

new city known by the Chinese as Dadu (meaning "Great Capital").

Kublai's new government was headed by a large ministry, the Secretariat, which oversaw six smaller ministries. Since the Mongols were relatively few in number (there were only about 1.5 million), the khan initially allowed the local people to rule themselves — but under Mongol supervision.

Conquest of the Song

Kublai's highest priority was to conquer the richest part of China — the Yangzi River valley. But defeating the Southern Song was no easy task. The network of waterways and rice paddies in the south made the traditional style of Mongolian warfare — frontal attacks by armed horsemen — nearly impossible. Besides, the Song cities were defended by stout fortifications and well-armed troops.

Back in the days when Genghis Khan first invaded northern China, the top Song ministers had debated for many long hours how to best respond to the Mongol presence. Some urged the policy of sending tribute, which had kept the Jin forces at bay. Others proposed aggressive military action,

feeling confident that they could defeat the Mongols with their superior weaponry and their excellent navy. But nothing was ever decided, so no actions were ever taken.

The first Mongol forays into the south were easily repulsed by the exploding missiles of the Song. But the tables were turned when the Mongols learned how to make gunpowder. Kublai hired Muslim engineers to construct huge, counter-weighted catapults that could throw a barrage of rocks weighing up to a hundred pounds each against the high, thick walls of the southern cities. The Mongols also seized a few Song warships and used them as models to build their own fleet. Well aware that his kinsmen were warriors, not sailors, Kublai hired Chinese boatmen to navigate them. The ships were broad enough to transport squadrons of horses and riders. A ship could easily make it to the riverbank at any time and let down a ramp. The horsemen could then gallop down the ramp to fight on the land.

In 1268, the newly equipped Mongol forces attacked Fanchang and Xiangyang, two cities on the Han river that were key to control of the Yangzi valley. After a five-year siege, the constant pounding of the walls

Many stories that have survived about Kublai Khan. In one, his chief adviser, a former Buddhist monk named Liu Bingzhong, remarks that although the empire has been conquered on horseback, it cannot be administered on horseback. In other words, force might be the means to achieving power, but governing depends upon thoughtful negotiation and management.

and launching of gunpowder-filled shells brought about the fall of Fancheng. When the commanders in Xiangyang heard the news, they immediately surrendered. The route to the Yangzi valley was now clear.

As word arrived in Hangzhou about the looming Mongol threat, the Song officials continued arguing about what to do. The emperor (Gongzong) was a child, with his grandmother (Empress Dowager Xie) serving as regent. Since there was no effective leadership, the fate of the dynasty was left in the hands of the the military.

In 1275, a huge Mongol force began making its way down the Yangzi. It soon encountered a Song fleet of 2,500 ships. The Mongols put their cavalry ashore on both banks of the river, covering them by barrages of missiles aimed at the enemy vessels. The horsemen easily mowed down the defending Song soldiers, forcing them to retreat.

As the invaders proceeded eastward, the Empress Dowager appealed to the local people to rise up and defend their homeland. But there was no stopping the Mongols. They smashed through the walls of Changzhou, a city on the Grand Canal 100 miles north of Hangzhou, brutally slay-ing most of the 100,000 inhabitants. The bodies were piled up and covered with dirt, creating a mound over 40 feet high that stretched across nearly an acre of land. This sent a terrible message to other Song strongholds planning to resist.

As the Mongols approached Hangzhou, the Empress Dowager wisely surrendered the city before any blood was spilled. The dynasty of the Southern Song had officially come to an end. Gongzong and his family were later sent to Dadu, where Kublai saw to it that they were treated with respect. The former emperor would live out his life in the Mongol capital, in his later years becoming a Buddhist monk.

But although the Song government had surrendered, many southern Chinese continued to resist the Mongols. A motley crew of scholars, poets, peasants, and bandits rallied around the emperor's younger brothers — Duanzong (whom they now called emperor) and Bingdi — as a last hope to preserve the Song dynasty.

Three years later, the court of the acting emperor boarded a fleet of warships and escaped to the safety of the sea, just as Gaozong had done over a century earlier. By now, Duanzong had died (some say of

Kublai's favorite wife, Chabi, was an intelligent, well-read woman. She strongly supported his policy of conciliation, personally taking care of the defeated Song royal family when they arrived in Dadu. Kublai had four wives, but Chabi was the only one with a major influence on him. Of his 12 sons, only hers attained eminence.

fright) and Bingdi had assumed his title. The ships carrying the court joined the rest of the Song fleet and sailed south. They maneuvered into a defensive line off the island of Yaishan (present day Hong Kong). The commanders assumed the Mongols would attack immediately, and they were confident they could hold them off. But the Mongols waited for several days. Then, under cover of night, they surrounded the Chinese vessels, cutting off their supply of fresh water.

Two weeks later, the Song sailors and passengers were dying of thirst. This is when the Mongols attacked with a panoply of rockets, flaming arrows, and grenades. Most of the Song ships were sunk, although a few of the lighter vessels escaped. Thousands of men flung themselves into the water to avoid being taken captive by the dreaded Mongols. One minister tried to save Bingdi by jumping overboard with him in his arms. But the boy, weighed down by his yellow robe and the imperial seals of gold that were strapped to his waist, slowly sank beneath the surface of the sea.

So ended the Song resistance. The literati who had remained in the southern cities would continue their own form of passive resistance to the Yuan dynasty. And although southern China was now in the hands of the Mongols, Hangzhou would remain a center of Chinese culture for

The Yuan Empire in 1279

many centuries to come.

Cultural Differences

For the first time in history, all of Inner China was in the hands of a non-Chinese ruler. This would have an enormous effect upon the traditional way of life. The Chinese, as you know, had long considered their homeland the center of the world (the Middle Kingdom) and their civilization the standard by which all others were judged. The Mongols, however, had dealt with many cultures throughout Asia and eastern Europe. They regarded China as only one part of their vast empire and

Chinese civilization as only one among many.

Furthermore, the basic lifestyles of the Mongols and the Chinese were worlds apart. Since their origins on the steppes, the Mongols had been a robust, physically active people, who loved to hunt when they weren't engaged in warfare. They scorned the more sedentary ways of the Chinese. For their part, the Chinese generally viewed the invaders as uncouth and undisciplined barbarians who smelled badly. The differences between nomadic hunters and settled farmers were magnified when both groups found themselves living together.

Of course, Kublai Khan was not a typical Mongol. As you know, he valued Chinese culture and tried in many ways to adapt to it. He worked hard at managing his dual role as Chinese emperor and Mongolian khan. He dressed in Chinese robes on formal occasions, encouraged Confucian rituals, and sponsored performances of Chinese music and dance at his court. He hired Chinese scholars to translate the great classics and official dynastic histories into the Mongol language. He had a temple built to honor Confucius, and he even exempted Confucian scholars from paying taxes. Although he disbanded the civil service examination system, he allowed Confucianism to remain the foundation of Chinese society.

At the same time, Kublai saw to it that ancestral tablets were set up for Genghis Khan and his other Mongolian ancestors near the palace grounds, and he followed the traditions of the ancient religion of the steppes. Every August, for example, he performed the Mongol ritual of scattering mare's milk, while bowing to the heavens and calling out the name of his revered grandfather, Genghis. This was intended to bring good luck for the coming year. Kublai loved to hunt, and he had screens of ermine skin placed in his sleeping chambers to remind him of the joys of the chase in Mongolia.

A New Social Order

To compensate for the fact that the Mongols were outnumbered nearly one to ten and to reinforce his own authority, Kublai divided all of his subjects into four classes. The Mongols, of course, formed the top class. They ran the military. The second class was made up of miscellaneous foreigners, mostly from western and central Asia, although a few came from as far away as Italy. Many of the foreigners were well educated, and Kublai appointed them to high-level government positions. Muslims

The Yuan court, fearful of its own non-Mongol officials, increased the authority of the Censorate to spy on the bureaucracy and to report abuses in the government and the military.

also enriched Yuan society as architects, physicians, astronomers, military engineers, merchants, poets and musicians. Ranked below the foreigners were the northern Chinese, the people with whom Kublai had grown up. The khan kept a few carefully selected Chinese scholars as advisers. And as you might expect, the lowest class of Yuan society was made up of the southern Chinese, former subjects of the Southern Song dynasty.

Kublai further separated the Mongols and foreigners from the Chinese by imposing a rigid set of social regulations. Chinese people were forbidden to congregate in public and could not own weapons — they were even prohibited from dealing in bamboo because it could be used for making bows and arrows. All Chinese were subject to stricter punishments than non-Chinese. For example, Mongol criminals could often avoid imprisonment by paying a large fine, whereas Chinese criminals were automatically imprisoned (with the sentence of a slow death ordered for especially hardened offenders). The Chinese and the Mongols were further required to use their own languages, dress, and customs. Intermarriage between them was prohibited.

Kublai was tolerant of other religious beliefs as long as they did not conflict with his own interests. (His mother, who became a Christian, had encouraged such open-mindedness.) He and his favorite wife, Chabi, were Buddhists. Kublai granted the Tibetan lama (leader) jurisdiction over the province of Tibet and contributed funds and land for the building of Buddhist temples and monasteries. Muslims were free to worship as they wished throughout China, and Daoism remained a strong influence in all levels of Chinese society.

Kublai's Gleaming Capital

China's rich resources enabled the Mongols to live in a luxurious style they had never known in their homeland. Dadu became Kublai's showcase. Like a traditional Chinese city, it was built on a square that was aligned with the four cardinal directions. It was surrounded by a high earthen

---

Kublai Khan encouraged the production of treatises on mathematics, cartography, astronomy, and water conservancy. Chinese astronomer and mathematician Gho Shoujing was employed to build 27 observatories, of which the observatory at Gaocheng zhen is the oldest surviving example. A Persian astronomer, Jamal-ad Din, was summoned to court in 1267, bringing a new more accurate calendar and several globes of the world. The Muslim Institute of Astronomy was established, and Persian doctors worked in newly founded hospitals as well as the Imperial Academy of Medicine. Kublai also authorized the compilation of the Basic Elements of Agriculture and Sericulture.

wall and entered through twelve gates, three in each of the four wall segments. Nine streets going east-west intersected nine others going north-south, forming a grid. The grid of streets divided the city's residential area into 50 neighborhoods, called *fangs*.

Beyond the residential area was a huge park surrounded by another square wall. In the park were ponds stocked with exotic fish and gardens filled with trees and shrubs transplanted from many parts of Asia. One tract of land was planted with steppe grass to remind the khan of his Mongolian homeland. A man-made mound of earth 100 paces high was crowned with an ornamental pavilion.

In the middle of the park stood Kublai's magnificent palace complex. It had 400 rooms, one being so large it could hold 6,000 dinner guests. The rooms were furnished with tables and chairs made of carved ebony, rosewood, and teak, and the walls were hung with huge silk paintings. The palace roofs were covered with gilded and varnished cane, which glittered in the sun as though they were made from solid gold.

Canals and Highways

The city of Dadu quickly grew until it had half a million people, and the local food supply was no longer sufficient. Additional grain and other produce needed to be brought in from the south. The question was how. Roads in the region were poor, and the Grand Canal did not extend as far north as the city. Besides, the canal had fallen into disrepair when the Jin ruled the north. At first, shiploads of food were brought to Dadu by sea, but frequent storms often hampered deliveries. In 1286, Kublai assembled a work force of nearly three million laborers to restore the Grand Canal and extend it 135 miles north, linking his capital with the rice fields to the south. Muslim engineers constructed a section of waterway over a small mountain using a system of locks.

The improved canal system solved the problem of food supplies, but there remained the issue of communications between the central government and the towns and cities throughout China. Kublai had a wide, stone-surfaced imperial highway built to connect Dadu with Hangzhou, 1,100 miles to the south. Do you remember Genghis Khan's postal relay system? Kublai

Despite the luxurious comfort offered by the palace, many of Kublai's sons and their cousins opted to live in yurts pitched on the imperial grounds amid the grass that had been transplanted from the steppes of their homeland. They scorned Chinese robes and wore their traditional garb of furs and leather.

expanded it until the network of roads linked his capital not only with other parts of China but also with major cities throughout the sprawling Mongol empire.

Overland Trade

The post roads were open to merchants and other travelers, but only those carrying a *paizu* (an official "tablet of authority") could take advantage of the supplies and other amenities offered at the stations. A paizu was a foot long and three inches wide and was made of wood, copper, or gold. It was inscribed with the words "By the strength of the eternal Heaven, sacred be the name of the Khan. Let him that pays him not reverence be killed."

The roads connected with the Silk Road, the network of trade routes dating back to the days of the Han dynasty. Trade along the Silk Road had been disrupted during the centuries of the Song, when nomads controlled parts of central Asia. But now the Mongols held all the land along the entire length of the Silk Road; for the first and only time, the overland route between China and Europe was under one authority. The slow-moving caravans of camels, laden with heavy loads of silk, tea, gems, and other products, were carefully monitored by Mongol patrols, and local governors were held responsible for their safety. This led one Chinese writer to remark, "A maiden bearing a nugget of gold on her head could wander safely through the [Mongolian] realm." While his boast is somewhat exaggerated, historians refer to this period of free and open trade as the *Pax Mongolica* ("Mongol Peace").

China was now part of an integrated Eurasian international community, and this led to many more contacts with the West than ever before. A steady stream of traders and diplomats traveled to Dadu along the improved system of roads, and the capital city soon had resident communities of merchants from as far away as Russia and Constantinople.

Marco Polo

The most famous traveler of the Silk Road was Marco Polo. In 1260, his father and uncle, both merchants of Venice, had visited China. Their ability to speak Turkic dialects enabled them to communicate directly with Kublai Khan. (The Turkic peo-

Throughout the vast road system were 10,000 stations, stocked with 300,000 horses. The stations stocked were located every 25-30 miles along major routes and every 35-40 miles in areas without roads. Urgent messages were carried from one station to the next by riders (*bukhia*) of great courage and stamina. They were very much like the Pony Express riders of the American West. And in Siberia, trained dog teams pulled messengers from one station to the next.

ples were the nomads who roamed the steppes of central Asia and Mongolia since early times.) The Polos returned home a year later with a message of friendship from the Great Khan addressed to the Pope, along with a request for for 100 learned priests and some oil from the lamp burning over the Holy Sepulcher at Jerusalem. The two men were issued tablets of authority (paizu), so they were able to stop at the postal stations on their journey.

The Polo brothers returned to China in 1275, but without the priests. (Pope Gregory had sent only two Dominican friars, and they had abandoned the journey at the first sign of physical hardship.) They *did* have a flask of the oil, however. But of greater importance, they were accompanied by Niccolo's 17-year-old son, Marco. He took detailed notes in his journal, thoughtfully describing their long, difficult trek through the rugged terrain of the Silk Road. The travelers arrived in China in May 1275 and were immediately granted an audience with Kublai. Marco so impressed the Great Khan with his knowledge of business, his powers of observation, and his proficiency with languages that he was invited to become a foreign adviser.

The three Italians remained in China for 17 years. Marco was sent on several fact-finding missions in China, Burma, and India. During these expeditions, he was very observant of the local customs he encountered, and he later described them in a book. (More about that later.) He was intrigued by the bits of paper with which "you can buy anything," having never seen a paper currency before. He was amazed by the public bathhouses located in every town and city and the fact that people actually bathed several times a week — some even on a daily basis. (Europeans tended to bathe only occasionally, and often not at all during the cold months.) He noted how the bathhouses and many private homes were heated by "stones that burn like logs." (These stones were coal, a fuel not used in Europe until 400 years later.)

Marco was impressed by the imperial messengers who sped along the post roads, and he discovered that there was also a lower priority service, in which messages were carried in 3-mile segments by foot-runners. He marveled at the size and complexity of the Chinese iron industry and the amount of salt collected (30,000 tons a year in one province alone). In the

---

In 1340 Italian traveler Francesco Pegolotti compiled a guidebook for travelers of the Silk Road, giving details of stopping places and the distances between them. He also listed the duties levied on particular products of trade, including such exotic items as salted sturgeon tails, nutmeg, Slavonian squirrel skins, amber, and "dragon's blood."

more remote regions, he observed people who covered their teeth with gold, men who tattooed their entire bodies, and "loaves" of salt that were used as money. At one seaport, he watched sailors test the strength of the wind before embarking on a sea voyage by sending a man up in a kite.

Marco spent some time studying a segmental arch bridge that stretched over the Yongding River in Dadu. This style of bridge was invented by the Chinese in the 7th century. The bridge in Dadu had a succession of 11 segmental arches of stone and was 700 feet long. It was wide enough for ten mounted men to ride abreast across it. The balustrades that ran along each side of the bridge were decorated with 283 marble lion heads. Built in 1189, the bridge is still used today and is known as the Marco Polo Bridge.

Marco described Hangzhou as "without doubt the finest and most splendid city in the world... where so many pleasures may be found that one fancies oneself to be in Paradise." He marveled at the great carriages with silken curtains that moved along the tree-shaded roads and the brightly painted barges that were poled about West Lake, while the passengers sipped wine and admired the view.

Marco was particularly impressed by the power and wealth of Kublai himself. At one ceremonial banquet, the Great Khan appeared in a costume of solid gold and his

courtiers dressed in silk clothing with golden threads which had been provided by their host. The company was entertained by magicians and a troop of acrobats, while a trained tiger purred at the khan's feet.

In late spring, Kublai and an entourage of about 20,000 servants, concubines, and courtiers escaped the stifling heat of Dadu by traveling 160 miles north to Shangdu. The summer palace compound was a marvel to behold, with its its sumptuous halls and pavilions, fountains, gardens, and streams. It was surrounded by a huge game preserve, where Kublai and his kinsmen used to hunt as they once had in Mongolia. In his later years, Kublai had become rather fat, and he no longer pursued the athletic activities of his youth. Marco wrote, "Kublai goes on four elephants, on which he has a very beautiful wooden room, which is all covered inside with cloth of beaten gold and outside it is wrapped round and covered with lion skins." He added, "Kublai stays in the room when he goes hawking, [being] troubled by gout, and he sees the hunt always sitting in his room lying on his couch."

The Great Khan kept a herd of 20,000 snow-white horses at Shangdu. (A white horse was considered a symbol of power and purity by the Mongols. Do you remember how Temujin raised his standard adorned with white horse tails when he accepted the title of Genghis Khan?) The horses at Shangdu were selected from the 100,000 animals presented to Kublai each New Year by his subjects. The koumiss made from the milk taken from the mares in this herd could not be consumed by anyone outside the royal family, save for members of a certain tribe who had been granted this favor long ago by Genghis Khan as a battle honor. The white horses were so revered that even the highest-ranking travelers would detour around the herd or wait patiently for it to pass of its own accord before proceeding on their way.

The khan would remain at Shangdu for three months. Then, on a day appointed by his astrologers, he would make a sacrifice of mares' milk to the spirits so that they would "guard all his possessions, men and women, birds, beasts, crops and everything else besides." Having completed this traditional Mongol ceremony, he and his retinue would depart for Dadu.

After his many years of service, Polo left China with his father and uncle. Their mission was to sail to Persia as escorts for a Mongolian princess who was to be married. During the trip, Kublai died, and the Polos decided to proceed home to Italy. They arrived in Venice in 1295.

Marco was later captured during a war between Venice and Genoa. While in prison, he recounted his experiences, such as the ones you've been reading about, to a cell mate. This resulted in his book, *The Travels of Marco Polo* or, as Marco preferred to call it, *The Description of the World*. It began with these words: "Since God first created man, no Christian, Pagan, Tatar, Indian, or person of any other race has explored every part of the world as thoroughly as Marco Polo, nor seen as many of its marvels." It became the bestseller of the times.

Marco's colorful accounts of his travels so astonished Europeans that they could scarcely believe him. Many insisted he had made the tales up. Even today, some people argue that Marco Polo never visited China, basing their contention on the fact that he failed to describe such important aspects of Chinese culture as calligraphy, the tradition of drinking tea, or footbinding, nor did he mention the Great Wall. They laugh at his flights of fantasy, such as his description of giant birds that dropped elephants from a great height and devoured their broken carcasses. And they point out that his name did not appear in the Annals of the Empire (the official directory of the Yuan which recorded the names of foreign visitors). And yet, despite the fact that he was often called in his lifetime *Marco Milione* (an Italian reference to the million lies he supposedly told), he insisted, as he lay dying at the age of 70, "I have only told the half of what I saw!"

East-West Exchange

Marco Polo's book sparked a great interest in China among Europeans and led to a dramatic increase in trade and travel along the Silk Road. Westerners now learned about movable type, the magnetic compass, playing cards, kites, eyeglasses, the decimal system, wheelbarrows, gunpowder, the mass production of books, and China's numerous other inventions. There was also an active exchange of knowledge in the field of medicine, of religious beliefs, and of styles in art and architecture.

The intricate metalwork and the brightly painted ceramic tiles imported from the Muslim world inspired Chinese artists to add more elaborate design to their pieces of porcelain, and shipments of cobalt oxide (a metallic element used to make blue paint) from Persia, enabled Yuan craftsmen to develop "blue-and-white" porcelain, which became highly prized by collectors in the East and the West. (It was Marco Polo who gave porcelain its name: the translucent purity of the vases and dishes he saw reminded him of the cowry shell, which, in Italian, is *porcellana*.)

Protest Through Art

And yet, within Yuan society creativity was often stifled. Despite Kublai's support for Chinese traditions, most Mongols had little regard for the native scholars and artists, placing them in a category with beggars and tramps. The literati, for their part, resented the Mongols for destroying their way of life and derided them as "unwashed barbarians." They withdrew from public life and kept largely to themselves. Many lived as recluses on their estates, entered Buddhist of Daoist monasteries, or taught in private academies. The scholars were reluctant to write about their feelings, fearing that the Mongols might take affront at their words and sentence them to unpleasant punishments. One southern scholar lamented that all the poets had vanished, and he likened himself to a horse that "strolls back and forth, neighing mournfully when passing by its old stable."

Painting, however, provided a subtler and safer means of protest against the Mongol rule. Many literati painted wistful scenes dominated by stalks of bamboo.

When Marco Polo died, he left behind the order that his Mongolian servant be given his freedom. He also left a collection of embroidered silk, carved jade, and other objects mentioned in his book, as well as the golden tablet (paizu) that had been given him by Kublai Khan on his departure from Dadu. But his greatest legacy was the book itself. Two hundred years later, Christopher Columbus read a copy of it and was inspired to sail west across the Atlantic Ocean to find the places Marco had written about.

Traditionally a favorite subject of artists, bamboo now became a popular symbol of the scholars' predicament. Like the graceful and resilient plant, which bends under heavy snow and springs back when the snow melts, the scholars preserved their dignity and integrity in troubled times (by refusing to collaborate with the Mongol court) and waited for the return of the traditional way of life. Wu Zhen chose bamboo as the theme of an album of 20 paintings.

The plum-tree was another popular symbol. Even before it has its leaves, the plum tree puts forth its blossoms. It is the first tree in the spring to do so. Yuan artists depicted the blossoming tree, often with snow on its branches, to suggest the noble retired scholar, who kept Chinese culture alive during the "barbarian winter."

Birds were also effective symbols. One artist, whose name is unknown to us, painted a hanging scroll of the bird-and-flower genre featuring a large hawk perched on a pine tree.(The pine tree was a symbol of perseverance.) The hawk is ignoring a pheasant, one of its favorite prey, which has wandered to the foot of the tree, unaware of the danger it is in. The hawk symbolizes the literati who refused to serve the Mongols, thus rejecting the opportunity to make an easy living at the cost of losing their own principles.

The Mongols showed little interest in pictures of bamboo and plum blossoms, much to the relief of the artists who painted them. They preferred hunting scenes and paintings of horses. Zhao Mengfu was a southern scholar, who was distantly related to Gaozong, the founder of the Southern Song dynasty. Kublai pressured him and some of his friends to come to the Mongol court to paint. Zhao finally agreed to move to Dadu in 1286 and was immediately appointed to the prestigious Hanlin Academy. He became a close adviser to the khan.

Zhao had spent years studying the art of earlier Chinese masters. Like many of his peers, he often copied the styles of earlier painters, not only to express his reverence for the past masters, but to indicate his longing for the days when China was not in the hands of the foreigners. While he was in the north, Zhao had an opportunity

A famous painting of the times depicts an orchid with no soil around its roots: it represents the Chinese people, whose land had been stolen by the Mongols.

to gather paintings and ceramic sculptures of horses created by Tang artists. These inspired him to paint a series of prancing and high-spirited horses in very realistic settings.

Zhao was scorned by his former friends in the south because of his "betrayal," and later historians excluded him from the ranks of the great painters. Zhao offered a discreet apology for serving the Mongols in his painting of a sheep and a goat: the goat was said to represent Su Wu, a captured general of the Han dynasty, who remained loyal to his emperor while guarding sheep for his captors. (Interestingly enough, Zhao's wife, Guan Daosheng, was one of the greatest of the bamboo painters.)

Of a different ilk was Qian Xuan. Rather than work for the Mongols, he preferred to live as a hermit. He painted scenes of horses and other subjects, which often carried the message of resistance. Among these was a painting of Yang Guifei, the concubine of Tang emperor Xuanzong. According to the historical records, the aging Xuanzong had become infatuated with Yang Guifei. She had taken advantage of her elevated position to promote the interests of her own favorite, a general of Turkish descent named An Lushan. The general later led a civil rebellion, forcing Xuanzong and his concubine to flee the capital city on the backs of mules. (En route, they were captured, and Yang Guifei was strangled with a silken cord.) In Xuan's painting, the pampered concubine is being helped onto her horse for a riding party, while the old emperor, already mounted, watches her, thoughtfully. The artist has implied a parallel between Xuanzong, who would later be driven from power by a barbarian, and the Song dynasty, which was crushed by the Mongols. Adding to the impact was the inscription: "Why was it that the august persons here seated on fine horses were later obliged to travel on muleback when fleeing from the devastated capital?"

Chinese Drama

While certain literati expressed their resentment of the foreign occupiers through their paintings, others turned to writing plays. Their efforts led to a great revolution in Chinese drama.

Theater was nothing new in China. Since very early times, clowns, jesters, acrobats and dancers had entertained the members of the imperial court, often acting out scenes from well-known folktales. A more structured approach to drama began with the Tang dynasty, when two actors performed in plays called *canjunxi*, exchanging dialogue to the accompaniment of string, wind, and percussion instruments. Emperor Xuanzong, who once shared his love of performances with his beloved concubine Yang Guifei, established the first academy of dramatics in his Pear Garden at his palace in Chang'an. (Until recently, "Young Folk of the Pear Garden" remained a polite term for actors in China.)

Dramatic narrative evolved further during the Song dynasty. A popular form was the *zaju* ("variety play"), in which actors played several roles in a particular sequence, or series of scenes. A sequence consisted of dancing, acrobatics, a short play based upon a well-known story or satirizing government officials, comic routines, and a musical conclusion. Gradually, drama spread to the general population, as troupes of actors began performing in permanent theaters in many cities and even toured the countryside.

But it was not until the Yuan dynasty that plays as a distinct literary form appeared. Unlike the traditional poetry and philosophy, which were written in the elegant tongue of the highly educated elite, the plays were written in the everyday language of the people. The main reason for this was that the Mongols could not understand the local dialects. Over 170 plays have survived from the period. (The most famous of the playwrights, Guan Hanqing, wrote at least 60.)

The plots of these popular plays were sketchy and melodramatic. They were usually based upon legends and historical events, and they offered their audiences everything from military battles to family conflicts and love stories. (A favorite subject was the famous story of Xuanzong and Yang Kuefei.) The plays usually consisted of four acts and a prologue. They had a limited number of character-types, such as a scholar, war hero, judge, rebel, or concubine, and the actors specialized in one of

Kublai attempted to conquer Japan twice (1274 and 1281), but each time he was driven back by fierce Japanese resistance and bad weather. On the second occasion a typhoon, referred to by the Japanese as *kamikaze* (a "divine wind") caused the destruction of half the Mongol force. This gave the Japanese the belief that their country was protected from foreign attack by the "divine winds." Two Mongol invasions of Java (1281 and 1292) also failed.

these. Few props were used on stage, but the performers more than compensated for this by wearing bright, gaudy costumes and plenty of painted make-up. Once on stage, they entertained the audience with a lively mixture of dialogue, song, dance, pantomime, and acrobatics. Musicians accompanied them with flutes, drums, and clappers.

Skillfully woven within the plots and characterizations were numerous references to the Mongols, so the theater provided an outlet for the feelings of frustration and discontent felt among all classes of Chinese. Ironically, the Mongols were big patrons of the theater. They enjoyed the color and spectacle, fully unaware that they were the targets of political satire.

Decline of the Yuan Dynasty

By the end of the 13th century, Kublai was getting old. The huge Mongol feasts of rich meats and unlimited drinking had taken a toll on the Great Khan's health. The official portraits reveal how the athletic young man of 1260 had become grotesquely fat. His gout condition made his feet swell so much that he had to wear very wide shoes sewn from Korean fish skins. His great weight and foot problems are the reason why Marco Polo observed him viewing a hunt from his giant "room" on the back of an elephant. Adding to Kublai's physical torments was the grief he experienced upon the death of his favorite wife, Chabi, followed by that of his favorite son. These events sent him into a dark despair from which he never fully recovered. When he died in 1295, his body was returned to Mongolia. It lies today in an unknown grave.

Like the Qin dynasty of Shi Huangdi, the Yuan dynasty was basically a one-man show. While Kublai was alive, he held China together by the sheer force of his personal charisma. But his policy of staffing his government with foreigners had always grated upon the nerves of the literati, and his favoritism toward wealthy traders had drawn protests from many social classes. Although Kublai considered himself emperor of China and supported many aspects of the local culture, he and his kinsmen were never truly more than alien over-

---

The Chinese despised the Mongols' "uncouth" manners, including their "barbarian" use of steel knives at the table. (A Mongol cut his meat into large chunks and then used the same knife to spear each one before stuffing it into his mouth.) And they were appalled by their banquets of uncontrolled gluttony and drinking. Without the activity of steppe life, such excesses (apart from offending the Chinese) naturally led to serious obesity and alcoholism. Kublai Khan's physical decline was, therefore, rather predictable.

lords rulers of a resentful body of subjects. And once he was gone, what had always been a quiet rumbling would grow into a mighty roar of protest.

Kublai was succeeded by his grandson, Temur Oljeitu, who managed to maintain the status quo during his short reign. After Temur died in 1307, the foundations of the Yuan dynasty were fatally undermined by a quick turnover of rulers — seven in 26 years. Some of these were Chinese-educated men, who promoted the traditional arts and culture. Others showed no interest in Chinese civilization at all and ruled like nomadic chieftains. The pendulum swung back and forth until the last Yuan emperor, Toghon Temur, came to the throne in 1333. He would rule for 35 years.

A weak ruler, Toghon left most matters to his ministers. His chief minister, Bayan, was convinced that Mongol authority was waning because of previous attempts to be soft on Chinese culture, so he went to great lengths to be tougher. All Chinese subjects were forbidden to learn Mongolian (something that few cared to do, anyway), the theater was banned (Bayan was aware of the rebellious undercurrent in the plays), and all weapons, horses, and iron tools were confiscated from their Chinese owners. Bayan even suggested the extermination of all Chinese families having the five most popular names. This would have led to the execution of a vast majority of the population! Even the Mongols found Bayan's policies too extreme, so he was replaced. But no one in the government could stem the growing anger of the people. And while the Mongol military commanders fought with one another for supremacy, the emperor spent much of his time designing a huge pleasure boat for his lake.

The Final Straw

In the 1340's, the Yellow River flooded, destroying huge amounts of wheat and killing many people. The floods caused the sections of the Grand Canal in that region to silt up, closing off part of this vital artery and thereby cutting off the supply of rice from the south. The Yuan government ordered thousands of northern farmers to work on a massive but necessary project, which involved rerouting the Yellow River by building huge embankments and dredging the Grand Canal. The farmers had no choice (the Mongols never took no for an answer!), and they were reportedly treated very poorly by their overlords. Meanwhile, the peasants in the southern regions were forced to pay even higher taxes to support the project.

Before long, rebellions were breaking out in throughout the countryside. Such a scenario often occurred in the final years or months of a dynasty, and it was a good indicator that this cycle of history was nearing an end. The current ruler had proven himself unworthy of the Mandate of Heaven. The spirits had revealed their disapproval through natural calamities, and the people were taking the law into their own hands. In this case, the Chinese had the extra incentive of booting the barbarians out of their country.

The Red Turbans

In this turbulent atmosphere, many groups, among them secret societies with a strongly religious cast, vied among themselves to lead the people in a major assault against the Mongols. The White Lotus, which had been founded under Southern Song, drew many recruits. Members of this Buddhist society expressed their protest by refusing to pay their taxes or to contribute labor for public work projects. The White Cloud Society had similar goals. The Red Turbans were a secret society made up mostly of peasants, who wanted to restore the Song dynasty. Their vision included the coming of a new Buddha, who would bring peace to the country.

The Red Turbans were led by a charismatic Buddhist monk named Zhu Yuanzhang. Zhu's entire family had died of famine and disease when he was 17. He found a home with Buddhist monks, who taught him to read and write. In 1352, Zhu joined a Red Turban band, and he soon rose in its ranks. He married the band leader's daughter, and when his father-in-law died, he took over his position and began building up his rebel army. By toning down the religious aspect of his society, he was able to enlist the support of many literati.

In 1356, Zhu's forces crossed the Yangzi River and captured Jinling (present-day Nanjing). Using the city as a base for campaigns against other local strongmen, he gradually gained control over all the rebel bands in the southeast.

The Chinese Triumph

Zhu's vision had grown considerably from his earlier goal of driving out the Mongols. He now aspired to become the legitimate leader of China. In 1363, he defeated the leader of the southern half of the Red Turbans and proceeded to conquer all of his other rivals.

On January 23, 1368 (the beginning of the Chinese New Year), Zhu declared the founding of a new dynasty, which he named Ming ("Brilliant"). Toghon Temur, last of the Yuan emperors, fled north with his family to Mongolia. The Middle Kingdom was back in Chinese hands.

The Mongol Empire held together for about a century – then fell apart; the longest lasting khanate was that known as the Golden Horde in south Russia, where Batu's descendants ruled for about 200 years.

Review Questions:

1. How did the Mongols sustain themselves on the steppes?

2. What was a Mongol warrior's most prized possession?

3. How did Genghis Khan organize his army?

4. Where did Kublai Kahn spend his boyhood, and how did this affect his ideas as ruler?

5. What enabled the Mongols to defeat the Song?

6. After the Mongols, what was the most important class in Yuan society?

7. How did the Mongols influence the development of transcontinental trade?

8. What contributions did Kublai Khan make to China?

9. How did Marco Polo spend most of his time in China?

10. What was Shangdu?

11. How did the literati protest Mongol rule?

12. In what important ways did the plays written during the Yuan dynasty differ from other literary works?

13. How would you characterize the Mongol rulers who came after Kublai?

14. What was the goal of the Red Turbans?

15. What did Zhu Yuanzhang name his new dynasty?

Projects:

1. Make a timeline of the Yuan dynasty.

2. Many historians refer to the Yuan dynasty as the Mongolian interlude or interruption, claiming that the Mongols took much and gave little. Do you agree? Write an essay expressing your views.

3. Find out what happened to the Mongols in the centuries after the Yuan dynasty. Make a timeline of their later activities, or write a short report.

4. Kublai Khan's magnificent summer palace north of Dadu was the inspiration for "the stately pleasure-dome" evoked centuries later as Xanadu, by English poet Samuel Taylor Coleridge's "Kubla Khan." The poem is based on Marco Polo's account of the place he called Shangdu. It begins with the words, "In Xanadu, did Kubla Khan/A stately pleasure-dome decrees,/Where Alph, the sacred river, ran/Through caverns measureless to man/Down to the sunless sea." Find a copy of Coleridge's poem and read it carefully. Think about what you've learned about Marco Polo's descriptions of Shangdu. Do you think Coleridge took any "poetic license?" Read the poem to your classmates and share your own interpretation of some of its lines.

6. Make a Venn diagram comparing the cultures of the Mongols and the Chinese.

7. Today Mongolia is divided into two parts: Inner Mongolia, which lies within Chinese borders, and Outer Mongolia, which is an independent country. Find out more about the people who live in Inner Mongolia and compare them to what you know about the Mongols. Write a short report noting similarities and differences. Or write a report about modern Outer Mongolia.

8. In the 1340's, Moroccan explorer Ibn Batuta visited China. Find out about his journey and write a report.

9. Timur (1336-1405), known as Timur Leng ("the Lame") because of a limp, was a chief of one of the Turkic tribes which had been allied with the Mongols. (In the West he is known as Tamerlane.) In the 1360's he gained control of Kashgar and Khorazm, and subsequently began to enlarge his domains rapidly. By 1385 he had conquered all of eastern Persia, and went on to overrun virtually all of western Asia, including Asia Monor. Only his death early in 1405 prevented a planned attack on China. Find out more about this man and write a report. One useful resource is *Tamerlane: The Ultimate Warrior* by Roy E. Stier.

10. Marco Polo had a counterpart in Rabban Sauma of Dadu. In the 1280's, he traveled across Asia to Persia, then to Constantinople, and eventually to Italy, where he talked with the Pope. He also went to France, where he met King Philip IV and visited the University of Paris. During this period, the first Christian missionaries arrived in China. They were supported by the Mongols. Reports carried back West by the missionaries added to the lively image of China that emerged in the West with Marco Polo's writings. Consult some books and/or the Internet about Rabban Sauma and write a short report.

11. Toward the end of the Yuan dynasty, devastating epidemics killed thousands of people in eastern Asia. It was possibly the Black Death, which had broken out among Mongol soldiers in Crimea and later traveled to Europe. Find out more about this epidemic and share your findings with your classmates.

12. Write a poem about the life of Kublai Khan. It can be humorous.

13. Study the bamboo paintings of the Yuan artists. Then, using a brush and black paint on large pieces of white paper, create your own bamboo paintings.

14. Consult several books about Chinese drama. Then write a report about the plays written and performed during the Yuan dynasty.

15. Find a recent edition of Marco Polo's famous book. Select five sections that you find particularly interesting and share them with your classmates.

16. Using felt, popsicle sticks, clay, and cardboard, make a model of a yurt in its natural setting in Mongolia. Include a few horses made of clay or plastic.

17. Read *Marco Polo: A Journey Through China* by Fiona MacDonald.

**Important Happenings Elsewhere In The World
(1260 – 1368)**

Philip IV crowned king of France — 1285
Inca Empire expanding in Peru — c. 1290
The Arabs conquer Acre, ending Christian rule in the Middle East — 1291
Roger Bacon teaching philosophy — 1297
Mayan Empire flourishing in Chichen Itza — c. 1297
Kingdom of Benin emerges in Nigeria — 1307
Dante writes *The Divine Comedy* — 1309
Hundred Years War begins — 1337
Black Death reaches Europe — 1347
Ottoman Turks enter Europe — 1353
Tamerlane conquers Persia, Syria, and Egypt — beginning 1364

Chapter 5
The Ming Dynasty
(1368 — 1644)
The Tightening of Imperial Authority

Zhu Yuangzhang was the second man in China's long history to rise from peasant origins to the role of emperor. (The first was Liu Bang, who founded the Han dynasty 1,500 years earlier.) Zhu named his period of reign *Hongwu*, which means "Boundless Martial Spirit," and he is known as the Hongwu Emperor. He would rule for thirty years, laying the foundations of what proved to be the most durable dynasty in Chinese history. It would also be the last native government to rule imperial China.

A Brilliant Dynasty

Hongwu restored the Chinese bureaucratic traditions that had lapsed during nearly a century of alien rule and set the stage for a long period of peace and prosperity. During the "brilliant" dynasty, the population would expand to about 160 million, the Forbidden City would be built, Chinese mariners would visit Africa, popular novels would be read by millions, Jesuits would become courtiers, and the Chinese elite would enjoy a higher standard of living than any other people on earth.

Recovering the Empire

The Ming government was headed by three ministries: the Chancellery, the Bureau of Military Affairs, and the Censorate. The emperor's right hand man was the prime minister, who ran the Chancellery.

Soon after he was crowned, Hongwu sent an army north to drive the remnants of the Mongol court from Dadu. His soldiers easily took over the city, which was renamed Beiping ("The North is Pacified"). A year later, they overran Shangdu and pushed north well beyond the Great Wall. Ming forces burned the old Mongol capital

---

Highlights of This Chapter

Hongwu Reestablishes Order
The Nine-Rank System
The Yongle Emperor
The Sea Explorations
The Forbidden City
The Ming Tombs
Ming Porcelain
Trade With the Europeans
Painting
Chinese Gardens
The Chinese Novel
Matteo Ricci and the Jesuits
The Manchus

The Ming Empire (showing provincial borders)

at Karakorum, then chased the retreating Mongols as far as the Yablonoi Mountains. This is the furthest north any Chinese army has ever marched. In a reversal of Yuan policy, the new emperor forbade any Mongols who remained within his borders to marry within their own ethnic group. (Can you explain why?)

Hongwu now turned his attention to the heartland of China. Within four years he controlled all the territory once held by the Tang dynasty at the height of its power. However, he had no authority in Central Asia, where the Mongol khanates remained strong. Envoys were sent to Korea, Japan, Vietnam (Annam) and Tibet, announcing Hongwu's rule and inviting them to send him tribute. Japan refused, stating that there was "more than one ruler on earth."

Nanjing

Hongwu set up his capital in Jinling, a city well situated at a juncture of the Yangzi River and the Grand Canal. (An adviser recommended this strategic site, referring to it as the place where "the dragon coils and the tiger crouches.") He was the first emperor to rule a united China from a city south of the Yangzi River. The city was renamed Nanjing ("Southern Capital").

The old city wall was extended east so that at least part of the capital would lie south of Mount Zhong. (According to the Daoist principles of *feng shui*, an important site should be "guarded" on its northern side by a mountain.) The wall was massive — 40 feet high and 25 feet thick. Its foundations were made of huge slabs of stone to prevent enemies from placing charges of gunpowder beneath it, and every gate could be closed against intruders by portcullis barriers that slid down into place from above. The Nanjing wall was now 24 miles long, making it the longest city wall in China.

Lofty wooden palaces and government buildings were constructed within the protective wall, as were new dwellings, ranging from the elegant townhouses of the wealthy to the cramped apartment buildings of the common people. The population of Nanjing grew rapidly as Chinese from all walks of life — craftsmen, merchants, laborers as well as scholars and army officers moved in. Before long, there were over a million people living there.

Return of the Literati

Hongwu was determined to wipe out all reminders of the the Mongol occupation and to restore China to its former glory. He reminded his subjects to follow the rules of Confucius — to "observe proper behavior, respect elders, instruct children, and be peaceful." The literati, once again valued for their scholarship and cultural refinement, resumed their high place in Chinese society.

Hongwu revived the civil service examinations and placed the scholars in government posts. The Hanlin Academy was an academy of scholars set up during the Tang dynasty to aid the emperor and his court in clerical and literary matters. The scholars wrote letters, treaties, and historical documents, and they composed poetry for state occasions. (*Hanlin* literally means "the forest of writing brushes.") This learned institute had lingered on during the dark days of the Mongols. (As you know, Kublai appointed artist Zhao Mengfu to the academy after he coaxed him to come to Dadu.) Hongwu now expanded it and drew upon its members to serve him in his new government.

A Confucian school was founded in Nanjing, which would later become the prestigious Imperial Academy. Smaller schools were reestablished in all prefectures and counties of the empire.

The Nine-Rank System

All civil and military officials of the Ming court were divided into nine ranks. They wore badges on their robes to indicate the rank to which they belonged. (See the figure on the opposite page.) Hongwu got the idea of the badges from the Mongol

courtiers, who had worn large plaques decorated with animals and flowers on their robes as symbols of rank. The Ming badges were squares of silk embroidered with brightly colored images of birds and animals. Civil officials wore bird badges, while military officials wore animals. Why birds and animals? A bird could fly into the mystical realms of the heavens, just as the mind of a scholar soared to the highest levels of understanding; animals were tied to the earth, where they defended their young and hunted prey, just as the army defended the Middle Kingdom and drove off enemy invaders.

Each of the creatures depicted on the badges was shown looking up towards a

Civil officials wore badges embroidered with the following birds — first rank: crane; second rank: golden pheasant; third rank: peacock; fourth rank: wild goose; fifth rank: silver pheasant; sixth rank: egret; seventh rank: mandarin duck; eighth rank: quail; and ninth rank: paradise flycatcher. Military officials wore badges embroidered with these animals — first rank: qilin (mythical); second rank: lion; third rank: leopard; fourth rank: tiger; fifth rank: bear; sixth rank: panther; seventh rank: rhinoceros; eighth rank: rhinoceros (a different one); ninth rank: sea horse.

The caps of officials were crowned with finials indicating their rank. For the first rank, the finial was of transparent ruby; second rank: opaque coral; third rank: transparent sapphire; fourth rank: opaque lapis lazuli; fifth rank: transparent crystal; sixth rank: opaque jade; seventh rank: plain gold; eighth rank: worked gold with a *shou* (longevity) character; ninth rank: worked gold with two *shou* characters. The shou character is pictured to the right.

red sun, a reference to the ancient proverb, "keep your eye on the sun and rise high." (The sun was associated with the *yang* and symbolized physical vigor and imperial authority.) The background of a badge was filled with natural features — clouds, waves, rocks, trees, and mountains — and auspicious (lucky) symbols — such as peaches, peonies, and bats. (A bat is considered lucky because the Chinese character for it [*fu*] sounds the same as the character for good fortune.) An official's wife wore a smaller version of her husband's rank badge on her robe. Even members of the imperial family wore badges. Theirs were round in shape and were embroidered with (of course) dragons.

A Ming official also wore a silk cap. The material and color of the finial (knob) at the crown of the cap corresponded with his rank.

A Civil Courtier Wearing his Badge of Rank

Dealing with the Eunuchs

The court eunuchs played an integral role in the history of imperial China. An emperor could not control his palace and his harem of wives and concubines without the eunuchs. However, these men had to be carefully supervised, since they were liable to abuse their positions for personal advantage. You learned in Chapter 1 about the eunuchs who became very powerful during the Tang dynasty. At one point they actually ran the government!

Hongwu was very aware of the dangers posed by the eunuchs. He ordered that they be kept illiterate, and he forbade them to take any part in government — upon pain of death. A large metal tablet was hung prominently in the palace, incised with the words, "Eunuchs must have nothing to do with politics." As long as the throne was occupied by a powerful ruler, this order was obeyed, and the eunuchs were kept out of the political arena. But as you've seen, not every emperor had the talents and the inclination to be a strong leader.

Aid to the Countryside

The Mongols had strongly encouraged trade with foreign nations, and the Yuan dynasty had become very wealthy as a result. Hongwu, however, adhered to the Confucian view, in which the peasants were seen as the backbone of society and ranked just below the scholar-officials in the social hierarchy. Merchants, on the other hand, were seen as greedy parasites, who lived off the labor of others. For this reason, the emperor, undoubtedly influenced by his own humble upbringing, took steps to improve the condition of the farmers.

His first act was to resettle uprooted families on land that had been abandoned during the rebellions that had brought about the downfall of the Mongols. He decreed that nobles who had unfairly taken land anywhere in China during the civil unrest would be punished unless they gave the land back. He ordered that all dikes and canals be repaired and that marshes be drained, with the water collected in reservoirs. These measures stabilized life in the country and greatly increased the amount of farming land. Within ten years, there was a great surplus of grain. Some of this was stored in public granaries for use in times of famine.

Over the centuries, much of the countryside of eastern China, from Beiping to Hangzhou, had been denuded of trees. The wood had been used primarily for fuel, housing, and, in more recent years, for shipbuilding. To address this problem, Hongwu launched a major reforestation project, requiring each family on the newly settled land to plant 200 each of mulberry, jujube and persimmon trees. The trees helped prevent soil erosion, added to the beauty of the landscape, and produced food for the silkworms (the mulberry leaves) and fruit for the market. It has been estimated that nearly a billion trees were planted during the early years of the Ming dynasty. Certain forests in southern China were set aside as timber for shipbuilding.

Local Government

Closely tied to the land reforms were Hongwu's policies toward local government. He ordered every village and town to draw up its own charter and empowered the older men to decide local disputes that arose. Each household was issued with a registration certificate, which recorded such details of family members as age and occupation. These records were compiled in public registers known as the "Yellow Books."

In 1391, toward the end of Hongwu's reign, over 50 million trees were planted in the Nanjing area alone.

The entire population (currently about 100 million) was divided into the categories of gentry, farmers, soldiers, and (at the bottom, of course) merchants. No one was allowed to change status without special permission. (Can you see where this impinged upon certain basic rights?)

The Great Wall

The Great Wall, the long stone barrier that had been built by Shi Huangdi and extended by his successors, had little significance during the Yuan dynasty. In fact, the Mongols, more concerned with openings than closings, added the white marble gateway known as "Cloud Terrace Pass" about 35 miles north of their winter capital.

Now, with the Mongols reverting to their nomadic lifestyle back in the north, the wall was again considered a barrier between the barbarians and the settled communities of China. Hongwu began a long project that involved reinforcing parts of the wall and reconstructing others. He stationed soldiers at strategic spots along the wall. They were allowed to farm the local land when they were needed to fight. By giving the men free use of the land, the government avoided the expense of paying them salaries. The army commanders were instructed to repel invasion but not to pursue an enemy beyond China's borders.

This defensive policy would be followed by most of the Ming emperors. It allowed them to concentrate their energy and funds on internal matters. Although the wall did not always keep out invaders, it did serve as a psychological dividing line.

Distrust Breeds Contempt

Hongwu was a very capable leader and an efficient bureaucrat. And yet, beneath the confident facade lingered great feelings of insecurity. His peasant upbringing and lack of education often made him feel self-conscious in the company of the learned Confucian scholars. He was also quite ugly, having a protruding lower jaw, tiny eyes, and a pockmarked complexion. (Some said he had a porcine (pig-like) appearance. Ironically, his family name "Zhu" sounds like the Chinese word for pig!)

After over a decade on the throne, the emperor's feelings of insecurity began to fester. He worried that others were secretly laughing at him or even plotting against him. In 1380 he accused his prime minister, Hu Weiyong, of conspiracy and had the man beheaded. (It appears that Hu was innocent, his only mistake having been to build up a personal power base in the government.) Hu's death was followed by the execution of everyone in his family and then of anyone who had been remotely connected with him. Thousands of his supporters were targeted to die. With Hu out of the way, Hongwu eliminated the office of prime minister — and the entire department of the Chancellery over which the minister presided. He would take over their tasks himself.

In his quest for security, Hongwu created the imperial "Embroidered Brocade Guards" — a secret police empowered to seek out and arrest anyone who did not support him. (As their name implies, they wore elegant silk uniforms.) Needless to say, all secret societies were banned. The least suspicion of treachery now brought brutal punishment. Anyone found guilty of receiving a bribe was decapitated, his head was spiked on a pole, and his corpse was skinned, stuffed with straw, and hung in the office of his successor — a grisly reminder to tow the line! Lesser offenses led to beating (flogging with long bamboo staves) in a public place — a punishment that was embarrassing as well as painful.

Hongwu oversaw four waves of political purges during his reign — over 100,000 officials were killed or beaten on his orders for largely imaginary acts of disloyalty. (The emperor once remarked that he felt driven to rid the world of evil people.) A few fortunate political prisoners were saved by the intervention of the emperor's wife, the kind-hearted Empress Ma.

A Tireless Worker

By isolating himself and killing off most of his advisers, Hongwu found himself surrounded with a monumental amount of paperwork. It has been estimat-

When Empress Ma fell ill, she refused to see a doctor, knowing that if he failed to cure her Hongwu would have him killed. Attended only by her servants, she soon died. The emperor was inconsolable after the loss of his beloved wife.

ed that in one eight-day period he had to deal with 1,600 dispatches. He also followed a punishing schedule of audiences (official meetings). Working a ten-hour day, he managed to get through much of the work previously done by his top ministers. No emperor since Shi Huangdi had held such personal power and borne such a burden of daily office work. Toward the end of his life, exhausted and stressed to the limit, Hongwu wrote in his journal, "for 31 years I have labored to discharge Heaven's will, tormented by worries and fears without relaxing for a day."

The Question of Succession

The contrast between Hongwu's useful reforms and his terrifying acts of cruelty was very unsettling for his subjects. Many longed for a new, more tolerant ruler. So Hongwu's death, just four days short of his 70th birthday in 1398, was greeted with considerable relief. He was buried in a large tomb complex on the slopes of Mount Zhong, in the northeastern suburbs of Nanjing.

Hongwu had 26 sons and 16 daughters by his various wives and concubines. To limit sibling rivalry at court, he had created hereditary principalities in the provinces for his sons and forbidden them to come to the capital. This kept the brothers from squabbling among themselves in Nanjing, but it also enabled them to build up a good deal of power — and military might— in the countryside. Can you see where this might pose a threat to the central government?

Hongwu's eldest son and heir had died in 1392, so his 21-year-old grandson inherited the throne, taking the reign name of Jianwen ("Civil Virtue"). The new emperor was a gentle, scholarly fellow, who loved to talk about philosophy and poetry. But he lacked his grandfather's administrative talents. Many wondered why Hongwu had chosen someone so unskilled in politics as his heir. Jianwen *did* listen closely to his Confucian tutors, and he revoked many of the despotic measures made by Hongwu. (Ministers no longer had to worry about losing their heads.) But his political naivete led him to make one very major mistake.

The Prince of Yan

Hongwu's fourth son, Zhu Di, had always been his favorite offspring, probably because he showed an unusual love for the military. In fact, he arranged for the boy to spend time with some of his best generals. But, much to Hongwu's disappointment, Zhu Di was not eligible to succeed to the throne, because his mother had been a secondary wife. (The heir was chosen from among the sons of the empress.)

When he became a young man, Zhu Di was given the principality of Yan, which contained the city of Beiping. As the Prince of Yan, he had the responsibility of defending China's northern borders. In 1390, Hongwu sent him beyond the Great Wall to capture some Mongols who were organizing an attack. Zhu Di and a handful of soldiers marched through a huge snowstorm and caught the enemy by surprise, forcing their surrender. Hongwu was extremely impressed with his son's accomplishment. For the next eight years, the prince continued to monitor the activities of the Mongols, ably defusing any serious threats to China's borders. In the process, he built up a good-sized army.

When Hongwu died, none of his sons were expected to attend his funeral, since they were forbidden to enter Nanjing. The Prince of Yan, however, defied this order and traveled to the capital. Clearly rattled by his sudden appearance, Jianwen's ministers ordered him to leave at once. After he was gone, the ministers warned the young emperor that unless he undermined the power of his uncles the throne would be in jeopardy. This is when Jianwen made his major mistake. He removed his uncles' titles and sent his secret police to spy upon them. Several were arrested (on false charges). But it was the Prince of Yan Jianwen was really concerned about. When

he sent a delegation to arrest him, the prince had the men killed, later remarking that it was his duty to kill evil men. Civil war was now inevitable.

In 1399, fighting broke out between the forces of the Prince of Yan and the imperial army. Although the prince's soldiers were outnumbered three to one, they were far better trained — *and* they had a superior leader. After three years of battles, the prince entered Nanjing with his troops and burned the imperial palace. One of the bodies was identified as that of Jianwen. It was immediately buried. The prince then proclaimed himself the new emperor of China. He was destined to become the greatest of the Ming rulers.

Yongle Takes Charge

Zhu Di took the reign name of Yongle (Yong lee, meaning "Eternal Happiness"). He immediately ordered the execution of the supporters of Jianwen, as well as their families and associates (friends, neighbors, teachers, students, and even servants). Then he saw to it that all evidence of his nephew's reign was blotted from the history books and replaced with descriptions of how *he* had directly succeeded Hongwu. He even changed the records to show that his

According to legend, Jianwen disguised himself as a monk and fled from Nanjing to a monastery in Sichuan, where he lived for forty years — reading great books and composing poetry.

mother was the Empress Ma.

Yongle created seven ministries to replace those Hongwu had dismantled. He also set up a cabinet of learned scholars recruited from the Hanlin Academy to advise him. These men came to be known as the Grand Secretaries. They would have greater power than the imperial ministers. Yongle reversed his father's discriminating policies toward eunuchs, appointing many of them as advisers. The eunuchs could usually be relied upon to do the emperor's bidding without asking questions, unlike the strongly principled Confucian officials, who often argued against what they felt to be improper decisions. Yongle viewed the eunuchs as loyal watchdogs, and he even encouraged them to keep files on the government officials.

With these changes, Yongle set up a situation in which the top level of government was divided into two camps — the Inner Court (the emperor and his close advisors, the eunuchs and the Grand Secretaries) and the Outer Court (the imperial ministers). As long as there was a strong leader on the throne, the state would function smoothly. But what would happen when the ruler was weak?

The Mongol Threat

Yongle moved the capital from Nanjing to his old power base in the north, building a new city near the ruins of Dadu.

He named the city Beijing, which means "Northern Capital." By being only 40 miles from the Great Wall, the new capital gave the emperor tighter control over the troops stationed there and greater knowledge of what was going on further north. He had good reason to worry, since the Mongols had regrouped and were beginning to pose a major threat. In 1408, they crushed a Ming expedition sent to drive them further beyond the Great Wall.

The following year, Yongle himself led a force of nearly half a million soldiers. He crossed the Kerulen River, deep in Mongolia. This was further than any Chinese emperor had ever ventured with a personal command. His campaign was successful. The Mongols were defeated and forced to sign a treaty. Peace was restored in the north, a least for the time being.

Scholarly Pursuits

Yongle's interests were not limited to warfare, however. He had received an excellent education, and he took great pleasure in scholarship and the arts. He enjoyed the study of history, and he had written a number of philosophical essays. He was also a skillful calligrapher.

As emperor, he sponsored several literary projects. One was the compiling of the Confucian classics and more recent literature into a massive work known as the Yongle Encyclopedia. More than 2,000 scholars worked for over five years to produce the 11,000 volumes, which were carefully arranged according to subject. The encyclopedia was originally intended to be published in book form, but its vast size (it contained 50 million words!), made this an impractical task. Instead, three handwritten copies were made on scrolls. Two were kept in the palace in Beijing, and the third was sent to Nanjing.

Other scholars produced the *Great Compendia*, a compilation of learning required for the civil service exams. One part consisted of extracts from the great Confucian works — the *Five Classics* and the *Four Books*, with the commentaries by Zhu Xi. The other part contained Neo-Confucian writings. The compendia were printed and distributed to schools throughout the empire.

The Sea Explorations

In 1403, Yongle ordered the construction of a large fleet of ocean-going ships. As you know, the Chinese had made a number of advances in shipbuilding in the days of the Southern Song. But until now, fighting and trading vessels had generally remained in eastern waters. This was about to change.

The emperor appointed Zheng He, a court eunuch, to command the fleet. In July of 1405, he set sail on the first of seven expeditions that would take him far beyond the horizon. Zheng carried personal messages from Yongle requesting the states he visited to accept Chinese suzerainty (which meant pledging loyalty and sending tribute to the Ming). In return, the foreign states would be given permission to trade with China.

The main vessels of the fleet were 62 "treasure ships." They were the largest ships that had ever been built, measuring up to 440 feet in length and 180 feet in width. (The Santa Maria, the flagship of Christopher Columbus on his famous expedition later that century, would be only 85 feet long.) The huge ships carried four to nine masts up to 90 feet high and were steered by stern-post rudders. Like the smaller trading junks you learned about earlier, these ships had rectangular sails with bamboo ribs and folded up like accordions when they were lowered. A dozen water-tight compartments made the vessels even more sea-worthy. In good weather, they could sail at a speed of about 8 knots per hour.

Each treasure ship had up to 50 luxuriously appointed cabins for the imperial envoys and sleeping quarters for as many as 500 people. Its hold was filled with the treasures — the finest silks, porcelain, lacquerware, and pieces of carved jade. The treasure ships were protected by 225 warships and patrol boats. The warships comprised the largest display of naval power the world had ever seen. A crew of 26,800 soldiers and sailors were assigned to man the fleet. Zheng had a personal staff of 70 eunuchs, 180 medical personnel, and 5 astrologers.

The fleet sailed south for nearly 400 miles, stopping about every ten days to restock supplies. From Taiping it set out across the great expanses of the Indian Ocean. Within a year of its departure from China it arrived at Calicut, the most important trading post in India. From there, it stopped at several other Indian ports before returning home.

Over the next three decades, Zheng He commanded six more expeditions, venturing as far as the Red Sea and Persian Gulf. Detachments from his fleet explored the African coast as far south as Kenya and visited such exotic places as Egypt and Mecca. The average voyage lasted about 20 months. The Chinese products were exchanged for gold, silver, pearls, rhinoceros horn, incense, medicinal herbs, and spices. One ship brought back a giraffe for the imperial zoo in Beijing. But the major purpose of the trips was diplomacy. In most cases, Zheng He was greeted in peace and his terms were accepted. Thanks to his efforts, 36 nations agreed to a tributary relationship with China. There were exceptions. When the king of Sri Lanka and two Sumatran chieftains defied Ming authority, they were forcibly taken to China to submit to the emperor in person!

The Northern Capital

While Zheng He was traveling to distant ports, major construction was going on at the new capital, Beijing. Yongle intended to create a city of great splendor to symbolize Ming imperial power. This ambitious enterprise would take 14 years, involving over 100,000 skilled workers and a million laborers.

Before the work started, plans had to be made to bring the men and building materials to the site. Although Hongwu had overseen the repair of dikes and canals in southern China, many of the waterways of the Grand Canal further north still suffered from neglect. Yongle had them dredged, widened and deepened. These improvements enabled a great number of boats to travel through the canal system, but they also created very fast currents and an unsteady flow of water. Boating accidents soon became a great concern, as did the possibility of floods. In 1411, an engineer named Song Li tackled the problem by

None of the large ships of Zheng He's fleet has survived, but in 1957 near the site of the dockyard a huge wooden rudder post was discovered. It is believed to have been fitted with a rudder blade measuring over 20 feet in both dimensions.

designing a mile-wide dam. When this was constructed, water backed up behind it, forming a large reservoir. Fourteen sluice gates in the dam could be opened or shut to control the flow of water. With the Grand Canal revitalized, work on the new city began in earnest.

Beijing was laid out according to the ancient plan — it was a square, the four sides lined up with the cardinal points of the compass. The city was protected by a 40-foot high wall of earth and bricks that measured nine *li* on each side (a *li* is about a third of a mile). Watchtowers stood at the four corners; three ceremonial gates faced each direction except north, which had four.

Within the protective outer wall, Beijing resembled a set of nested boxes. At the very center (the smallest box) was the imperial palace compound. This was, of course, the most important sector and contained the ceremonial halls as well as the emperor's living quarters. It was enclosed by a high wall and moat.Outside the palace compound was the "imperial city," where the government officials lived. This, in turn, was enclosed by another wall and surrounded by "greater Bejing," where ordinary people went about their daily lives. The streets of the city formed a grid, with nine major avenues running north-south, and another nine going east-west. Of course, the buildings faced south.

The Forbidden City

The imperial palace compound came to be known as the Forbidden City, since common people were not allowed to enter it. (A curse was put upon anyone who disobeyed this command.) This would be the home of the last 24 emperors of China. Yongle personally supervised work on the buildings. Most of those standing today were reconstructed in the 17th or 18th centuries, but they followed Yongle's original plans. (Since Chinese buildings were made of wood, few have survived from ancient times. However, whenever an important building burned in a fire or was destroyed in some other way, it was always rebuilt according to its original plan.)

Let's take a closer look at Yongle's Forbidden City. The compound covered 250 acres of land. It was divided into two main areas — the front area, consisting of three large halls used for official ceremonies, and the rear section, containing three large residential palaces, a few smaller palaces (for concubines), and the Imperial Gardens.

The Forbidden City was entered through the beautifully carved "Meridian

---

The Grand canal is over 1100 miles long, making it the world's longest artificially created waterway. It is still in use today.

Gate." Apart from the emperor, the only people allowed to enter this gate were the empress on her wedding day and the scholars who had passed the highest level civil service examinations (the *jinshi*). Just inside the gates were five elegant marble bridges arching over a stream of water (the "River of Golden Water"). Only the emperor could cross the central bridge. The number of bridges symbolized the five Confucian virtues (benevolence, righteousness, proper conduct, wisdom, and trustworthiness). The stream served a double purpose: it fulfilled the traditional Daoist requirement (*feng shui*) of having water to the south of an important building complex, and it served the practical purpose of providing running water for the imperial household. (The water was carried to the palaces by an underground pipe.) An artificial hill was raised to the immediate north of the city, since, as you know, an ideal site had a protective mountain on that side to shield it from the forces of cold and darkness.

The bridges led to a courtyard of fine pebbles. Beyond this, the Gate of Supreme Harmony opened onto another, larger courtyard. At the far side of this courtyard stood the three ceremonial halls, where the emperor conducted state affairs. The halls were lined up one behind the other along the central north-south axis, facing (of course) south. The buildings were simple and symmetrical in design. They were made of timber imported from far-off Sichuan and Yunnan provinces. Each of the halls stood on a white marble terrace, which was mounted by a short flight of steps. (White symbolized purity.) The steps were uneven in number. (The masculine and imperial force *yang* is associated with uneven numbers.) The bricks and stone slabs of the steps and terraces were glued together with a sticky mixture of steamed glutinous rice and egg white.

Chinese buildings were constructed very differently from those in the West. The builders first made the framework of the roof, and this determined the positions of the columns that would support it. Usually there was a massive pillar in each corner of a building and smaller pillars along each side supporting the beams and brackets that held up the roof. The walls of a building were merely screens and were not used for support.

The walls and pillars in the Forbidden City were painted red. (Red was the color associated with *yang*.) They were decorated with intricate carvings and gold leaf. The roofs were covered with bright yellow glazed tiles. (Yellow, of course, was

---

The Forbidden City remains as the largest complex of ancient buildings in the world today. Over 3.1 billion bricks were used for the buildings and the surrounding wall.

The Hall of Supreme Harmony

the imperial color.) The edges of the roofs curved up, to deflect evil spirits who moved in straight lines rounded ones. Perched along the edges were figures of mythical animals, whose purpose was to frighten off any forces of evil that might be hovering nearby.

The first of the three buildings was the largest. Known as the Hall of Supreme Harmony, it was 121 feet long, 210 feet wide, and 88 feet high. The roof was supported by 72 red pillars. Inside the building, rich yellow carpets covered the floor of glazed bricks. High on a platform in the center of the hall was the emperor's "Dragon Throne," the heart of imperial power. It was was made of gilded rosewood

Large audiences took place in the square courtyard in front of the Hall of Supreme Harmony. Civil and military officials would assemble there and line up according to rank. There are no trees in the courtyard. There were several reasons for this. Most important, the Chinese believed that nothing (not even a tree) should tower over the site where the emperor sat upon the Dragon Throne. From a practical point of view, trees could offer cover for would-be assassins. And there was the matter of symbolism: a tree in a square was the Chinese character for the word "trouble." No one wanted any trouble in the Forbidden City! Houses in Beijing had to be single-storied because nobody could overlook the Forbidden City.

and decorated (of course) with dragons. The throne was flanked by six golden columns, also adorned with dragons. From this lofty perch, the emperor held his grand audiences, announced state edicts, appointed generals, presided over traditional ceremonies, announced the results of palace exams, and conferred degrees on the successful candidates. Two dragons carved on the ceiling just above the throne appeared to be playing with a pearl. (The pearl was made of glass and painted with mercury.) The Chinese believed that these dragons could sense the presence of a usurper of imperial power. If anyone who was not the true Son of Heaven descended the throne, they would drop the pearl and it would strike him dead!

The emperor entered the Hall of Supreme Harmony to the accompaniment of music dating back to the time of Confucius. As he took his seat, gongs and chimes sounded from the gallery, while the thick smoke of incense rose from bronze cranes standing beside the throne. (The crane was the symbol of long life.) Heralds then summoned the high officials, who slowly entered the hall with heads bowed and performed the ceremonial kowtow — touching their foreheads to the ground nine times to express their supreme reverence for the Son of Heaven. Only after these formalities were completed could the business of the day could begin.

Just behind the Hall of Supreme Harmony was the much smaller Hall of Middle Harmony. Here the emperor prepared himself for entry into the larger hall or received ambassadors. Once a year, a special ceremony took place here in which the emperor was given plowing implements and fresh seeds to carry out the ancient ritual of sowing the first seeds of the planting season. (This ritual dated back to the days of the Shang dynasty.) The Hall of Protective Harmony, just beyond the second hall and resembling it in design, was the setting for the New Year Banquet. This is where the emperor would interview successful candidates of the imperial exams.

The stairs leading to each of the halls had a marble ramp in the center, which was carved with dragons and other creatures, mythical and real. The emperor was carried along a central path and up (or down) these ramps in a litter. Needless to say, no one else was allowed to set foot on it! And, except for the empress on her wedding day, no women were *ever* allowed in the ceremonial halls of the Forbidden City.

The only building in the Forbidden City with a roof of black tiles was the royal library. There was a good reason for this. For the Chinese, black represents water among the five elements (gold, wood, water, fire, and earth). Water can overcome fire, which was a constant danger for the collection of books inside.

Just beyond the three halls stood an ornate gate, which separated the official part of the compound from the private sector. On the far side of the gate, steps led to the living quarters of the imperial families, concubines, servants, and eunuchs. There were thousands of rooms, including more than 100 offices, archives, libraries, artists' studios, storerooms, and a three-story theater, not to mention the elegant halls and chambers of the emperor. The building interiors were decorated by the tribute gifts brought from distant places as well as domestic art — paintings, statues, carved furniture, and pieces of porcelain made by order of the emperor. Beyond these buildings was the Imperial Flower Garden, where the emperor and his family could stroll along paths leading past strange shaped rocks, clumps of peonies, and artificial ponds filled with goldfish.

A Warning From Above?

By 1417, the walls and major buildings of the Forbidden City were sufficiently completed for Yongle to move in. Five years later, all the work had been done, and there was a great celebration to mark the "grand opening" of the imperial palace compound. On February 2, 1421 (New Year's Day), thousands of officials, foreign representatives, and military officers gathered in the palace courtyard. They bowed and kowtowed to the emperor and wished him a long and prosperous reign in his new official quarters.

But three months later, lightning struck one of the three great halls during a spring storm, and fire spread rapidly throughout the wooden structures. Silk curtains and canopies burst into flames, and tile roofs collapsed in the intense heat. The gilded copper pots filled with water

---

While the Forbidden City was under construction, Yongle oversaw the building of a huge religious complex known as the Temple of Heaven. It had three sections: the Hall of Annual Prayers, the Hall of Heaven (which housed tablets bearing the names of deceased ancestors), and the Altar of Heaven.

Once the Temple of Heaven was completed in 1420, the emperor would visit it each year at the time of the winter solstice to honor his imperial ancestors and to pray to Heaven for a good harvest. All traffic in Beijing stopped and all windows and doors were closed while the emperor's magnificent procession made its way from the Forbidden City to the temple complex. After meditating in the Hall of Heaven, he fasted for a few days until the solstice. Then, with the appearance of the first rays of the sun, he donned special robes and ascended the steps of the Altar of Heaven. Kowtowing nine times, he asked the spirits for help and blessings for the empire.

that had been placed throughout the complex proved of little use against the raging inferno. Not even the magic of the dragons and the creatures on the roof could fight back the power of the flames. Many people in the living quarters were killed. Fortunately, Yongle escaped injury, but he wept in despair when he viewed the damage done by the fire.

Building the Forbidden City had been a costly project. Now certain officials who had opposed the expense all along said the fire was caused by angry ancestral spirits in order to punish the emperor for his extravagance. Yongle had his harshest critics imprisoned or banished. However, he *did* change his spending habits. He made no attempt to restore the damaged buildings (that task was left to his successors), and he undertook no new projects.

The Ming Tombs

Yongle died in 1424 while leading an expedition against the Mongols. He was buried with his wife and 16 concubines in a secluded valley nestled in the Tianshoushan Mountains, about 31 miles northwest of Beijing. The entrance to the valley is "defended" on both sides by the Dragon and Tiger Mountains. Yongle had planned the layout of this royal necropolis. (A necropolis is cemetery, or more literally, "city of the dead"). It became the final resting place of 13 of the 16 Ming emperors. No

A Stylized Lion Guarding the Sacred Way

other dynasty left such a complete set of tombs in a single burial ground.

Yongle's tomb remains the most impressive of these. It is approached by the Sacred Way, which winds for 4 ½ miles across the valley floor. Guarding the last mile of the path are eighteen pairs of gigantic carved statues of animals — elephants, camels, horses, lions (like the one above), and mythical beasts — as well as figures of military and civil officials representing the imperial court.

The road ends at the Dragon and Phoenix Gate, which opens onto a series of landscaped courtyards. Beyond these is Yongle's tomb. A grand pavilion standing atop a triple white marble terrace is an exact replica of the Hall of Supreme Harmony. This and two other smaller halls nearby were used for sacrifices to the emperor's spirit. Beyond them, another courtyard leads to the round artificial hill planted with trees covering Yongle's underground burial chamber. To the east and west are the tombs of the 16 imperial concubines. They were allegedly buried alive to serve their emperor in the next life. (Ritual execution had been common practice during the very early dynasties but was unusual at this period of history.)

Yongle's Successors

Yongle was succeeded by his eldest son, Hongxi. The new emperor was very fat and, like Kublai Khan, suffered from gout. He disliked any sort of physical activity, so much so that he was known to abandon military campaigns when the exercise made him uncomfortable! Hongxi was a good administrator, however, and quite scholarly. He was especially intrigued by astronomy. Several of his paintings of the sun, showing sunspots, have survived to modern times.

Hongxi died within a year of becoming emperor and was succeeded by his eldest son, Xuande. The new emperor combined a talent for military matters with administrative ability. He also had a social conscience, which he demonstrated by opposing the death penalty and the imprisonment of the poor for being in debt. Xuande was a patron of the arts, being a talented poet and painter himself, and an avid collector of luxury items (such as carved jade) and exotic animals. He embellished the Ming Tombs with beautiful columns and the largest marble archway in China.

Xuande made the mistake, however, of extending the power of the eunuchs. He established a palace school for them and even appointed eunuchs as military supervisors. As you know, many eunuchs already worked closely with the emperor as advisers. Now they were being trained for much more influential positions. In the years to come, emperors would rely increasingly on the eunuchs. The eunuchs, in turn, would make the most of their opportunities. Their greed became legendary.

The Ming ministers still worried about the nomads to the north and spent a

Unlike other ancient burial sites such as those in Egypt, the Ming imperial burial ground was undisturbed for centuries. Little was known about the contents of the tombs until 1956, when archaeologists opened the burial site of Emperor Wanli. They discovered an underground palace with six chambers. Among the 3,000 beautiful objects found there were a golden crown, gold wine vessels, porcelain vases, embroidered silk clothing, and 26 chests of "miscellaneous" treasure.

large part of the imperial budget on defense. This cost, added to the constant drain on the treasury caused by the emperors numerous hobbies and projects, prompted the decision that the expense of Zheng He's sea expeditions could no longer be justified. The treasure ships returned home in 1433, never again to venture forth from China's ports. The sailing personnel were dispersed, the ships were left idle to rot in their moorings, and, for reasons that are unclear, the navigation charts were burned by a minister of war (Liu Daxia).

A Captive Emperor

Xuande's eldest son, Zhengtong, came to the throne in 1436 when he was only seven. His grandmother served as regent, and for the next decade the government bureaucracy hummed along efficiently and the economy flourished. But in 1448, a Mongol army managed to get through the Great Wall and raced toward Beijing. It defeated a Chinese force just west of the city. Zhengtong, now 22, followed some rather poor advice from his tutor, eunuch Wang Zhen, and led a counter-attack. The emperor had no military experience, and his army was poorly prepared. The Mongols had no difficulty

ambushing his troops and slaughtering them by the thousands. (Wang Zhen was among those killed.) Buoyed by their easy triumph, the tribesmen seized the emperor and returned with him to the north, plundering the countryside as they went.

The Mongols had hoped for a large ransom in exchange for their imperial prisoner, but they were disappointed. The Ming ministers decided to avoid bargaining with the enemy by simply deposing Zhengtong and making his half brother, Jingtai, emperor instead. Zhengtong, having lost his value as a hostage, was released a year later. When he returned to Beijing, he was placed in confinement in the palace. He lived as a prisoner for seven years, until Jingtai fell ill and he was finally restored to the throne.

Zhentong's kidnapping made the Chinese more wary than ever of the nomads living in the north. The restored emperor added a second line of defense to the Great Wall — an interior wall, running south of the main one to the northwest of Beijing. Work on this wall as well as the renovation and reinforcement of the Great Wall itself would continue throughout most of the Ming dynasty. Actually, the Great Wall now standing in the region around Beijing is mainly a Ming construction. It follows the

---

The Great Wall was also known as "the Wall of Ten Thousand Li." Its actual length was 2,485 miles. Today, it is considered one of the great architectural wonders of the world, the only manmade structure observable from outer space. What remains is only half the length it reached under the Ming.

lines of the Qin and Han walls but was built several miles to the south. Unlike the original barriers of ancient times, which were solidly constructed from rocks and stones, the Ming walls have a tamped earth interior encased in a facing of bricks. (The kiln-fired bricks were mass-produced in the imperial factories.) Most of the system of walls and watchtowers that can be seen today was built by the Ming in the 15th and 16th centuries.

An End to Sea Travel

The treasure ships were not the only vessels to be grounded. By the 1440's, the imperial shipyards had been abandoned, and even private citizens were prohibited from venturing overseas. China's long coastline was now left unprotected against Japanese pirates and anyone else who was out on the high seas. Gradually, the Ming government closed off the empire to the rest of the world. No Chinese person could sell goods to foreigners or travel to foreign lands without official permission. A small number of merchants defied government orders, however, and continued to trade with countries in Southeast Asia. Modern historians continue to debate why China turned inward at this time. What reasons would you give?

Ming Porcelain

For a long time, a major product in China was porcelain. As you know, porcelain had long been produced in the south, where there was a good supply of kaolin (the white clay used by porcelain potters). Hongwu set up imperial kilns at Jingdezhen (in Jiangxi province), and this became the center for porcelain production. The kilns were conveniently situated near Poyang Lake, so the porcelain could be shipped by lake and river to Nanjing and by the Grand Canal to Beijing. Certain kilns supplied less expensive porcelain for ordinary Chinese citizens, for trade abroad, and for bricks like the ones used on the Great Wall.

As the porcelain industry expanded, workers were organized to perform specific tasks. These included molding the wet clay, refining its shape on a potter's wheel, glazing the clay vessel, firing it, painting it, glaz-

Ming craftsmen produced beautiful pieces of cloisonné — bronze vessels decorated with colorful enamels. The technique involved outlining patterns of flowers or leaves with thin copper wires and soldering them onto the vessel. The individual shapes were called *cloisons* ("cells"). The craftsman painted each cloison with a different color of enamel (a mixture of molten glass and metallic oxides which provide color). He fired the object at a low temperature to harden the enamel, then rubbed the surface smooth and polished it. Finally, he coated the outlines of the wires with gold. The resulting object — usually a box, plate, or incense burner — had the richness of a jewel.

ing it again, firing it again, polishing it, and finally wrapping it up. An imperial kiln was a marvel of mass production. New kilns built on the slopes of hills around Jingdezhen could fire thousands of pieces at the same time. Among the most common objects produced were rounded bottle bases, wide-mouthed fish bowls, elegant stemmed cups, and vases specially designed to hold the branches of flowering plum blossoms.

During Yongle's reign, potters developed a technique called *anhua* ("secret decoration"), in which figures were painted on the white clay and covered with glaze. The figure was just scarcely visible (hence secret) unless the vessel was held up to the light. Some of these vessels were so thin (like an eggshell) that they seemed to consist of nothing but the glaze itself.

Many pieces of porcelain were painted in bright colors, such as deep red, ruby, jade green, bright yellow, and peacock blue. Porcelain used by the emperor was decorated with five-clawed dragons, which were often flying through the sky above a sea of waves or diving through clouds and flames. No piece of porcelain was ever signed by a potter, although beginning at the time of Yongle each vessel bore the mark or seal of the reigning emperor.

Most highly prized of all Ming porcelain were the "blue and white" vessels made during the reign of Xuande. Blue-and-white pieces had been produced during the Yuan dynasty, but Ming potters perfected the style. Artists decorated the bone-white dishes and vases with a profusion of delicate lotus scrolls and vines using blue paint made from ground up cobalt. Popular flower motifs represented the seasons: peonies (spring), lotus blossoms (summer) chrysanthemums (autumn), and plum blossoms (winter). A combination of pine, bamboo, and plum blossoms symbolized everlasting friendship. There was a special magic associated with the firing process of the blue-and-white porcelain. The design disappeared completely when the opaque glaze was applied, but when the piece was fired, the glaze vitrified and became translucent, allowing the figures to reappear.

The Ming court ordered at least 10,000 pieces of porcelain every year for palace parties. A single order in 1433 specified 433,500 pieces of porcelain decorated with dragons and phoenixes. Each piece had to meet the highest standards. In recent years, archaeologists have discov-

---

Only the imperial dragon had five claws, which represented the five directions he governed — north, south, east, west, and center. Robes, dishes, and other objects of high officials were decorated with four-clawed dragons. The dragons of lower officials had three claws.

ered huge piles of shards (broken pieces) of imperial porcelain that was deliberately smashed because they failed to meet the proper standards of form, design, or color. (They could not be sold to ordinary people because of their imperial markings.)

European Traders Arrive

In one of history's more intriguing ironies, it was just after the Ming ceased their sea-going activities that the Europeans began their maritime exploration of the world. The Portuguese were the first to sail down the western coast of Africa, around the Cape of Good Hope, then on to India and the "spice islands" of the East Indies. From here they began to explore routes to the south China coast.

In 1514, the first Portuguese trading ships arrived at Guangzhou. Although it was illegal to trade with the Chinese, the local officials were easily bribed and smuggling became rampant. The Portuguese later managed to obtain permission from the Ming to dry their cargoes on the small island of Macao (muh kow) near Guangzhou. The island was gradually set-

tled by traders, and in 1557 the Chinese officially leased it to Portugal as a trading base. They tried to restrict all foreign trade to that single port, but this simply encouraged more smuggling.

Zhengtong tried to protect the imperial monopoly on fine porcelain by banning the manufacture of the most valuable wares for sale, including the famous "blue-and-white." But despite his efforts and those of his successors, large quantities of porcelain were smuggled out of China to markets in Japan, Vietnam, the Philippines, and to ports in the West. Porcelain had become a more valuable trading commodity than silk.

Civil Service Exams

By the middle years of the Ming dynasty, the civil service examinations had become extremely narrow in regard to intellectual and literary content. (Even more so than before!) Preparation for the exams had always involved strict memorizing, and the emphasis on a single scholar's interpretations of the Confucian Classics (that scholar being Zhu Xi) certainly dis-

Although the glass-like glaze of imperial vessels had to be flawless, slight imperfections on the surface actually appealed to many overseas customers. A glaze with small pittings was called "orange-peel," tiny pine-holes were called "palm eyes," a wrinkled glaze was called "wind-ruffled," and small raised creases were nicknamed "chick skin." The tea masters of Japan sought out wares whose glazed surfaces had tiny holes caused by broken off pieces of glaze. They called these rough spots "insect nibbles," because they looked like holes left by worms eating through paper.

couraged any creative thinking. In 1487, the examination process itself became more rigid when the the "right-legged" essay was introduced as the prescribed way of answering questions. This essay was divided into eight sections, and the style and even the number of characters in each section had to conform to specific standards. Writing such an essay involved incredible precision.

The Ming added a lower tier to the examination system. A new test given by the provincial education officer in a local city led to a degree of *shenshi* ("flowering talent"). Successful candidates could wear distinctive caps and sashes, were exempt from labor service, and were sometimes given stipends. Their titles gave them standing as community leaders and entry into educated circles, although the degree did not secure entry into the bureaucracy. Simply passing the exam and advancing in social status was the ultimate goal of some men of financial means. After achieving it, they retired from any further professional pursuits to look after the family estate and lead a life of culture and privilege. A *shenshi* in more modest circumstances could use his title to secure a job as a tutor in a wealthy family.

The next exam was held every third year in the provincial capital. It now took place in a special examination compound honeycombed with tiny cubicles, in which candidates sat for nearly a week as they wrote their essays. A cubicle was furnished with only three long boards, which served as shelf, desk, and seat (and bed). Each candidate brought his own food, bedding, and writing materials (ink and brushes), which the proctors searched as a precaution against cheating. He also brought a curtain to hang across the doorway to his tiny cell. Each man was identified by a number. Those who passed the exam at this level (about 10 percent) received the degree of *juren* ("recommended man") and were entitled to greater privileges than the *shenshi*, including eligibility for appointment to lower-level government posts.

The most prestigious exam was offered in the capital a few months later. This test consisted of three sets of essay questions. Once a candidate started writing, he could not make any corrections or cross out any characters. He was watched throughout the exams by a guard. When he completed the test, clerks recopied his answers so that no one's handwriting would be recognized. Finally, three judges read each answer. Only those candidates who passed this grueling test — about one in twenty or thirty — were invited to the palace for a final exam, which was held in front of the emperor in the Hall of Protective Harmony. This was strictly a formality in which the successful scholars were ranked in order of academic achievement. Each man then received the degree of the *jinshi*, ("presented scholar") — the highest honor, which entitled him to one of the loftiest positions in the government. Those who were ranked first and second became the superstars of the literati, and the common people considered them incarnations of the gods.

The new *jinshi* were feted at an official banquet, and a few days later they attended a ceremony in their honor at the temple of Confucius. The top palace graduates went straight into the Hanlin Academy and could expect to become one of the Grand Secretaries. However, the new degree did not automatically bring appointments for all candidates, since there were not enough jobs for those who were qualified. For many, it meant becoming part of a pool from which appointments were made.

Art and Culture in the South

There were many educated men of independent mind who chose not to participate in the rigid exams. They organized private academies, where people of similar political persuasions met to discuss "unorthodox" philosophies. In 1537 the government outlawed these academies, but the law was not thoroughly enforced and so many academies continued to function.

Southern China remained the center of free-thinking scholars who shunned government service. In beautiful cities like Nanjing, Yangzhou, Hangzhou, and Suzhou, well-off literati devoted most of their time to reading, writing, and other creative pursuits. It was the private art collectors in this area, rather than the Ming emperors, who preserved the great works created during the Song and Yuan dynasties. And it was here that the greatest artists of the Ming dynasty lived and worked. Foremost among these was Shen Zhou.

Ming Landscape Painting

Shen Zhou was born in 1427 to a wealthy family in Suzhou. His father had a very extensive collection of paintings and calligraphy. Shen spent most of his life on the family estate, enjoying the benefits of his wealth and the company of a circle of scholars and art collectors. But most of all he enjoyed painting. (Consult an art book to find illustrations of his two paintings entitled *Walking with a Staff in the Mountains* and *Watching the Mid-Autumn Moon.*)

Shen Zhou mastered the techniques of the Southern Song artists and of the painters who lived in the south during the Yuan dynasty. But he did not merely copy the works of the old masters, he reworked their techniques to create a style that was uniquely his own. He created many small, pleasant landscapes of his country estate and larger scroll paintings, which he filled with the tall mountains, gnarled trees, and great expanses of water. These are elements you'd expect to see in a Chinese landscape, and yet those of Shen Zhou have a gentle, whimsical quality.

Human figures are often the focus of a scene. Like the earlier artists, Shen Zhou intended for the viewer to identify with the figure and be drawn by him into the picture itself. An excellent example is the vertical scroll entitled *Walking with a Staff in the Mountains*. A mountain stream cuts through a gorge, winding its way from the center of the painting into the foreground. Large, rugged boulders rise above one side, and a small bridge crosses from right to left. An old man approaches the bridge, carrying a long staff. The long sleeves of his scholar's robe fall to his knees, and he wears a hat with a wide brim the keep out the sun. A group of slender trees shade the banks in the foreground, the central tree rising high above the others and dividing the lower parts of the painting into two neat halves. This symmetry is most unusual in Chinese painting, and it adds an intriguing dimension to the work. A massive set of hills rise beyond the trees and water. Unlike the misty peaks of the Southern Song paintings, the bulkiness of these hills contrasts dramatically with the delicacy of the foreground trees, the bridge, and the old man himself.

Shen Zhou's handscroll entitled *Watching the Mid-Autumn Moon* is a far more intimate picture. Here the artist and three friends have gathered to dine and drink wine in a small shed, which is open in front to allow them to gaze at the moon. In the right foreground several trees bend toward the shed as though they were eavesdropping on the men. Just beyond the shed to the left, the river bank drops abruptly, and beyond is an unbroken expanse of light wash in which water and sky seem to blend together. High in the left corner shines the moon. The artist, who was 60 at the time, described the melancholy musings the scene invoked:

> "When young, we heedlessly watch the mid-autumn moon, seeing this time as all other time.
> With the coming of age, respect has grown, and we do not look lightly every time we raise the deep cup to celebrate the feast..."

Shen Zhou was considered the greatest of the 'Four Great Masters of the Ming." These men formed the Wu School of Painting, named for the Wu district in which they lived. Let's meet the other three — Wen Zhengming, Tang Yin, and Qiu Ying. (Try to find copies of the following paintings: Wen Zhengming's *Old Trees by a Cold Waterfall*, Tang Yin's *Fishermen on an Autumn River*, and Qiu Ying's *Spring Morning in the Han Palace*.)

Wen Zhengming was the greatest Ming artist of the 16th century. He sat for the civil service exams ten times, and ten times he failed. (Perhaps his mind was too creative for the constraints of the exam questions!) However, he was summoned to the capital and spent a few years at the Hanlin Academy, compiling the official history of the Yuan dynasty. He returned to Suzhou in 1527 and devoted the rest of his life to his art and scholarship. Wen collected and studied the works of the old masters; his studio became an informal academy, where he passed on his ideas to his many pupils.

Wen painted his finest work, a large vertical scroll entitled *Old Trees by a Cold Waterfall*, when he was 79. A dense tangle of pine and cypress trees fills most of the painting. Beyond, a narrow waterfall plunges from the upper third to the bottom right of the picture. The crowded forms of the trees and explosive energy of the tumbling water create a sense a turmoil, something most unusual in a Chinese landscape. This work is a far cry from the spacious openness in the landscapes of earlier times, don't you think?

Tang Yin was a friend of Wen Zhengming. As a young man, he seemed a promising scholar. He took first place in the provincial examinations, then set off for the capital to take the imperial exams. Again he passed — in first place. But his destiny changed when he was drawn into a scandal involving a rather disreputable friend, who was accused of using bribery to get advance information about an upcoming examination. Although he was probably innocent of any wrongdoing, Tang's hopes for a career in the government quickly dissolved. Since he lacked the means to live in the private elegance of many literati, he dwelled in a humble abode, painting landscapes and selling them to pay for his living expenses.

One of Tang's most charming paintings is entitled *Fishermen on an Autumn River*. It features two scholar-fishermen, relaxing in their small boats as they slowly drift side by side along the river. One trails his foot in the water while playing a flute, the other keeps time by clapping his hands. In the right foreground stands a tree, its leaves turning a seasonal red. Many of the leaves have fallen into the water and are drifting with the current, while others pile up on the rock below the tree. On the far side of the river, rocky boulders line the shore, while a waterfall tumbles in the background. You can almost hear the sounds of the flute, the splashes of the waterfall, and the rhythmical clapping of the man's hands. And do you sense the coolness of the autumn air?

Qiu Ying was born to a peasant family and lacked the scholarly education of his peers. In fact, he seems to have envied the lifestyles of those born to a higher social status. His paintings of palaces and pavilions skillfully portray the leisured life of the elite. A fine example is his handscroll entitled *Spring Morning in the Han Palace.* In one section of the picture, a court artist is engaged in painting the portrait of an empress (or perhaps an imperial concubine), while her curious servants cluster around her. Two eunuchs stand guard in the hallway. Such fine details as the embroidery of the women's robes, the paintings on the walls, and the designs in the carpets add a realistic touch to this intriguing glimpse into life in the imperial palace during the Ming dynasty.

The Image of the Scholar

Since the times of the Song, the classic image of a scholar had been that of a dignified, sedentary man. He never ran, jumped, or swam. He didn't even travel by horse (which required some athletic ability) but by sedan chair or litter. A scholar spent most of his time reading, reflecting, writing, chatting with friends, playing the lute, sipping wine, or playing a game of chess with another scholar. Fishing was considered an appropriate pursuit, and many paintings depict the scholar sitting tranquilly in his reed boat, contemplating the ever-changing surface of the water. (Tang Yin's *Fishermen on an Autumn River* is an excellent example.) So was bird-watching. Often, the scholar simply sat in a pavilion and gazed at the scenic view, gathering images he would later describe in his poetry or depict in a painting.

Scholars were actually encouraged

Dong Qichang was a painter, an art critic, and a historian of the 16th century. He divided Chinese painters into two categories, which he called the Northern and Southern Schools. Into the Southern School he lumped the great landscape painters of the Southern Song, the displaced literati of the Yuan, and the Ming painters you've just read about. These artists, he said, were thoughtful men, whose wide reading enabled them to understand the nature of the world about them. (Qiu Ying would be an exception, since he lacked a proper education.) Dong claimed that the amateur status of the artists of the Southern School enabled them to freely express their feelings and intuitions through their paintings.

In the Northern School he placed the imperial court painters who, he believed, compromised their talents by following rigid formulas and creating decorative pieces to please the passing whims of the reigning emperor. Their precise bird-and-flower paintings and imperial portraits were not great art, in his opinion. Dong Quichang succeeded so well in convincing others of his views that many books about painting written in China after his time were strongly influenced by them.

As for his own paintings, they tend to be dark, austere landscapes, with no human presence at all. There is a brooding quality about them.

to walk with a shuffling gait, bent in a stooped position known as the scholar's posture. (When an actor assumed this position, the audience of a play immediately knew he was portraying a scholar.) He cultivated the sensitivity of his fingers by rolling smooth stones or metal objects in his hand, so that he could judge the quality of fine porcelain. He grew the nails of his little fingers as long as possible as proof of his unfamiliarity with manual labor. (The was an old custom. Remember, the Song scholars did this, too.) The image of the scholar had certainly changed since the days of the Tang dynasty, when court officials commonly played polo and hunted wild boar!

The Gardens of Suzhou

Many of the scholars who lived in Suzhou transformed their courtyards into elegant gardens that reflected, on a small scale, the panoramas of landscape paintings. They hired workers to dig ponds and heap up piles of dirt and pebbles to create "mountains." (In Chinese, the art of designing landscape gardens is known as "piling up stones!") These "mountains" were interspersed with strategically placed rocks (often dredged out of the bed of nearby Lake Tai), uniquely-shaped evergreen trees, and clumps of flowers. Goldfish swam in the garden ponds, while lotus flowers floated on the water's surface.

Strolling along the narrow, winding paths of such a garden was like letting your mind wander through a landscape painting. Graceful bridges over man-made streams offered unique views, as did small pavilions with curved roofs and brightly painted pillars. Garden scenes could also be viewed from balconies and through round openings in the surrounding wall, known as "moon gates." Visitors to a garden often wrote short verses about particular scenes and placed them along the walkway or in a pavilion, just as an inscription might be written in the open space of a painting.

The Garden of the Master of the Fishing Nets had been laid out in Suzhou the 12th century and was tended by generations of homeowners. It covered a little over an acre of land. A visitor could stroll along the a covered walkway and peer into the garden through one of many latticed windows. Each window framed a particular view, often of a carefully placed tree or rock. As he progressed along the walkway, each "framed" picture would offer a new per-

The city of Suzhou was located on the Grand Canal and beautiful Lake Tai. Renowned for its beautiful setting, it was paired with Hangzhou, which lies just to the south, in the famous saying, "In Heaven there is Paradise, on earth there are Hangzhou and Suzhou." Marco Polo was very impressed when he visited Suzhou and remarked on its 6,000 stone bridges. During Ming times, the city was a center for artists, scholars, and wealthy merchants.

spective. In addition to several pavilions, the garden had a small library, where the scholars would gather for literary competitions. A portion of this famous garden has been reproduced in the Metropolitan Museum in New York.

Between 1631 and 1634, Ri Cheng wrote *The Craft of Gardens*. It may have been the first manual on landscape gardening.

A Most Peculiar Emperor

As was so often the case in Chinese history, many of the men who came to the throne in the later years of the Ming dynasty lacked the talent and ambition of their predecessors. (How would you explain this? Isn't it more challenging to found a new dynasty than to simply inherit the throne? Don't some people get complacent when the living is easy?) Some of the later Ming rulers were downright incompetent. Zhengde is a good example. He became emperor in 1506 when he was only 14. His father had worried about his character, noting on his deathbed that the boy was " intelligent but loved ease and pleasure." That was an understatement!

Zhengde's main interest was in having fun, and he filled his court with magicians, acrobats, and wrestlers. He had a cluster of buildings known as the "Leopard House" constructed on the palace grounds and took up residence there. Zhengde loved role-playing, whether dressing up like a Tibetan monk or pretending to be a merchant in the eunuch-run shops he had set up in the Forbidden City. He often put on a disguise and slipped out of the palace compound to wander the streets of Beijing. And he became so fascinated with the military that he would often "play soldier," drilling a unit of eunuchs in a palace courtyard.

Zhengde had little interest in politics and met with his ministers only in the evenings — if at all. He preferred the flattery of his eunuchs to the sage advice of his Confucian advisers, many of whom he had transferred to distant posts. With such a man on the throne, the eunuchs easily gained control of the government.

In 1517, when an army of Mongols raided a Ming outpost north of the Great Wall, Zhengde took personal command of the frontier forces. Although the Ming soldiers defeated the enemy, their casualties far exceeded those of the Mongols. Two years later, Zhengde made plans to tour the southern provinces as Supreme Military Commander. When 146 officials knelt in

---

Although a Chinese garden is asymmetrical, it represents a balance of the two forces of nature, *yin* and *yang*. The "mountains" and evergreen trees represent *yang*, while the water represents *yin*.

the courtyard of the Hall of Supreme Harmony, begging him to call off the journey (it was a tremendous expense), he ordered them punished with thirty strokes of the whipping club. (Eleven of them eventually died of their injuries.)

As soon as he arrived in Nanjing, Zhengde announced to the local people that they were forbidden to raise hogs, since the word for that animal sounded like his family name, Zhu. (Remember Hongwu?) A few months later, the fishing boat he was on capsized. Although he was rescued, he never fully recovered from the experience. Early the next year, Zhengde, perhaps China's most eccentric emperor, died in the Leopard House.

The Daoist Emperor

Because Zhengde had no sons, the throne passed to his adopted son, Jiajing. From the start, he didn't seem any more promising than Zhengde. He avoided official meetings whenever he could, focusing his attention on religious matters. Jiajing was the only Ming emperor to become an ardent Daoist.

You learned earlier how Daoism evolved from an elitist philosophy of ancient times to a popular religion. Daoists now worshiped of a multitude of deities, the most important being the Jade Emperor and the Queen Mother of the West. Daoists also practiced meditation, slow dance-like movements, and breathing exercises to balance the forces of *yin* and *yang* in their bodies. And the priests were still experimenting in hopes of creating a potion that would make them immortal. (Do you remember how the formula for gunpowder was discovered?)

During the Tang dynasty, folk tales about Eight Immortals became popular among Daoists. The Immortals were ordinary human beings who gained immortality through their efforts in meditation, performing good deeds, and making sacrifices. They lived on high mountain peaks above the clouds, but they kept their human forms and remained in touch with people on earth. By the Song dynasty, the stories about the Immortals were widespread throughout China. Daoists worshiped them, believing they would show them the way to achieving immortality themselves. The Immortals represented people from all walks of life in Chinese society, and they all wore a distinctive garb and special emblems. They were often depicted in paintings as a jolly group, enjoying cups of fine wine or helping deserving causes.

Emperor Jiajing was fascinated by the beliefs and rituals of Daoism. He ordered the construction of many new Daoist temples, and he spent huge amounts on precious materials (pearls and gold) for his priests to concoct an elixir of immortality. When he died, he was succeeded by his son, Longqing. Like his father, he had no political skills or interests. He never spoke a court audiences, avoided his ministers whenever he could, and sought out the eunuchs for company. His major act was to rid his court of all Daoists! After a reign of five years, Longqing died and was succeeded by Wanli. The new emperor would rule for 47 years — the longest reign since Wudi of the Han dynasty in the 2nd century BC. You'll learn about him later in this chapter.

The Chinese Novel

One of the great legacies of the Ming dynasty was the development of the Chinese novel. Like the plays of the Yuan dynasty, most novels were written in the vernacular, the everyday language of the people.

The tradition of storytelling dates back to very early times in China, when people gathered around the hearth to hear the tales that were passed down orally from one generation to another. During the Tang dynasty, certain scholars began writing short stories to entertain one another — in the elegant style of the educated elite. After the invention of printing and the mass-pro-

duction of books created a wider spectrum of readers, storytellers from the lower classes began writing down rough sketches of their tales — to refresh their memories and to provide a working text for others. These are known as *hua pen* ("story roots"), and they formed the core of many of the first novels.

People have always enjoyed stories of good versus evil, and the Chinese novelists catered to this interest. Tales of daring and bravado described the exploits of the public-spirited rebel fighting a corrupt regime, while other accounts mocked the flashy glitter of merchant wealth or the hypocrisy of certain wayward bureaucrats. The stories often contained ribald passages in their colorful descriptions of everyday life, passages that contrasted sharply with the philosophical musings of the more scholarly writings. Many of the stories were even written by literati, although they disguised their identity by using false names (pen names).

By the Ming dynasty, four major works — the first true novels — had emerged. They are *The Romance of the Three Kingdoms, The Water Margin, Golden Lotus,* and *The Monkey King*.

In early Chinese novels, chapters open with the invocation, "Reader, you will remember that in the last chapter…" and end with "Reader, if you want to know what happened to [so and so] in these circumstances, please listen to the next installment." These phrases clearly echo the words of the storyteller as he gathers or dismisses his audience.

The Romance of the Three Kingdoms

The Romance of the Three Kingdoms was written by Luo Guanzhong in the 14th century. It serves as a link between the more erudite writings of the literati and the evolving popular novel, being written in a refined literary style but containing the elements of "the people's literature." The book is a fictionalized history of the three kingdoms — the Wei, Shu, and Wu — that fought for dominance after the fall of the Han dynasty in the 3rd century BCE. The story is based on material that was compiled during the Song dynasty from legends and folktales. Although the Wei kingdom eventually absorbed the other two and was given legitimacy in official government records, the folktales were partial to the Shu, which came to represent good as opposed to the evil Wei. (The third and smallest kingdom, the Wu, actually plays a minor part in the drama.)

The novel begins with the hero, Liu Pei, ruler of the Shu, taking the "Peach Orchard" oath of loyalty with his close friends, Guan Yu (a general) and Zhang Fei (his prime minister). The three men swear to defend one another to their deaths in their fight against Cao Cao, ruler of the Wei. The story follows the struggle for power between the two kingdoms, leading up to a famous battle in which the Shu defeat Cao Cao and his army.

While the novel follows the events of recorded history, many of its dramatic episodes probably never took place. It is a highly entertaining tale, one that became so popular that the major characters are still household names throughout China. Liu Bei is generally viewed as the very model of the bold and handsome freedom fighter, and Guan Yu (depicted as a nine-foot giant with a red face and a forked beard) has been immortalized as a powerful defender of the weak. (Guan was later worshiped as Guandi, a god of war, during the Qing dynasty.) Liu Bu's scholarly minister, Zhuge Liang, symbolizes political cunning, and Cao Cao will always be remembered as a selfish bully.

This novel was revised into its final form by Mao Zonggang in the late 17th century. Today, well-known episodes are often performed by the Beijing Opera.

The "Peach Orchard" in *The Romance of the Three Kingdoms* is a reference to the Daoist Queen Mother of the West. She grew peaches in her orchard that, when consumed, made a person immortal. Peaches became symbols for immortality or permanence in Chinese culture. The "Peach Orchard" oath of the three heroes was, therefore, one that could never be broken.

The Water Margin

Luo Guangzhong and Shi Naian compiled another series of legends that had been circulating for years to produce *The Water Margin*. This vast novel — it originally had 120 chapters — was written in the vernacular. It depicts the events of a minor rebellion that took place at the end of the Northern Song dynasty. The heroes are a group of honest men, who have been driven to become outlaws by the injustices of the government. The novel's title comes from the marshy and mountainous country where they have their hideout. The bandits stage a number of assaults in a valiant effort to right the wrongs of society and to aid the weak and poor — like Robin Hood and his Merry Men. They struggle against the unsavory and cowardly provincial authorities, but as their legend grows, so, too, does the government force that is moving against them. By the end of the story, each of the bandits has met his death.

This lively tale revels in the nobility of its virile heroes, who fight to the death to defend their beliefs. Less attractive is the portrayal of the women, who appear as bossy, complaining stumbling blocks to the heroes' exploits. And isn't it interesting to see the Confucian officials, who in theory were very virtuous and scholarly, depicted as corruptible hypocrits? (The true image of a Ming official is probably somewhere in between.)

The Water Margin was revised in 17th century and cut to 70 chapters. It is still popular today. It was translated into English in 1933 by American author Pearl Buck under the title *All Men Are Brothers*.

Golden Lotus

Golden Lotus was written in the late 16th century by an unknown author. The story contains material from existing plays and novels. In fact, two of the characters, including the main one, a concubine named Golden Lotus, appeared in *The Water Margin*.

Like *The Water Margin*, the story is set during the Northern Song dynasty. It describes the adventures of a merchant, Ximen Qing, who becomes wealthy by manipulating a number of unsuspecting government officials. Of greater interest to us is the colorful and rather scathing portrait it paints of the everyday life on a large country estate in one of the provinces. It concludes with the conquest of the Northern Song by "barbarians," the message implied being that the Chinese are being punished for their low morals.

Monkey

An all-time favorite novel in China is *The Record of a Journey to the West*, better known as *Monkey*. It was written by Wu Cheng'en, about whom little is known.

(Perhaps he used a pen name.) This humorous story of travel and adventure was loosely based on the actual 7th century pilgrimage of a Chinese Monk, Xuan Zang. He traveled to India to obtain Buddhist scriptures for translation into Chinese. In the novel, he is joined on his travels by Monkey, a mischievous rascal, and two other amusing characters, known as Pigsy and Sandy.

The first part of the book relates the early adventures of Monkey, the sly trickster who has acquired magical powers. He can jump 108,000 *li* in one bound, and he is able to summon aid when in a tight spot by plucking out one of his own hairs, chewing it up, and spitting out the pieces, which immediately turn into an army of monkeys! Monkey defeats all the forces the Jade Emperor (Daoist ruler of the heavens) sends against him. In one episode, he steals the banquet feast of the gods and makes himself immortal by eating the peaches of immortality (picked in the Peach Orchard of the Queen Mother of the West).

Monkey is finally curbed by Buddha himself and given the task of accompanying the monk on his pilgrimage to India. The rest of the novel follows the numerous adventures of Monkey and his friends on their journey, as they encounter an assortment of demons, ogres, monsters, and fairies. The sober-minded pilgrim tries to keep the group focused on their quest, but Pigsy is always looking for something to eat, Sandy gets confused, and Monkey is always getting into trouble.

The clever but mischievous Monkey has become a popular figure in Chinese culture. Also known as the Monkey King, he is frequently portrayed on stage by agile actors, who perform dazzling acrobatics. Every Chinese child is familiar with Monkey, and thanks to the television special, *Big Bird Goes to China*, American children know him, too.

Wanli, the Spendthrift

Wanli, the 14th Ming emperor, came to power in 1573 and ruled for nearly half a century. If only the quality of his reign had been as impressive as its longevity, this would have been a golden age. But such was not the case, and Wanli's lack of political acumen contributed to the decline of his dynasty.

Like several of his predecessors, Wanli neglected his state duties from the beginning. Eventually, he stopped appearing at state audiences, leaving his ministers and foreign envoys to kowtow to an empty throne! Any communication with him had to come through the eunuchs, who ran the imperial palace. In time, the eunuchs would be running China.

With so much time on his hands, Wanli was able to indulge himself in his favorite pastime — spending money. He ordered vast quantities of ornate jewelry and elaborately embroidered silk robes for himself and his family. He spent a fortune on the weddings for his two daughters and the placement of his numerous sons on huge estates in the provinces. This emperor loved parties and banquets, and he had food brought to the Forbidden City from all over China. Delicacies like plums, bamboo shoots, and shad were packed in ice and shipped over 1,00 miles along the Grand Canal from the south. Wanli consumed food and drink with such abandon that he eventually grew extremely fat — so fat that he could not stand unaided!

The emperor spent vast sums on rebuilding two palaces that had burned down. But this was nothing compared to the costs of the construction and furnishing of his tomb. It amounted to one half of an entire year's national income! In 1956, archaeologists opened the burial site and discovered an underground palace that had never been robbed. The rooms were filled with fabulous funerary objects, gold ingots, porcelain vases, golden chopsticks and goblets, exquisite jade objects, and the black silk hat with a golden rim and the strings of precious stones worn by the emperor on his official journeys. They also unearthed the "phoenix headdress" of the empress, made of kingfisher feathers adorned with 5,449 pearls, and 26 chests of treasure. Besides these, there were beautiful robes and vast quantities of the finest woven embroidered silk, each bolt marked with the date and place of origin and name of the pattern and responsible foreman. Near the entrance of the tomb was a blue-and-white porcelain vase filled with oil and a wick. It was intended to provide light for a thousand years, but the flame had gone out soon after the tomb was sealed for lack of air.

Matteo Ricci

In 1583, Jesuit missionary Matteo Ricci arrived in China with the intention of converting those whom he met to the Christian religion. He was an intelligent, scholarly man, and he soon realized that in China merit was equated with knowledge of the classics. He decided the only way to influence the Chinese people was to meet them on their own ground. So he studied the Chinese language and mastered enough characters to be able to express himself and to understand what others were saying. He even created a Chinese dic-

During Wanli's reign, new crops from America, such as corn, sweet potatoes and peanuts, increased food production in China. The sweet potatoes and peanuts were especially valuable since they could be grown on hilly land that was previously uncultivated.

tionary and grammar for English speakers.

Ricci eventually became friendly with the local literati, who were greatly impressed by his ability to quote from the Confucian classics. He sometimes amazed them by such feats of memory as reading a page of 500 characters once and then, without looking, repeating them in perfect order. Ricci took the Chinese name of Li Madou and started dressing in the silk robes of a scholar. (Li was the nearest family name to Ricci. There is no "r" in Chinese, and family names are of one syllable. Madou was the Chinese translation of Matteo.)

At the time, Latin was the language of the Catholic Church and also the language of scholars throughout Europe. So Ricci translated the Five Confucian Classics into Latin. It was he who came up with the Latin name, Confucius, for the esteemed Chinese philosopher *Kong Fuzi*. Ricci even wrote a series of books in Chinese. The first one, *The True Meaning of the Lord of Heaven*, explained the basic beliefs of the Christian religion using many Confucian concepts. For example, he employed the concept of "self-cultivation" to explain how a "superior man" could cultivate and broaden himself by worshiping God. His book on friendship, which took the form of a dialogue between himself and a Chinese scholar, became so popular in China that it was reprinted many times. Ricci also translated the first six books of Euclid into Chinese and constructed a huge map of the world, giving the Chinese their first view of the American continent.

Ricci was not allowed in the Forbidden City until 1598. Even then, he did not see Wanli. (Remember, the emperor didn't *do* audiences!) He had brought a number of gifts for the emperor, and these were quickly carried out of sight by the eunuchs. Most were religious objects, such as a crucifix and a statue of the Virgin Mary. But it was a chiming clock that truly charmed the emperor. Ricci returned to the palace every day for three days to instruct the eunuchs on the workings of the clock's mechanism. During this time, he was bombarded with questions sent from Wanli about conditions in Europe. In order to prolong his contacts with the emperor, Ricci retained the key to the clock, so that he had to be summoned weekly in order to

Ricci later became the patron deity of Chinese clockmakers and was worshiped until the 19th century in Shanghai as Buddhist Bodhisattva Ricci. (A bodhisattva is someone who has become "enlightened" but has chosen to remain among the living to help others attain *Nirvana*.)

wind it. The eunuchs were extremely impressed by the priest's knowledge of music, mathematics, and geography, and, of course, they relayed everything he said to Wanli. The emperor instructed him to teach the eunuchs to play the clavichord, and when he heard of the map Ricci had made of the world, he ordered a copy made as a screen for his palace. Although Wanli never agreed to see Ricci, he was rather curious about what the man looked like. So he sent the court artist to paint his portrait.

In time, Ricci was named science tutor to the emperor's son. He was allowed to settle in Beijing, where he founded a small mission and worked for the rest of his life to establish the Roman Catholic religion. The priest saw no problem with a Chinese Christian convert continuing to worship his ancestors. This issue, however, would lead to a major controversy in the Catholic Church in later years.

Ricci thoughtfully described the Chinese beliefs and customs he observed in the letters he wrote to Jesuits and others back in Europe. These opened the eyes of many Westerners to the rich civilization of China, and they are an invaluable source of information about the later years of the Ming dynasty. When he died in 1610, Matteo Ricci was buried outside the Fucheng Gate of Beijing by order of Wanli.

Ricci's work was continued by Jesuits Adam Schall von Bell and John Schreck, who arrived in Beijing in 1622. They brought the first telescope to China. Their astronomical skills impressed the court of the next emperor (Tainqi). After predicting an eclipse more accurately than the Chinese astronomers, they were given the task of reforming the imperial calendar.

The Eunuchs Take Over

As you've seen, the eunuchs had become very powerful by the later years of the Ming dynasty. Their sheer numbers were huge — there were no less than 70,000 eunuchs living in the palace during Wanli's reign. Their access to the emperor enabled them to exert tremendous influence on him, particularly when the emperor had little political savvy. Wanli heard only the news the eunuchs decided to relate to him. And these men were quick to exploit their privileged position for their own personal advantage at the expense of the government — and the people. The eunuch secret service created by Yongle had slowly evolved into a powerful organ of terror that was difficult for even the emperors to control. It provided unlimited opportunities for blackmail and corruption, leaving many government officials helpless in the face of false accusations.

The relentless in-fighting between the eunuchs and the literati at the highest levels of government was crippling the dynasty. The authority of the bureaucracy reached an all-time low in 1621, when 15-year-old emperor Tianqi entrusted all his government affairs to Wei Zhongxian, a eunuch who had been butler to his mother. While Tainqi devoted his time to carpentry, Wei became virtual dictator of China. Using the secret service as his personal police force, he purged all his enemies from among the government officials. Then he began raising taxes to an exorbitant level, using most of the income to erect temples in his own honor! He was eventually banished, and the last Ming emperor, Chongzhen, came to the throne in 1627.

But by then, the dynasty was crumbling. The eunuchs controlled the court, the civil service was divided into factions, and royal expenditures continued to exceed income. There was suffering everywhere. With the lack of government leadership, soldiers often did not receive pay for months, even years. Many of these deserted the army to join the rebel bands that were springing up all over China. The bureaucracy was slowly grinding to a halt — posts were left unfilled, there were no promotions, and prisoners languished and died in prison for lack of a judge to try them. And just when it seemed things couldn't get worse, there were ominous rumblings coming from just beyond the Great Wall.

The Manchus Build A Power Base

The Manchus were descendants of the Jurchen tribesmen who had once ruled northern China under the Jin dynasty. They lived in Manchuria, a region of wide, fertile plains and densely forested mountains lying east of Mongolia. During the later part of the Ming dynasty, southern Manchuria was a frontier region, where Manchu and Chinese families farmed adjacent fields and mingled socially. In the late 1500's, a chieftain named Nurhachi (Ner HAH chee) unified the Manchus in this region under his personal rule. The Chinese, alarmed by Nurhachi's rise to power, immediately created a boundary line between the Manchu lands and those of the Chinese farmers.

Nurhachi erected a strong fort as his base of operations and began forging the military and political framework of a new state. He organized his people into groups of 300 households. Each group made up a company, and 50 companies formed a banner. The name "banner" referred to the patterned flag belonging to each group. Every

---

Beginning with Hongwu, every direct descendant of a Ming emperor was given some kind of title and salary. Towards the end of the dynasty, the total number of imperial clansmen ran into tens and even hundreds of thousands – with a resulting financial burden that was huge!

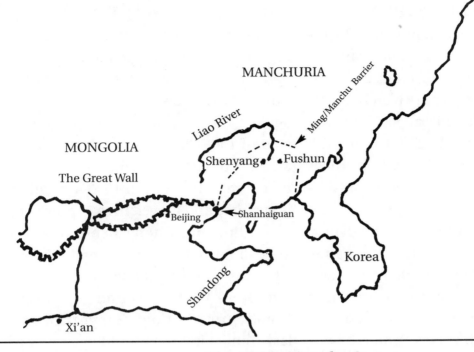

The Rising Manchu State

banner head had to provide fighting men whenever called upon. But a banner did not fight as a unit. During a military campaign, each squadron was made up of men from different banners. This promoted the "national" spirit and eliminated the danger of one banner defecting or challenging the authority of the leaders. During peacetime, the banner leaders managed the local government.

Nurhachi hired Chinese scholars to help him to convert his confederation of tribesmen into an efficient bureaucracy. He had the Ming law code and Confucian classics translated into Manchu. In 1616, he and his son, Abahai, founded a dynasty, reviving the old name of Jin.

Two years later, Nurhachi seized the Chinese trading post of Fushun, which lay just over the Manchu borderline, and lured the commander of the post into his own army. The following year, he entered the Chinese town of Shenyang and made it his capital, renaming it Mukden. The Ming sent an army of 200,000 into Manchuria, but it was easily defeated by the Manchu. By the time Nurhachi died in 1626, his forces had conquered all the land that had been held by the Ming east of the Liao River in Manchuria.

The Manchurian State

Abahai now ruled alone. In 1629, his warriors crossed the Great Wall, captured four Chinese cities, and reached the walls of Beijing before they were driven back. By 1635, he had extended his rule as far south as Shanhaiguan, where the Great Wall reaches the sea. He had also made alliances with the Mongol tribes to the west and subjugated Korea to the east.

In 1636, Abahai dropped the dynastic name of Jin in favor of a Chinese name, Qing, meaning "Pure." (The name was intended to be a challenge to the Ming ["Brilliant"] dynasty.) He set up Six Ministries to lead his government, with official posts going to Manchus, Mongols, and Chinese. He appointed a prominent Chinese scholar-official, Fan Wen Cheng, as Grand Secretary. (Fan had been captured by Nurhachi and, like many others, ended up collaborating with him.) Abahai introduced a Confucian civil examination system, wooed even more Chinese into his government, and organized his Chinese and Mongol troops into banners.

By 1642, Abahai had united most of Manchuria and controlled all areas northeast of the Great Wall. When he died the following year, his throne went to his six-year-old son. His brother, Dorgon, served as major regent.

The Fall of Beijing

While the Manchus were establishing a powerful state, conditions in China had grown from bad to worse. Growing numbers of people had begun to rebel against the corrupt, inefficient and harsh rule of the Ming government. Li Zicheng, an army deserter, became a powerful leader of a group of rebels. In 1643, he gathered a huge force and moved in to capture Beijing.

Emperor Chongzhen sent a desperate call for help to his general, Wu Sangui, who was guarding the easternmost pass of the Great Wall. Uncertain whether help would arrive in time, Chongzhen called a last council in the Forbidden City, at which "all were silent and many wept." As Li Zicheng's rebel army approached, two-thirds of the imperial troops guarding the capital fled or surrendered. Soon the rebels were pouring through the Beijing, although the Forbidden City was still protected by its own wall and the imperial guard.

The emperor helped his two sons to escape in disguise, then ordered the empress and dowager empress (the widow of the previous emperor) to commit suicide in order to avoid capture. When they were dead, he attempted to kill his daughters and concubines with a dagger. (Only two survived his attacks.) The following morning, April 25, 1644, Chongzhen arose at dawn and dressed in his yellow imperial robes. Then, accompanied by his faithful eunuch attendant, Wang Chengen, he climbed the hill behind the now silent palace and hanged himself from the beams of a pavilion. Thus ended the Ming dynasty. (Ironically, the place where he died had been known as the Pavilion of Imperial Longevity.) Wang then dutifully took his own life. (He would later be buried beside Chongzhen in the Imperial Cemetery.) Later that morning, the imperial ministers searched for the emperor. When they could not find him, they assumed the worst. Hundreds took their own lives.

The next day, Li Zicheng, wearing pale blue robes and mounted on a black warhorse, led a procession of his followers into the imperial city, the section of Beijing where the government officials lived. Crowds of fawning eunuchs, military leaders, and officials (those who had chosen not to commit suicide) met him with heads bowed and escorted him to the gates of the Forbidden City. Li entered the Hall of Supreme Harmony and eyed the Dragon Throne. Most people assembled around him assumed that he would be the new emperor. But for the next few days, Li's attention was drawn more to the riches waiting to be plundered than to claiming the Mandate of Heaven.

The Manchus Take Over

Let's not forget about Wu Sangui, the general to whom Chongzhen had sent his desperate call for help. Believing his own forces were not sufficient to fight the rebel forces, Wu had turned to the Manchus for assistance and signaled them through the gate of the Great Wall. And in they came, by the thousand! Working with the Ming forces, the Manchus easily defeated the rebel forces in the countryside. On June 6, 1644 they entered Beijing and drove out Li Zicheng and his followers.

The Manchus were now in control of northern China, and they weren't about to leave. They claimed Beijing as their capital and declared Nurhachi's six-year-old grandson, Shunzhi, emperor of China. The Middle Kingdom was once again in the hands of foreigners.

Review Questions:

1. Where did Hongwu set up his capital?
2. What was the Hanlin Academy?
3. Who was the highest official in Hongwu's early government?
4. How did Hongwu keep the eunuchs in line?
5. What were the "Yellow Books?"
6. What was the purpose of the Great Wall?
7. Why did Hongwu start killing off his staff?
8. Why was the Prince of Yan able to defeat the imperial army?
9. How did Yongle deal with the eunuchs?
10. What was the purpose of sea voyages of Zheng He?
11. Why did Yongle make his capital in Beijing?
12. What were the purposes of the great halls of the Forbidden City?
13. What was the Sacred Way?
14. What was Xuande's big mistake?
15. Why did the sea explorations end?
16. What did the high officials do when their emperor, Zhengtong, was captured by the Mongols?
17. What was the importance of the island of Macao?
18. What was the most prized type of porcelain during the Ming dynasty?
19. What was an eight-legged essay?
20. What was a "flowering talent?"
21. How would you characterize the paintings of Shen Zhou?
22. How was a garden like a landscape painting?
23. Use three adjectives to describe Zhengde.
24. Who were the Eight Immortals?
25. What did the three great Ming novels have in common?
26. What was Wanli's favorite pastime?
27. In what ways did Matteo Ricci meet the Chinese on their own terms?
28. What factors made it easy for the eunuchs to become powerful?
29. Why were the Manchusrian groups called banners?
30. What mistake did Wu Sangui make?

Projects:

1. Make a timeline of the Ming dynasty.

2. Historians have praised and condemned Hongwu — praised him for having expelled the Mongols and founded the Ming dynasty, condemned him for having been a tyrant. Make a chart, listing Hongwu's reforms and his abuses of power. Then write an essay expressing your views about whether Hongwu should be remembered as a mainly positive or negative force in Ming history.

3. During the early Ming period, the Chinese were probably the most skillful sailors in the world. Find out more about the expeditions of Zheng He. Make a map

showing the routes of several of his voyages and/or draw a picture of one of his treasure ships.

4. Yunnan a rugged mountainous land on Chinese frontier with Vietnam, Laos and Burma. Its timber was hauled all the way to Beijing to build the imperial palaces of the Forbidden City. Today, the forests shelter elephants, pandas and parrots, and the vegetation is more varied that that of any other Chinese province. The climate ranges from icy cold to tropic heat, depending on the height above sea level. Find out more about this remote part of China and write a report.

5. History has proved that the Yongle made a mistake when he moved his capital to Beijing the capital. Think about what you have learned about the history and culture of the Ming dynasty. Then write an essay supporting or opposing this statement. Give specific reasons for your point of view.

6. Make a diorama or a model of a Ming garden.

7. Zhengde has been compared to Caligula, a very eccentric Roman emperor. Find out more about these two men. Write a report comparing them, or write a play in which they encounter one another.

8. The literati despised military men. They considered the army a gathering of brutish men of very little brain. Imagine a conversation in which a soldier encounters a scholar in the countryside. Write a dialogue. Then present your playlet to your classmates.

9. Make a model of Beijing during the Ming dynasty or of the Forbidden City.

10. Consult several books on Chinese porcelain. Write a report about the "blue-and-white" pieces produced by the Ming dynasty which were imported to other parts of the world. (This is known as the China trade.)

12. Make a Venn diagram comparing Genghis Khan and Nurhachi.

13. Read *The Record of a Journey to the West*. Then, choosing a few major episodes, write a short play. Choose a group of classmates to perform it.

14. Read *The Examination* by Michael Bosse. This is a humorous tale about two brothers. It is filled with interesting details about life during the Ming dynasty. One brother is a brilliant scholar, who is ill-equiped to deal with the ways of the world. The other, less intellectual but far more savvy, finds ways to raise the funds so that his brother can travel to Beijing to take the

imperial civil service examination. Choose an episode and write a skit about it.

15. Find out more about the Eight Immortals. Make a poster, describing the attributes of each Immortal.

16. Matteo Ricci was a fascinating man. Consult at least three books or other sources about him and then write a short report.

17. Remember Yongle's tree-planting project? In May, 2002, China embarked on a $12 million, 10-year program to plant 170,000 square miles of trees. (This is an area roughly the size of California and is the largest reforestation project ever.) It is designed to stop the expanding deserts, chronic droughts, and deadly flooding due to stripping trees for timber and fuel and to produce more farmland. Sand carried from the spreading deserts in the north scour Beijing and other cities during the summer. The program include six separate projects, ranging from reforesting hillsides to creating protected grasslands and nature reserves for pandas, Tibetan antelopes, and rare orchids. One challenge is where to find enough trees! Find out more about this reforestation program and determine what progress that has been more so far. Share you findings with your classmates.

Important Happenings Elsewhere In The World
(1368 — 1644)

Mongol Tamerlane conquers Persia, Syria and Egypt — 1364 - 1405
Richard II crowned King of England — 1367
Joan of Arc burned at the stake — 1431
Thais of Siam take Angkor — 1431
Turks conquer Constantinople — 1453
Italian (High) Renaissance — c 1410 – 1550
Columbus Reaches America — 1492
Vasco da Gama rounds Cape of Good Hope — 1498
Nanek founds the Sikh religion — 1498
Protestant Reformation inaugurated by Martin Luther — 1517
Cortes conquers the Aztecs — 1519
Pizarro conquers Incas — 1531 -1533
Ankar Mogul emperor of India — 1556 -1605
Queen Elizabeth I — 1558 – 1603
Dutch purchase Manhattan — 1626
Louis XIV crowned King of France — 1643

Chapter 6
The Qing Dynasty
(1644-1911)
The Past Collides With the Future

China's new overlords, the Manchus, had every intention of preserving the rich civilization that had fallen into their hands. During the early years of the Qing dynasty, three talented emperors would make significant contributions to this civilization. Ironically, by strongly embracing the long-standing traditions of the Middle Kingdom, the Manchus would prevent the country from changing with the times and adapting to the modern world. This would prove fatal in the long run, when China's greatest opponents would come not from the rugged regions beyond the Great Wall, but from far across the sea.

Taking Over

It was Dorgon, regent for the six-year old emperor, Shunzhi, who established the government of the new Qing dynasty. He wanted very much for his people to be viewed as legitimate heirs to the Dragon Throne. But to ease the transition in government, he ordered the Ming officials to remain in office. They would continue to perform their duties — but under the eyes of their Manchu counterparts. The civil service exams were continued, and a pro-

gram of reforms that had earlier been proposed by the Ming ministers was put into effect. All state documents were to be written in both Chinese and Manchu. Given these accommodations, it appeared as though the new regime and the old guard of the Ming would share the governing of China.

But appearances can be deceiving. Before long, the balance of power shifted, and Manchus took over many of the top government posts. Chinese officials at every level soon found themselves playing second fiddle to the new arrivals. Many

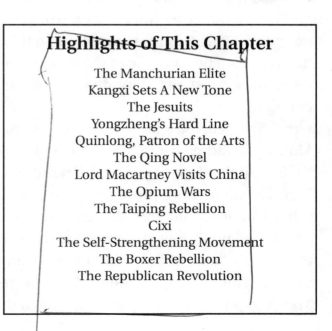

Highlights of This Chapter

The Manchurian Elite
Kangxi Sets A New Tone
The Jesuits
Yongzheng's Hard Line
Quinlong, Patron of the Arts
The Qing Novel
Lord Macartney Visits China
The Opium Wars
The Taiping Rebellion
Cixi
The Self-Strengthening Movement
The Boxer Rebellion
The Republican Revolution

even feared that they were being spied upon (as, indeed, they were).

The Manchus had reasons to assert themselves. Like the Mongols, they were dramatically outnumbered by the Chinese. (Their numbers would never amount to more than two per cent of China's population.) So once they took the dominant role in government, they looked for ways to make it clear that they were the masters and the Chinese their subjects.

For starters, every Chinese man was ordered to shave off the hair in the front of his head up to the crown and to wear the rest of his hair in a single braid (a queue) as a sign of submission to their overlords. (The style for the Ming man had been to grow his hair long and tie it in a knot at the top of his head.) In 1645, it was decreed that any Chinese man who did not shave his head and wear a queue within ten days would be executed. The Chinese, understandably, hated the queue, and one of the first acts of rebellion against the Qing dynasty was to cut off the long braid.

To keep their culture pure, all Manchu children were required to study their native language and traditions. Manchu adults were prohibited from marrying Chinese, and the women were not allowed to bind their daughters' feet. (Yes, the terrible "fad" of foot-binding had continued since Song times.) Nor were Manchus allowed to engage in the "degrad-ing" activities of trade or manual labor — that was left to the Chinese.

All Chinese families living in Beijing were forced to move into the southern, outer part of the city, and no Chinese farmers were allowed to settle in northern Manchuria, the tribal homeland. A willow palisade (actually, it was a big ditch with willows planted along it) stretched for several hundred miles marking the boundary beyond which the Chinese could not go.

The Manchu aroused further resentment by confiscating nearly a million acres of farmland in northern China. Most of this was assigned to the banners, and the local Chinese peasants were forced to work the land for them as their slaves.

The Ming Resistance

Many survivors of the Ming court refused to join the Manchus and settled in Nanjing. They tried to negotiate a peace settlement with the new regime, hoping to buy their freedom by paying off the enemy the way the Southern Song had done with the Jin many centuries earlier. Dorgon's response was to launch a vicious attack on the major cities of the south. His banner armies sacked Yangzhou, then crossed the Yangzi and seized Nanjing, driving the Ming court further south.

The fall of Guangzhou the following year (1647) officially ended the Chinese resistance to the new dynasty, although remnants of the Ming held out in various parts of southern and western China for several years.

The Lovesick Emperor

Dorgon ruled China as regent until he died in 1650. By then, the young emperor, Shunzhi, was thirteen. He was a conscientious and studious young man, respectful of local traditions and able to read Chinese. He replaced his Manchu household officials with Chinese eunuchs. Shunzhi spent a good deal of time with the Jesuits, eager to learn more about Western science and art. He later appointed Adam Schall von Bell, director of the Imperial Board of Astronomy, to tutor his sons.

Shunzhi's contemplative nature drew him to the beliefs and rituals of Buddhism. Perhaps this interest is what led him to fall deeply in love with a concubine, Xiao Xian, an ardent Buddhist. Whatever caused the spark, he was smitten, and he could think only of her. When Xiao Xian died suddenly, Shunzhi was so distraught that he wanted to end his own life. But to do so is unforgivable in the Buddhist religion (taking a life, even your own, is considered sinful), so he became a monk instead. The government was left in the hands of his ministers.

Shunzhi's own days were numbered. His health began to fail. He lost weight and spat blood (possibly he had TB), and he suf-fered uncontrollable rages. On one occasion, he attacked his throne with a sword! About this time, many members of the Qing court began succumbing to smallpox. (This disease was greatly feared by "outsiders" who, unlike the Chinese, had not built up any immunity to it.) Shunzhi, in his greatly weakened condition, contracted the disease and died — just four months after the death of his beloved Xiao Xian.

The Literary Inquisition

Shunzhi was succeeded in 1661 by his third son for a very practical reason: the boy had been infected with smallpox and survived. (This made him immune to any recurrence of the disease.) He took the throne at the age of six and is known to us as Kangxi (kahng shee). But until he came of age, China was ruled by four regents who did not share Shunzhi's openness. Their main concern was to strengthen Manchu authority, and their main target was the literati class.

As in the days of the Yuan dynasty, many of the wealthy Chinese living in the south strongly resented the presence of the foreign regime and expressed their loyalty to Chinese values by retiring to lives of classical scholarship. They viewed any collaboration with the current "barbarian" government an affront to the late Ming dynasty. The Manchus, ever suspicious of any criticism that might lead to rebellion, kept very close tabs on these men through a network of spies. In 1663, some of these spies snatched a history of the Ming dynasty that had been prepared in Hangzhou. it contained phrases that *could* be interpreted as critical of the Qing government.

This episode led to a wide-scale literary inquisition. Any published item suspected of expressing anti-Manchu sentiments was investigated and brought to the attention of the regents. "Suspicious" writings included such things as satirical poems, puns (making up puns had always been popular sport among the literati, and it was an easy way to mock those who were not "in the know"), and any historical reference that suggested a slight against the Manchus. If an item was judged subversive, not only were the author and sponsor of the publication punished, but also the printers, book sellers, and readers! In the most serious cases, the offenders were tortured to death (this was known as a "lingering death") and their family members —and even their students — were executed (beheaded), exiled, or enslaved. Even those who had since died were not free of abuse. Their bodies were dug out of their graves and desecrated.

Early Qing Artists

As in the days of the Yuan, certain literati expressed their feelings through art. Bada Shanren was a member of the Ming royal family, who was born in Jiangsu province in eastern China. When the Manchu forces attacked the south, he suffered a nervous breakdown, from which he never really recovered. (According to one account, when he heard about his father's death of the fighting he was struck dumb.) No longer able to speak normally, he would only shout bursts of words or laugh hysterically. Children would run after the ragged figure, taunting him so he would begin his raving. He retired to a Buddhist monastery, where he became known as Zhu Da.

In his earlier life, Bada Shanren had enjoyed painting, but with his mental affliction he stopped working in any traditional style. Now, when he was ready to paint (usually after drinking a great deal of wine), he would grab a brush, and, uttering loud cries like a madman, he would move the brush with a series of odd, twisting motions. (Consult an art book and look at some of his works.) His pictures of birds, fish, and flowers were formed by brushstrokes that seem careless and sloppy when compared with the elegant lines of other artists. Some of the fish look like rocks, and the birds are skinny, misshapen, and angry-looking, often perching awkwardly on one leg. And yet, the images clearly reflect the artist's unique vision of reality. His paintings would have an important influence on artists of the 20th century.

Like Bada Shanren, Shitao was a

member of the Ming royal family, who resisted the invaders and sought asylum in a Buddhist monastery. But unlike the unbalanced hermit, he spent most of his life surrounded by friends in Hangzhou or traveling around China. He enjoyed visiting and painting the mountains that were considered sacred to Daoists. Shitao even spent three years in Beijing, interacting with Manchu scholars and artists. In his later years, he settled in Yangzhou as a painter and designer of gardens.

Compared to traditional landscapes, Shitao's paintings are impressionistic — their thick lines, clusters of dots, and strange contours evoke a surreal quality. Shitao invented the "one-line method" of painting, which involved depicting a figure with a single continuous line. Among his most famous works are *The Peace Blossom Spring* and *A Man in a House Beneath a Cliff*.

Because of their innovative approach to painting, Bada Shanren (Zhu Da) and Shitao are known as the Individualist Painters. But while they were taking off in new directions, most Chinese artists stuck to the rules and traditions of the past. Best known among them were the "Four Wangs," four artists of the same name but no actual family connection. They continued in the footsteps of the great landscape painters of the Ming dynasty.

Kangxi Takes Charge

The very early years of Manchu rule were certainly oppressive ones for the Chinese. If things had continued in this way, there probably would have been a major revolt. Fortunately, when Kangxi took over the government in 1669, he made it clear that he cared deeply about his subjects and their cultural traditions. He was the first of three enlightened rulers who would give the country over a century of prosperity and internal peace.

But Kangxi could also be as tough as his ancestors. Early in his reign, he proved his mettle when three Chinese leaders challenged his authority. The three men were generals who had aided the Manchus in their overthrow of the Ming in 1644. They had been rewarded for their services with the title of prince and then commissioned to fight against the Ming resistance in the south. They ended up carving out huge territories for themselves in southern and western China, which they governed as independent "mini-kingdoms," or feudatories. (A feudatory is part of a larger realm under the control of the local ruler.) It soon became clear to the imperial ministers that these men had become too powerful.

In 1673, 18-year-old Kangxi tried to disband the three feudatories. When the princes resisted, civil war broke out between their armies and the imperial troops. Kangxi personally directed the campaign, relying upon Chinese commanders rather than Manchus. After eight long years of fighting, the Qing forces finally defeated the armies of the princes and the feudatories were broken up.

A Confucian Ruler

As a boy, Kangxi had been tutored by Confucian scholars as well as Jesuits. He had developed a deep respect for China's long history and was committed to being a model Chinese emperor. Once in power, Kangxi softened Dorgon's policies separating the Chinese from the Manchus. He made efforts to equalize taxes, and he prohibited any further confiscation of land. His ministers supervised plans to control the flooding of the major rivers (always a problem in China) and to establish storehouses throughout the countryside to hold grain for use in times of famine. Kangxi's Public Artwork Project led to the creation of 27 new imperial workshops in the Forbidden City for Chinese artisans. These included shops for metalwork, lacquerware, jade carving, painting, calligraphy, and porcelain decoration.

In 1670 Kangxi published the *Sacred Edicts*, official documents containing his Sixteen Maxims "for the guidance of daily conduct." These maxims, each seven characters long, conveyed the bare basics of Confucian belief as they pertained to the ordinary people. Once a month, the maxims were to be read by the local elders to gatherings of people in cites, towns, and villages throughout the realm. In very simple language, the maxims exhorted the people to be filial and thrifty, to value scholarship and avoid the unorthodox (any ideas that were not compatible with Confucianism), to respect the law, and to pay their taxes. The monthly readings of *The Sacred Edicts* bound the people together, reinforced traditional Confucian ideals, and promoted respect for the Qing regime.

Wooing the Scholars

Kangxi recognized that most of the country's intellectual talent was in the south. In 1678 he launched a program to encourage the literati living there to take the civil service exams so they could enter the upper levels of government. Of course, few had any interest in such an activity, but those who received an imperial "recommendation" to take the exam had no choice but to comply. (No one ever said "no" to the emperor!) Although a few of the recommended men threatened suicide, and a small number of others were excused for worthy causes (such as the need to care for an ill parent), most of the potential candidates reluctantly appeared at the examination halls. Of these, 50 ultimately succeeded in receiving the highest honor of *jinshi*.

But there was little celebrating until these successful candidates were told that their new job was to compile the official history of the Ming dynasty. This changed everything, and the scholars happily set about their huge task.

In the process of gathering information and writing about "the good old days" before the Manchus took over, the Chinese literati had many daily contacts with the other members of the Qing bureaucracy. Over the years, their dislike of the "usurpers" diminished as they developed friendships with them. Many later took up other official posts, and they did so willingly. Kangxi's strategy had worked extremely well. He had tended to the traditional task of recording the history of the previous dynasty while drawing the cream of the Chinese elite into his camp. In doing so, he softened the feelings of opposition that were gnawing away at many levels of Chinese society.

The Ming history was only the first of many projects commissioned by Kangxi that provided employment for the Chinese scholars. Others included writing additional histories, critiques on calligraphy and painting, an extensive treatise of geography, a complete edition of the writings of Zhu Xi, and a compilation of the poetry of the Tang dynasty. Kangxi, a scholar in his own right, wrote the prefaces to many of these books.

In 1700, the emperor ordered the compilation of a vast encyclopedia, *A Collection of Books and Illustrations of Ancient and Modern Times*. When it was finally published in 1728, the encyclopedia was the largest work ever printed. Another very ambitious project was the production of a huge dictionary of some 40,000 characters. It became the standard dictionary of the Chinese language for more than 200 years.

During the later years of Kangxi's reign, an important books appeared: *The Mustard Seed Garden Manual*. This was a manual published by Li Liweng on how to paint in the traditional Chinese style and included a series of color prints. The title refers to Li's garden in Nanjing, which was named after the famous saying "All Mount Sumeru in a mustard seed" — a metaphor for a microcosm or miniature. Like all Chinese gardens, Li's artfully arranged series of rocks, plants, and water represented the majestic scenes so familiar in landscape paintings. The metaphor can also be applied to painting, which is why Li chose it for the title: a viewer should sense in a scene depicted by an artist the essence (or *qi*) that pervades all the natural world. In 1685, an expanded version of the manual was published in Suzhou. It was later brought to Europe, and many of the prints included in it ended up in the British Museum in London.

The Emperor Kangxi

litter to the Palace of Heavenly Purity, which stood in the private area of the Forbidden City. This is where the emperor met with his closest advisers and handled most of his day to day business. As you know, the "Inner Court" of advisers became very influential during the Ming dynasty, often more so than the appointed officials, who made up the "Outer Court." As you will see, this trend would continue until the very end of imperial China.

Kangxi had a midday meal at 2 PM, then relaxed by reading (he was certainly a bibliophile), writing (poetry or essays), or painting. On special occasions, he would hunt in the imperial game park, where birds and animals were released just so he could shoot them. In the evening he returned to his paperwork, often dealing with official documents until late at night.

The Emperor's Day

Kangxi left behind many journal entries, edicts, and letters. These give us a clear idea of the kinds of issues he coped with from day to day as well as the routines of his work schedule. He rose each morning at 5 AM and had a cup of tea with milk. After a short period of prayer and contemplation at a small Buddhist shrine, he read extracts from the classics, histories, or other subjects. Then he was carried on his

The Grand Tours

Kangxi made six Grand Tours of southern China during his reign. These excursions enabled him to see for himself what conditions were like in this rich and fertile part of the empire and to impress his subjects with the full might of the Qing regime. He visited centers of Chinese learning and inspected the dike and water systems that were key to the transport of products in the south. As he traveled from place to place, he received local officials and discussed government policies with them, pardoned criminals, remitted taxes, visited temples, held poetry contests, attended banquets and theatrical performances, and simply admired the scenery. He once surprised a group of visitors by giving a personal demonstration of mounted archery. (Kangxi, like most Manchus, was an avid hunter, so his performance was most impressive!) On another occasion, he won the smiling approval of the local literati when he was heard reciting the words of Confucius well beyond midnight in his moored boat.

The Grand Tours were enormously expensive, since the imperial entourage had to be provided with "worthy" accommodations in temporary palaces en route. Kangxi ordered a series of handscrolls to be painted to immortalize his second visit of the Lower Yangzi in 1689. These vividly detailed paintings recapture the grandeur of the occasion — the emperor, splendid in his dragon robes, leading the procession of elegantly attired officials through the beautiful landscapes of the the Yangzi River valley.

Kangxi made a number of less grand visits to other parts of his realm and felt he got to know his country well. He once remarked in a letter to his eunuch, Ku Wenzhing, that he had traveled over 2,000 *li* in each of the four directions — north across the Gobi Desert to the Kerulen River, west to Shansi province, east through Manchuria, and south beyond the Yangzi. In 1684, he made a pilgrimage to Qufu in Shandong Province to visit the shrine of Confucius. (Qufu was the birthplace of the great sage.) He also climbed Mount Tai, the most revered of the Five Sacred Mountains of Daoism. Here he conducted sacrifices to the mountain spirits, just as earlier emperors had done since the time of the Shi Huangdi. He could not resist mentioning that no Ming emperor had ever performed this ceremony.

The Summer Palace

From the time the Manchus first conquered China, rulers and courtiers had longed for a summer residence that would offer an escape from the dusty, simmering heat of Beijing. Numerous scouting expeditions had been sent north in search of a site. The ideal setting was finally discovered at Chengde, along the Rehe River in Manchuria, about 150 miles north of Beijing.

In 1703 Kangxi began the construction of a summer palace at Chengde. He called the palace *Bishu Shanzhuang* ("Fleeing the Heat Mountain Villa"). His travels throughout China offered him an opportunity to collect unusual specimens of plants, animals, and birds, which he sent back to Chengde to join his "living collections" there.

Kangxi and the Jesuits

As you know, Kangxi enjoyed the company of the Jesuits, and he welcomed groups of the learned fathers to his court. He hired some as physicians and cartographers. He appointed Ferdinand Verbiest to head the court observatory in 1669 upon the death of Adam Schall von Bell. Father Verbiest had previously taught the Chinese how to cast cannons, and these weapons had been a major factor in the defeat of the war against the three feudatories. (The priest soothed his conscience after creating such destructive weapons by naming each cannon after a saint!) In his new position, Verbiest perfected a series of bronze astronomical instruments. These were kept on the terrace of the Imperial Observatory in Beijing.

In 1708 Kangxi dispatched groups of Jesuits to all regions of China to make a geographical survey of his empire. The results were recorded in *The Atlas of Kangxi*, which was an extremely accurate work for its time. It was engraved on copper plates and printed in 1718.

Although the Jesuits made many contributions in the areas of science and technology, their reason to be in China was to promote their religion. In 1692, Kangxi had given them official permission to preach Christianity to his subjects. He was inspired to take this action after the Jesuits had successfully treated him for malaria by prescribing quinine imported from America. By 1700, there were nearly 300,000 Christians in China, with churches at Macao, Guangzhou, and Beijing.

Matteo Ricci had believed the Chinese would only accept Christianity if it allowed the traditional worship of ancestors. The Jesuits who succeeded him agreed, seeing no conflict between Christian beliefs and the long-held rituals to honor the dead. However, in 1715 Pope Clement XI sent a letter to Kangxi demanding that Chinese Christian converts give up their practice of ancestor worship. Kangxi was furious at the Pope's attempt to interfere with his authority and with what he considered an attack on Confucian tradition. He ordered all Jesuits who were not willing to honor the "compromise" (allowing ancestor worship in the practice of the

---

Kangxi wrote about Chengde. "Several times I have traveled to the shores of the Yangzi and have seen the lush beauty of the south. Twice my way led me to Gansu and Shaanxi, and therefore I know the land in the west well. In the north I have crossed the Dragon Sands, and in the east I have wandered in the region of the White Mountains... I cannot count all the places I have seen, but I have chosen none of them. Here, in the valley of Rehe, is the only place which I desire to dwell."

Christian religion) to leave China. Many of the Jesuits, although torn in their allegiances, chose to remain in China. But the issue was far from settled.

Military Efforts

In 1683, the Qing forces conquered the last center of Ming resistance on Taiwan and brought the island into the empire. Other troops moved to reestablish China's dominance of Central Asia. They successfully battled the Russians, who had claimed Chinese territory along the Amur River in Manchuria, and drove them back. The Treaty of Nerchinsk, signed by Russian czar Peter the Great in 1689, established a dividing line between the two nations in Manchuria. Jesuit priests Gerbillon and Pereira acted as translators during the treaty negotiations. This settlement opened the way for trade between China and Russia.

In the 1690's, Kangxi personally commanded a large Chinese force that penetrated far into Mongolia. He pursued the powerful tribal leader, Galdan, like a hunter tracks down his prey. The Mongol warriors were no match for the heavy artillery of the Chinese, and they fell to defeat. This marked the beginning of the decline of the fierce horsemen who had dominated the steppes for so many centuries. Of course, many Mongols remained allies of the Manchus.

Toward the end of his reign, Kangxi sent Chinese troops to Tibet. The fighting was still going on there when he died in 1722.

The End of An Era

Kangxi had accomplished a great deal in his long reign of sixty-one years. He had skillfully and diplomatically won the support of the Chinese literati and quelled much of the anti-Manchu hostility among the general public. He had promoted scholarship and the arts, made the office of the emperor more visible to his subjects, and extended China's frontiers. He left to his successor a strong and efficiently run empire.

Enter Yongzheng

Kangxi's fourth son came to the throne as Yongzheng. Why a fourth son? Of Kangxi's 56 children, only his second son, Yinreng, was born to the empress, and her sons stood first in line to the throne. Kangxi was fond of Yinreng, and he saw to it that he was well educated. But he proved to be a lawless and mentally unstable young man. When Yinreng became involved in an apparent conspiracy, he was immediately demoted. Kangxi was so disturbed and disappointed by his son's feckless character that he refused to name a new heir until he lay on his deathbed.

After the old emperor died,

Yongzheng claimed that he had named *him* heir. Conveniently for him, were no witnesses to contradict his word. But many people considered his claim highly suspicious, even more so when Yongzheng eliminated all possible rivals and anyone who even challenged it. (Three of his brothers died in prison.) He edited documents written by Kangxi that had any reference to the question of succession in his own favor. (Does this remind you of the Prince of Yan?) Still, there were many doubts, although they were certainly not openly expressed. In 1730, the new emperor felt compelled to make a public statement that he had not murdered his father.

Yongzheng was a cold-blooded, heartless man, totally lacking Kangxi's sense of justice and humanity. Once he was securely on the throne, he ordered a "slow, lingering death" for anyone accused of writing anything that could be construed as anti-Manchu (or, of course, anti-Yongzheng). He had a book compiled and widely distributed that justified the Manchus' right to the throne. Throughout his reign, he ordered his secret police to spy on members of the government and to crush all opposition to his authority. Oddly enough, his official name, Yongzheng, means "Kind and Proper!"

More Power to the Emperor

Despite his ruthlessness, Yongzheng was an efficient ruler. He strengthened the authority of the Inner Court, creating a Grand Council of a half dozen of his personal advisors to replace the Grand Secretaries, and he ordered that all important decisions of state receive his personal approval. He brought the military branch more closely under his control by altering the laws that had previously given banner leaders authority over their own divisions. These reforms made him less dependent upon his bureaucracy (the Outer Court) and somewhat of an autocrat. (An autocrat is someone who takes power into his own hands.) Can you see where this could be a dangerous precedent?

Public Policies

Despite his harsh demeanor, Yongzheng pursued a number of policies that benefited China. He inherited a nearly empty treasury, due the expenses of Kangxi's campaigns, projects, and grand tours, and he took several steps to remedy the situation. He changed the tax structure, revised government salaries, and fought corruption in his bureaucracy.

Yongzheng sponsored projects to build more dikes to help prevent the flooding of the Yellow River and to ensure that rice was distributed to peasants in the years of bad harvest. He took effective measures to aid the people of Beijing and the surrounding region following a devastating earthquake in 1730.

Not surprisingly, Yongzheng promoted education and stressed such Confucian values as the total subjection of women, the indisputable authority of fathers, and the unquestionable loyalty of subjects to their rulers. Do you remember Kangxi's Sixteen Maxims? Yongzheng issued "amplified instructions," increasing the simple maxims to a length of 10,000 characters! He required scholars to recite the drastically expanded maxims twice monthly at every Confucian temple. During these long sessions, the aged (anyone over 80) were allowed to sit behind the gentry and be served tea, while the commoners had to stand and listen.

In 1742, the Pope in Rome forbad Christians to perform ancestral rites. This meant that Jesuits could no longer honor Kangxi's "compromise" allowing Chinese Christian converts to continue the traditional worship rituals of their ancestors. Although forbidden to teach their religion in China, the Jesuits were still welcome in court. Yongzheng later ordered all Jesuits not directly involved with the court observatory or other imperial functions to leave Beijing and resettle in the European trading colony on the island of Macao.

After only thirteen years on the throne, Yongzheng died quite suddenly. His successor was his fourth son, known as the Qianlong emperor. Although Yongzheng was an effective ruler, his reign is often regarded as an interlude between those of the two greatest Qing emperors — Kangxi and Qianlong.

Family Ties

Qianlong had been the favorite grandson of Kangxi. In fact, the old emperor had so admired the boy's inquisitive mind and moral courage that he invited him to live with him in the palace, so they could get to know each other better. When Kangxi died two years later, the bonds had been established that would strongly influence Qianlong in future years.

Like Kangxi, Qianlong combined military skills with the virtues of a Confucian scholar. And like his grandfather, he would win over the literati by reconfirming their place in Chinese society. His long reign would fill out the remaining two-thirds of the 18th century (1735 — 1799). It is considered one of the most glorious periods in the history of China.

The Empire Expands

Qianlong was just 24 when he became emperor. He continued his father's autocratic approach to government, allowing the Grand Council to become more powerful than ever. On the military front, he launched a series of campaigns leading to the conquest of Xinjiang, a huge territory in the west. It was made a Chinese

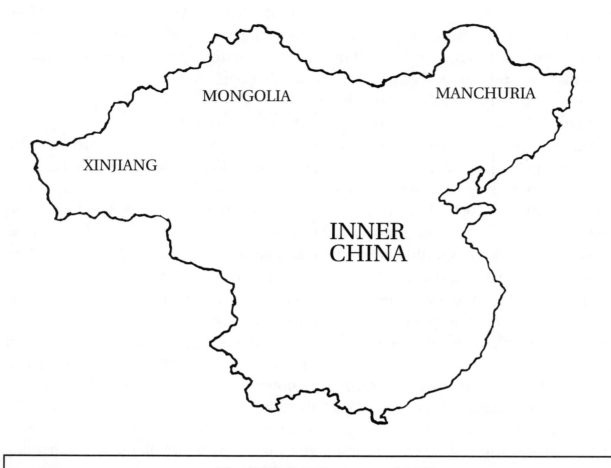

MONGOLIA

MANCHURIA

XINJIANG

INNER
CHINA

The Qing Empire around 1800

province, and political prisoners were sent to settle the region. This was just the beginning of an ambitious plan of expansion. Gradually, Qianlong took over more and more land until China's frontiers were wider than they have ever been. By 1759, the Qing empire covered nearly 4 and a half million square miles, including Mongolia and territories that are now part of Russia. The increase in the size of the Qing empire was accompanied by a dramatic increase in population. The number of people living in China Proper alone more than doubled between 1749 and 1793. By 1800, China's population would be 310 million, more than twice that of Europe at the time.

Qianlong also extended the range of China's influence in eastern Asia. In 1750, he sent troops to restore order in Tibet, which was being torn by civil war, and then made that country a protectorate of China. Other east Asian states, including Korea,

Annam (Vietnam), Burma, Thailand, and the Philippines, formally recognized China's dominance and became tribute-paying vassals.

Scholarship and the Arts

While Qianlong is admired for expanding the imperial borders and maintaining peace at home, his reputation as a great Chinese emperor rests mostly on his scholarship and his patronage of the arts. He attracted artists, poets, and scholars to his court from all over the empire.

Qianlong oversaw was the publication of an imperial edition of the best works in the Chinese literary tradition known as the *Library of the Four Treasuries*. Over 3,450 complete works were collected and copied by 15,000 scholars in 36,000 volumes. They were divided into four categories: classics (*jing*), history (*shi*), philosophy (*zhe*), and belles letters — poetry, plays, and stories (*ji*). Seven handwritten copies of the Qianlong collection were housed in seven newly built libraries, four around Beijing and the other three in major cities in the south. (Only the emperor's copy has survived to our times.) The library project had a darker side. Qianlong ordered all of the books scrutinized for any disrespectful references to the Manchus. Over 2,000 titles were found to be offensive and were burned. This was a terrible loss of Chinese literature.

Qianlong was also an avid art collector. During his reign, the imperial art collection grew to a size and importance it had not seen since the days of Huizong. He was especially fond of carved jade objects and obtained 376 of these nearly priceless objects in a single year. As his acquisitions increased, he had a series of specialized catalogues created. The one devoted to the "arts of the brush" listed 10,000 paintings and works of calligraphy. Unfortunately, Qianlong had the habit of writing poems all over his treasured paintings (he was not a particularly gifted poet) and stamping the paintings with his large, conspicuous seals.

The Summer Palaces

Do you remember Kangxi's summer

Dai Zhen, one of the greatest Confucian scholars of the Qing dynasty, lived during Qianlong's reign. As a young student, he frequently asked questions his teachers could not answer. By the time he was 16, he had read and memorized all the Confucian classical texts and their commentaries. And yet, he could never pass the civil service exams. (Like many other scholars who failed the exams, he had a creative, inquisitive mind that made it difficult to adhere to the rigid rules of the examiners.) He taught school, then spent rest of his life producing scholarly works in variety of subjects – philosophy, mathematical history, astronomy, phonetics, and the criticism of learned texts.

palace in Chengde? It was in the halls of that pleasant imperial "get-away" that the young Qianlong had been instructed by his grandfather in such matters as the proper form of answering petitions and the joys of studying classical literature. Yongzheng had added to the complex, and Qianlong carried on his work until the summer palace was finally completed. Like the Forbidden City, the palace compound was divided into official and residential sections. (The throne room was used as a set for the film, *The Last Emperor*.)

The palace grounds covered 1,383 acres and were surrounded by a six-mile long wall. Qianlong added beautiful gardens, inspired by those he had visited in Suzhou, Hangzhou, and Yangshou. He also added Buddhist temples, pavilions and tea houses around the small lakes on the grounds. These resembled the small buildings he had seen on his visits to the shores of West Lake. A unique feature of the palace grounds was the series of "landscapes," which represented the scenery in 72 different regions of China. For example, a grassy

area in the northeast section recreated the Mongolian steppes. This is where the imperial family would gather with the Mongolian princes on certain occasions. They slept in yurts, hunted wild game, and competed in equestrian jousts and archery contests. Sometimes a throne was set up on a small hill for the emperor to view fireworks.

Chengde became a delightful second capital, where the Qing emperors would spend six months of every year with their courts. But even when the court was residing in Beijing, the emperor had a special place just beyond the city limits to which he could escape for some peace and quiet. This was *Yuanmingyuan* ("The Garden of Perfect Brightness"), a complex of palaces, pavilions, and temples strategically sited in a landscape of artificially created hills, lakes, and canals. Yongzheng had begun work on redesigning this former estate in 1730, but it was Qianlong who made it a truly magical place. He had the southern and western parts of the landscape refined into 40 "scenic spots" according to his per-

---

Like Kangxi, Qianlong undertook six Grand Tours in the south, as well as over 100 smaller tours to various parts of his empire. These were expensive, and extravagant, enterprises. Lush facilities — "temporary" palaces and gardens —had to be erected to house and entertain the emperor and his large entourage. Special roadways were built up certain mountains and hills so that his litter (and those of his mother, wife, and concubines) could be carried to their summits. The emperor commissioned paintings of his favorite scenic spots that were visited. He particularly delighted in the quiet beauty of West Lake and the peaceful gardens and canals of Suzhou.

sonal guidelines. (Think about the "scenes" viewed by a visitor to a garden in Suzhou.) Each scenic spot was painted by a court artist, and the emperor himself composed a poem for each of the paintings. (The verses were written in beautiful calligraphy on each one.) On the eastern shore of a lake stood the "Hut of the Beautiful Vie." Here Quinlong loved to sit and gaze at the water and the western hills that rose beyond.

In 1747, Giuseppe Castiglione, an Italian Jesuit missionary and court painter, was commissioned to design a palace "in the manner of the European barbarians" in the northeastern part of *Yuanmingyuan*. (Qianlong had been impressed by pictures he had seen of French chateaux and Italian villas.) Castiglione created a baroque palace of white marble, with horseshoe-shaped staircases leading to its grand entrance. It was a replica of the French palaces of Trianon and Versailles. Every detail, from molding and chandeliers down to the furniture, was carefully copied from French engravings. The walls were hung with mirrors and decorated with the Gobelins tapestries sent by the French court in 1767. But behind the two-story facade of the palace was the traditional single-story Chinese hall. (Qianlong once remarked that he had no desire to "live in the air" like European monarchs, who must be "very poverty-stricken and lack land" to have to build one story upon another!)

French Jesuit Michel Benoit designed a series of mechanical fountains in gardens surrounding the palace. They had water-spouting figures inspired by those at Versailles. Among them was a water clock flanked by 12 stone fountains, each in the form of a zodiac animal. The Chinese divided the day into 12 2-hour segments, with each assigned to one of the 12 animals of the zodiac. In the clock, water spouted from one of the animals (from the antlers of the deer, the mouth of the dog, or some part of one of the others) for two hours, so you could tell the time by finding the source of the water spouts.

The palace grounds even had a maze, formed from carefully clipped tall bushes, that was similar to those in France and England. During the Middle Autumn Festival, the emperor sat in a raised pavilion in the center of the maze. His court ladies, with torches in their hands, had to

---

Castiglione, designer of Qianlong's baroque summer palace, was also a talented painter. He produced several portraits of the emperor and taught many of the Chinese court painters about such western techniques as the use of color, light and shade, and linear perspective. This "realism," so at odds with Chinese traditional painting, would spawn a unique school of decorative painting in the 18th and 19th centuries.

find their way to him. The first to arrive received a special gift.

Home Improvements

The buildings of the Forbidden City that burned during the reign of Yongle had been rebuilt by his Ming successors. Qianlong renovated and extended many of these and added new structures at the sides of the palace complex. As you might predict, he added gardens, pavilions and artificial waterways. The most beautiful garden in the complex today is named for him.

In 1773, Qianlong ordered the construction of the Nine Dragon Wall — a long screen about 18 feet high and 90 feet long. The dragons painted on the ceramic tiles of the screen were intended to protect the entrance to the northeast section of the compound from evil spirits.

As you know, the central part of the walkway connecting the large halls of the Forbidden City was reserved for the emperor's litter. It was made of slabs of white marble, many of them sculpted with dragons in low relief. Qianlong had what became the largest of these slabs installed beyond the Hall of Protecting Harmony. It formed a ramp in the middle of a wide flight of steps. The marble block weighed an amazing 250 tons. Qianlong had it hauled about 40 miles from Fangshan by 20,000 laborers. They reportedly moved it in the winter on man-made ice. Every half mile or so wells were dug and water was pumped out onto the road to ice it up so the stone could be slid over it. Once in place, the marble was carved with figures of dragons playing with pearls. (Pearls were a symbol of wisdom.) Anyone caught touching this sacred stone

---

As you have learned, the Chinese associated odd numbers with *yang*, and therefore with dragons, the emperor, Heaven, and the empire itself. The number nine, being the highest odd unit, was the imperial number. It is the square of three, an important number in *The Book of Changes*. (The Chinese character for nine also has the same sound as the word for everlasting.)

There were 9,999 houses in the Forbidden City. The great wooden palace doors were studded with nine rows of nine bronze knobs. In the living quarters were nine separate housing complexes. There were nine mythical beasts on the roof of the Hall of Supreme Harmony and nine "dragon walls" in the palace compound. The towers guarding the four corners of the palace compound each have nine beams and 18 columns. Beyond the palace, the altar of the Temple of Heaven had three tiers and all its measurements, number of steps and columns were in multiples of nine! The upper terrace was made up of nine concentric rings of slabs; the first ring (the innermost) consisted of nine fan-shaped slabs; the second ring of 18 (2 x 9), the third of 27 (3 x 9), and the last ring (the ninth) was made up of 81 (9 x 9). The streets of the imperial city formed a grid — nine streets going east-west, nine others going north-south.

The number nine appeared everywhere. There were nine kinds of dragons, and the New Years Dinner for the imperial family had 99 dishes!

without due cause was immediately exe-cuted.

Courtly Attire

In 1759, Quinlong passed an imperi-al edict describing the code of dress to be worn at court. All high officials were required to wear silk robes embroidered with dragons and other symbols for all for-mal and ceremonial occasions. These are known as *longpao* (dragon robes). The Manchurian robes were A-shaped rather than free-flowing like those of the Ming. They tapered at the sleeves and had tight cuffs and narrow neck openings. The new, stream-lined style of the robes reflected the athletic lifestyle of the Manchus, who loved to hunt on horseback. (What a contrast to the shuffling, sedentary Ming scholars!)

Among the other symbols that might appear on a robe was the geometric design known today as the swastika. It represented good luck and the number 10,000. When it was placed beside another auspicious sym-bol, it multiplied its value 10,000 times. The shou symbol for long life was also com-monly used. (There is a shou symbol on page 104.) Imagine the longevity implied by a shou and swastika embroidered side by side! Diagonal stripes at the hem of a robe represented water, and above those were the rolling waves of the sea. Pointed moun-tain peaks represented the sacred moun-tains, and above them were clouds. The

An Imperial Dragon Robe

embroidery around the neck of a robe rep-resented the gates of Heaven.

The formal robes of the officials were dark blue. There were always nine dragons on the robes of the first through third ranks, eight visible and the ninth hid-den under the fold in the front. (Why nine? Look at the box at the bottom of the oppo-site page.) Officials of the fourth through sixth ranks wore robes with eight dragons, and the lower ranks had seven. The officials wore red robes (red being the color of joy, celebration, and good luck) for festivals such as the lunar New Year, birthdays, and weddings.

The emperor's robe was, of course, yellow. It bore the same symbols as those of the high officials, as well as the 12 signs of imperial authority. These were arranged in order of importance in three rings, falling at the neck, waist, and hem. They represented the sun, the moon, a constellation (symbolic of Heaven), a golden pheasant (a symbol of literary refinement), an axe (representing power on earth), a flame (intellectual brilliance and love of virtue), and a bowl of grain (indicating the emperor's responsibility to feed the people). Viewing the symbols of the imperial robe was like reading the emperor's job description. The empress and empress dowager also wore yellow robes. The heir to the throne wore apricot yellow, while the other imperial princes wore brown (a "lesser yellow").

An official wore a plain, front-opening surcoat over his robe called a *bufu*. It was made of dark blue silk and was decorated on the front and back with a square embroidered badge indicating his office and rank. The symbols on the badges were similar to those of the Ming officials. The *bufu* covered the dragon robe, leaving only the waves border visible at the hem and the horseshoe cuffs visible at the wrists. This, according to Qianlong, would remind the official that he wore his elaborate robe not for display but for the inner spiritual power that its symbols represented.

When women were summoned to court for an official function, they wore robes reflecting the rank of their husbands. Their "informal" robes were also embroidered with figures, many symbolizing longevity and beauty — cranes, butterflies, peonies, chrysanthemums, and lotus flowers — in addition to the required cosmic symbols. On her wedding day, a bride wore a pleated silk skirt and a short red robe decorated with a dragon and phoenix. (The dragon and phoenix, symbols of the emperor and empress, also signified man and wife.)

The embroideries for the imperial robes were designed in the palace. They had to be approved by the emperor before being sent to special silkweaving shops in Suzhou, Hangzhou, and Jiangning.

The Novel in Qing China

While many Chinese literati were engaged in the Qing bureaucracy, others were busily writing popular books. In fact, the novel, which had evolved during the Ming dynasty with the tales of the bandits, kings, and that mischievous Monkey, reached new heights during the reign of Qianlong.

The Scholars was China's first truly satirical novel. It was written by Wu Jingzi in the middle of the 18th century. Wu was a

---

There were three times when the emperor did not wear yellow robes. He wore pale blue robes for sacrifices to the moon at the autumn equinox; dark blue at the start of winter when he appealed for rain and a good harvest, and red for the sacrifice to the sun at dawn of the spring equinox.

scholar who had no interest in being a bureaucrat. In his book, he mocked the civil service examination system, which, in his opinion, stifled creativity and promoted incompetency. He was amused by those literati whose greatest goal was to pass the exams so that they could win government positions and gain social prestige. Wu believed the only truly virtuous scholars were those like himself, who devoted their lives to private study and meditation. His book is filled with amusing portraits of pompous bureaucrats and unimaginative exam candidates. One comic character is Fan Chin, a peasant who spends years taking the civil service exams, failing each time, much to the dismay of those around him. When he finally succeeds, his rise in provincial society is meteoric — suddenly, those who have previously belittled him begin fawning upon him, seeking his attention and his patronage. Even his father-in-law!

The year 1791 marked the publication of China's greatest and best-loved novel, *Dream of the Red Chamber*, by Cao Xueqin. It was a vast epic — over 100 chapters long. (Perhaps you've noticed that Chinese books tended to be rather lengthy.) Xueqin came from a Chinese family in Nanjing that had risen to great power and wealth as personal servants to Kangxi. Unfortunately, the family later lost favor at court and went bankrupt. The author drew upon his memories of his upbringing and tales told by his relatives to write the novel, although he set the story in the Ming dynasty.

Dream of the Red Chamber tells about the decline of the Jia, a wealthy extended family of the south. Most of the scenes take place in the sheltered living quarters and gardens of the the family compound and depict the daily life of the wealthy elite. (The red chamber refers to a special room in the house where the women would gather to talk, sew, or simply enjoy one another's company.) The central characters are three young people: the hero, Jia Baoyu, and his two female cousins — the frail, sensitive Lin Daiyu, and the capable, cheerful Xue Baochai. Both cousins come to live with Baoyu's family. He falls in love with Lin Daiyu, but he is prevented from marrying her by his doting (and meddling) grandmother, who wants him to marry Xue Baochai.

The happiest times for the three young people are the idyllic hours they spend together in the garden, amusing themselves by reading and composing poetry, playing word games, and sharing their deeper feelings. But the good times end when Baoyu is tricked into marrying Baochai. (He is told he is marrying Daiyu, but after the ceremony, he lifts his bride's heavy veil and discovers that he has been duped.) When Daiyu learns of his deception, she falls ill and dies of grief (or perhaps TB). The novel ends with Baoyu, having passed the highest level of the civil service exams (to please his father, not himself), renouncing the world of Ming society to become a Buddhist monk.

Apart from the very sentimental love story, the novel has numerous subplots and a host of minor characters from all walks of life. Cao Xueqin has often been praised for his sensitive depictions of female characters, not merely the two main heroines, but also Baoyu's grandmother, mother, sister, sisters-in-law, and the dozens of maids with whom they reside. As you know, women, even the wealthiest among them, occupied an inferior position in the male-oriented society of the Chinese. *Dream of the Red Chamber* is revolutionary in its implied criticism of the gender-biased conventions of this society.

A Poor Choice

Qianlong proved to be one of China's most enlightened and beloved rulers. But after serving for 40 years, the aging emperor began to lose his powers of judgment. Quick to take advantage of the situation was an unscrupulous palace guard named Heshan. Charming and highly intelligent, Heshan easily won the emperor's confidence and gained great power, serving as his chief counselor for nearly two decades.

Heshan took advantage of his rank to place members of his family in strategic high-level offices — he even married his daughter into the imperial family. With this family network in place, he was able to funnel much of the state treasury into his own pockets. On his death (he was later forced to commit suicide), Heshan's private wealth was estimated at one and a half billion modern American dollars!

Trade With the West

Throughout most of Qianlong's reign, China prospered. In fact, the imperial treasury became so full that the emperor cancelled the payment of taxes on four separate occasions. But the costs of Qianlong's building projects, his ever-growing art collection, his Grand Tours and smaller excursions, and the extravagance of the imperial lifestyle gradually put a squeeze on the treasury. This, of course, was aggravated by the siphoning of public funds by Heshan. The Qing government would have been in big trouble if the deficit had not been offset

---

In 1989 *Dream of the Red Chamber* was made into a serial feature film by the Beijing Film Studio. Entitled *A Dream of Red Mansions*, the narrative was so complex and included so many characters (150!) that it required two years of preparation and three years of shooting. The entire film runs for about 13 hours.

by the healthy income produced by trade with the West.

As you know, the Ming had tried to restrict all foreign trade to the port city of Guangzhou. Merchants there had to deal through a guild of Chinese officials, known as the Cohong. And when the annual trading season was over, all foreign traders were ordered to withdraw to the island of Macao. But despite these restrictions, many European nations, headed by Britain, were actively engaged in trade with China, eagerly bargaining for the products that had become sought-after luxuries in their homelands.

Prime among these products was Chinese porcelain. Tens of thousands of workers at the kilns in Jingdezhen produced a special type known as trade porcelain, or "china," to meet the demand. (See the box below.) Many pieces were elaborately decorated with landscapes and verses in calligraphy that resembled scroll paintings. Chinese artists even catered to the whims of their Western customers by painting ancestral coats of arms, views of European family estates, and Christian religious themes. Many of the fine objects imported from China ended up in the "porcelain rooms" of the great houses of France and Germany. In 1643, no fewer than 129,036 pieces of porcelain were sent to Holland. The cargo of a single Dutch East India ship, which sank off Singapore in 1752, contained over 150,000 pieces destined for sale in Amsterdam.

The English Discover Tea

Today, a hot cup of tea is the national beverage in England. But until about

---

Pieces of Chinese porcelain first made their way into Europe during the Middle Ages via the Silk Road. They were greatly coveted by a privileged few. Porcelain increased in popularity after 1604. In that year, two Portuguese ships carrying a cargo of 200,000 pieces of Chinese porcelain were captured by the Dutch. When the stolen pieces were put up for sale, the bidders included agents for Henry IV of France, James I of England, the the Grand Duke of Tuscany. The beautifully delicate vases, bowls, and dishes were soon in demand among the leading nobility. By mid-century, the Dutch East India Trading Company was importing Chinese porcelain objects by the millions. The European importers stamped the boxes of produce carried on their ships with the name of the country of origin. Of course, all porcelain was stamped "China." In time, the porcelain itself came to be referred to as "the china." Ever since, fine dishes and plates made of porcelain are known as china.

For centuries, European potters tried to produce similar pieces, but, lacking a supply of kaolin and the knowledge of the technical requirements, their efforts were unsuccessful. The process for porcelain manufacture was finally mastered in Europe in 1710 in Dresden, Germany. The European porcelain was sold amid much fanfare at the Leipzig Fair of 1713. Interest in Chinese porcelain began to wane as Europe was able to supply its needs from its own porcelain factories.

1640, Europeans were unaware of the pleasant taste of the steaming brew. Of course, the Chinese had been sipping tea for centuries — ever since Buddhist monks began preparing it to keep themselves awake during their long meditations. Tea was first consumed by the general public as a type of food. (The tea leaves were dried, mixed with flour, and packaged in hard cubes, which could be added to water and cooked as soup.) It was later brewed the way it is today as a social beverage, which had the added benefit of aiding digestion. Tearooms became very popular gathering spots beginning in the Tang dynasty.

Eventually, tea made its way to British shores on the cargo ships, but as of 1700 only very small quantities (five or six chests a year) were imported. During the first quarter of the 18th century, however, the idea of drinking hot tea caught on among the British public, and the amount increased to some 400,000 pounds per year. By 1800, the British East India Trading Company was annually importing no less than 23 million pounds of tea!

The popularity of tea threw the balance of trade completely off kilter, since the Chinese had little interest in the woolen and metal products the British had to offer. (They regarded the English wool as a "barbarian fabric," suitable only for Mongolian yurts and riding gear.) So the British had to resort to paying for most of their tea in silver. This was a boon for the Chinese economy, but it created a great drain upon the British treasury.

A Visitor from England

King George III of Britain was pressured to do something about the China trade by his financial advisers, who worried about the one-sidedness of the tea trade, and the British merchants, who hated the restrictions imposed by the Chinese. So, in 1792, the king sent an envoy, Lord George Macartney, to Beijing.

Macartney sailed on a warship, *The Lion*, which was equipped with 64 cannons. He was accompanied on his mission by his secretary, Sir George Staunton, Staunton's eleven-year-old son, a German tutor for the boy, two doctors, two artists, and a full complement of attendants, musicians — and soldiers. A second ship carried a cargo of presents for the emperor — 600 cases filled with scientific instruments, chandeliers, howitzers, some Wedgewood pottery, and all sorts of clocks and watches. (Timepieces had become popular in the Chinese court since Matteo Ricci first presented his clock to Kangxi). There were even a pre-fabricated planetarium and a hot-air balloon.

The ships arrived on the Chinese coast in July of 1793. Macartney was given an imperial audience on Qianlong's 83rd birthday at the summer palace in Chengde.

Before the audience, two Chinese officials attempted to teach the envoy how to kowtow to their emperor. The kowtow was a traditional sign of respect to a superior that involved kneeling and touching one's forehead to the ground. The more times this was done, the greater the respect. In the case of the emperor, one should kneel three times and touch the forehead to the ground nine times. Macartney found such behavior undignified — and uncomfortable (he was an older man, and his joints were rather stiff). He said he would honor Qianlong in the same way he did his own king — by kneeling on one knee and kissing his hand. The Chinese were aghast at the idea of kissing the Son of Heaven! In the end, a compromise was reached. Macartney would simply kneel on one knee and bow his head.

Macartney presented Qianlong with a gold box studded with diamonds. It contained a letter from the king. The emperor assumed the gifts the British had brought him were tribute and that the box was another example. He told Macartney that if the "King of the Red-haired People of England" continued to be as civil as he was evidently attempting to be, he (Qianlong) would be willing to consider his country (Great Britain) a loyal tributary state of the Chinese empire. This, of course, reflects the ancient assumption that those living beyond the borders of the Middle Kingdom should acknowledge the authority of the Son of Heaven.

Qianlong later read the letter in the box. It requested an exchange of ambassadors, with a permanent British representative at the Chinese court, as well as permission for English merchants to trade at ports other than Guanzhong. It also asked for a warehouse at Beijing and a British base of trading operations that was closer to the silk and porcelain-producing areas of Zhejiang province. Finally, it requested the removal of certain trade tariffs and duties.

The emperor responded to these requests ten days later in a letter to King George. (It was delivered to Macartney's

---

In 1790, during the 80th birthday celebrations for Qianlong, a theatrical troupe performed a new style of drama, known as *jingxi*. Familiar stories from history and literature were enacted by people playing four principal roles: *sheng* (male), *dan* (female), *jing* (painted face) and *chou* (clown). (Those without painted faces wore colorful masks.) The male roles included such characters as scholars and government officials. Each role was characterized by a set of distinctive speaking, singing, and acrobatic skills. The actors were accompanied by percussion instruments and two-string fiddles (the *erhu* and *huqin*). By the early 19th century, *jinxi* was the most popular form of theater in Beijing. It remains so today, and is known as Beijing Opera.

lodgings in a yellow silk armchair carried by six Chinese servants.) Qianlong wrote that the king's requests were impertinent. Conditions would stay as they were. He refused to end government restrictions on international trade, to establish diplomatic relations, or to negotiate a trade treaty between China and England, noting that such acts were "contrary to all usage of my dynasty and cannot possibly be entertained." He added that China "possesses all things" and therefore had no need of European trinkets. He accepted the king's gifts (as tribute), although he actually ignored those he could not understand and dismissed most as useless objects. Finally, alluding to Macartney's refusal to kowtow, he suggested that once the British had acquired a degree of civilization sufficient to make them understand proper etiquette toward the Son of Heaven, the king might send another visitor to honor him.

The old emperor's serene self-confidence was based upon conditions that no longer existed. Although the empire had reached a peak of power during his early reign, it was now being undermined by the expense of maintaining large armies, a population explosion, and an all-pervading web of bribery and corruption. The bureaucracy was further hobbled by its out-dated notions of world politics. As Qianlong sent his letter to George III, imperial China was on the brink of collapse. The European invasion that had started as a trickle during the Ming dynasty would soon became a flood. Before long, a Son of Heaven would be on his knees...

The White Lotus Rebellion

The White Lotus was a secret society that originated during the Yuan dynasty among the uneducated peasants in the region just north of the Huai River. It came to symbolize Chinese resistance to foreign domination. During the 18th century, the society appealed to the disgruntled farmers of the countryside by promising them that a new Buddha would descend to Earth, restore the Ming dynasty, and remove disease, natural disasters, and all other suffering. In 1796, the members of the White Lotus started a rebellion to protest the collection of new taxes in certain regions of

Macartney wrote in his diary: "The empire of China is an old, crazy, first-rate Man of War [warship], which a succession of able and vigilant officers have contrived to keep afloat for these hundred and fifty years past to overawe their neighbors merely by her bulk and appearance. But whenever an insufficient man happens to have the command on deck, adieu to the discipline and safety of the ship. She may, perhaps, not sink outright; she may drift sometime as a wreck, and will then be dashed to pieces on the shores; but she can never be rebuilt on the old bottom.

the Yangzi River valley. They had stockpiled food and weapons, and they hid in the mountains before imperial troops arrived to stop them.

During this unsettled time, Qianlong abdicated his throne. His decision had nothing to do with the rebellion. Although quite elderly, he could have ruled longer. But, out of respect, he did not want to exceed the 60-year reign of his revered grandfather, Kangxi. He died three years later at the age of nearly 90.

His successor, Jiaqing, continued the fight against the White Lotus and slowly gained control over the territory where they were active. He offered amnesty to any rebels who came over to his side and exhorted local villagers to resist efforts to draw them from their traditional way of life. By cutting off their source of recruits as well as their food supply, Jiaqing was finally able to defeat the White Lotus. But the troubling undercurrents remained, and more conflicts were inevitable.

The Opium War

Meanwhile, trade with Britain had become a one-way street, since ships bearing tea from China often returned eastward empty, the British paying for all of their tea in silver. In the late 18th century, the king's ministers came up with a solution to their silver drain. British vessels began picking up opium in India (where the opium poppy was cultivated) and exchanging it in China for tea as well as luxury goods like porcelain.

Opium was nothing new in China. For centuries, the Chinese had grown poppies to produce a drug they used as a medicine for cholera. The habit of smoking opium to achieve a sense of euphoria was introduced in China in the 17th century. This practice is highly addictive, and it became a popular means of escape from the harsh realities of the times. (Among other things, smoking opium dulled hunger pangs.) Yongzheng prohibited the sale and use of opium in 1729, but this apparently had little effect. The Portuguese had discovered that there was great profit to be made by selling the drug, and they established a thriving opium trade between India and China.

After Macartney's failed mission, the British gave up all hope of improving normal trade relations, and they took over as the main opium dealers. Opium soon represented a quarter of the goods being sent east from India. In 1796, Qianlong banned the importation of opium, but his efforts were no more effective than those of Yongzheng. Besides, many officials (over 20 per cent) smoked the drug themselves, and others were easily bribed to close their eyes to the illegal trade.

By the 1830's, there were 10 million opium addicts in China. The drug was now in such demand that the balance of trade shifted against China, and it was the Chinese who had to make up the deficit with silver. The Qing government tried again to ban the sale of the drug, but with so many corrupt government officials involved such efforts were futile. The British opium importers and Chinese distributers were making a killing. Well-armed boats known as "fast crabs" and "scrambling dragons," manned by up to 70 oarsmen, collected the chests of opium from the foreign ships just off the coast of China and delivered them to the distributers. There was little the government could to to stop the rampant smuggling.

In 1836, the emperor's advisers suggested a new tack. Why not legalize opium? They reasoned that if the drug could be easily obtained, the people would lose their obsession for it. The plan backfired. As soon as the foreign traders heard about it, they ordered huge supplies from India to meet the increased demand! China was now drowning in opium.

In 1839, the Emperor Daoguang sent an honest and well-meaning official, Lin Zexu, to Guangzhou to do whatever he could to stamp out the illicit trade. He was known to the Europeans as Commissioner Lin. He decided the best way to deal with the problem was to communicate directly with the ruler of Britain, so he sent a letter to 20-year-old Queen Victoria that has become famous, even though it never actually reached her. (Copies were kept in Beijing.) After praising the British people for their "politeness and submissiveness" and noting that the country had become wealthy because of its long trading association with China (!), Lin went on to inquire why the British were selling to the Chinese a product (opium) known to be harmful and strictly forbidden in their own country. He noted that all Chinese products sent to Europe were beneficial, pointing out that the British could not get along for a single day without China's tea and rhubarb. (He based this assumption on the fact that tea aids digestion and rhubarb acts as a laxative.) He concluded his letter by requesting the queen to send a prompt reply "regarding the details and circumstances of cutting off the opium traffic," adding, "Be sure not to put this off."

Commissioner Lin had other plans up his sleeve as well. He demanded the surrender of all opium stocks held by Western traders at Guangzhou and imposed the death penalty on anyone caught dealing in the drug. The British government representatives in Guangzhou took responsibility for the opium held by British traders and handed over 20,000 chests of it to the Chinese authorities. Lin had the opium dissolved in water and poured into the sea, much to the distress of most of the onlookers, and he refused to compensate the

British for their lost profits. The British angrily withdrew to Macao, where they resumed dealing with smugglers.

In July, 1839, a group of British sailors killed a Chinese man near Macao. When the British refused to surrender the sailors to Lin, a fleet of Chinese war junks sailed toward the British ships at Xianggang (Hong Kong), an island near Guangzhou. The British warships fired on the junks and sank them. Thus began the First Opium War. Between 1840 and 1842, the British captured several ports between Guangzhou and Shanghai. When they threatened Nanjing, the emperor conceded defeat.

In August, 1842, the Chinese were forced to sign the Treaty of Nanjing. It provided for the opening of five ports — Guangzhou, Xiamen, Fuxhou, Ningbo, and Shanghai — to British trade. (Shanghai would quickly replace Guangzhou as China's largest trading port.) The Chinese Cohong (the merchant guild that collected tariffs) was abolished. China had to pay Britain $21 million to cover the costs of the war *and* the value of the opium that had been destroyed by Commissioner Lin. China also had to cede Xianggang (Hong Kong) to Britain. Finally, Britain was given "most-favored-nation" status. This meant that the British would automatically receive any privileges that China might later extend to any other nation.

Curiously enough, no mention was made in the treaty of the opium trade, apart from words expressing the vague hope that smuggling would cease. So what was the war really about? On one level, it was a conflict between the Chinese and Western views of the world. The Europeans could not accept the emperor's claim of authority over everyone else (Qianlong had described himself in his letter to King George as "monarch of the world"), and they demanded relations based on equality. They also claimed the right to trade under what they considered reasonable conditions. The Chinese continued to view all foreigners as barbarians. Despite more than 300 years of contact with the West, they knew very little about its culture. The Jesuits had taught them a good deal about Western science and art, but little about politics and society. And the superior ships and weapons of the Europeans had taken the Chinese completely by surprise.

The Treaty of Nanjing was the first of several treaties between China and the West (America and France later joined Britain) that are known as the "unequal treaties," since the Western powers received benefits and China did not. Through these treaties, the European countries gained the rights to 1) establish self-governing treaty-port settlements for western residence and trade; 2) have access to the Chinese interior; 3) operate foreign ships between the treaty ports on the coast and on inland waterways; 4) spread the teachings of Christianity without obstruction; 5) limit Chinese customs duties; and 6) establish formal diplomatic relations in Beijing and in treaty port areas. British subjects living in the ports and the Chinese they employed were under the jurisdiction of the British consul, not Chinese law.

The First Opium War had begun a new era for China. No longer the proud Middle Kingdom, the country would now face great humiliation and a painful adaptation to a world in which it would, for the next century at least, play only a minor role.

The Second Opium War

In 1851, Emperor Xianfeng came to the throne at the age of 20. Well-meaning but incompetent as a ruler, he inherited a crumbling empire and vastly depleted treasury. Unable to cope with the political chaos, Xianfeng did just what you'd probably expect — he left much of the running of the government in the hands of his officials.

In 1856, new troubles arose over an incident with a Chinese trading ship, *The Arrow*. The ship was registered in Hong Kong (recently ceded to Great Britain) and so it flew the British flag. (A Chinese vessel with a British flag! Can you predict what might happen?) Chinese police boarded the ship, pulled down the flag, and arrested 12 members of the crew. The British consul was furious. He viewed this was an insult to

his country and demanded an apology. But when the Chinese governor of Guangzhou released the crew, he offered no apology.

A while later, the British attacked Guangzhou and captured it. Thus began the Second Opium War. The French joined in, having their own grievances with the Chinese. When the British moved against Tianjin, a northern port city near Beijing, the Qing sued for peace. The Treaty of Tianjina was another of the "unequal treaties," making more demands on China.

The situation heated up again in 1859. A Chinese court refused to ratify the Treaty of Nanjing, and four British ships near Tianjin were fired upon by the Chinese and sunk. The following year, the British sent a mission to Beijing to negotiate, but the Chinese arrested the negotiators, and even executed some of them. As hostilities continued to escalate, British troops marched into Beijing. The emperor (Xianfeng) fled to Chengde.

European soldiers entered *Yuanmingyuan*, the Summer Palace near Beijing, burning everything they could not carry off as loot. Rare silks were ripped from the walls and used to cart the spoils away. Queen Victoria was later presented with a Pekinese dog captured there, which she appropriately named "Looty." A French officer described the pillaging in his diary: "The second night we spent in the Summer Palace…every trooper had his bird, his musical box, his alarm clock ...bells were ringing everywhere." The looting ended with a fire, and the soldiers used tapestries threaded with silver to try to put out the blaze.

Fortunately, the European troops did not enter the Forbidden City, where the emperor's brother, Prince Gong, had remained. The prince met with the British and agreed to obey the terms of the Treaty of Nanjing. He then ratified the new Convention of Beijing, which made even more demands on China. The Europeans now had the right to travel anywhere in China, to sail their ships up the Yangzi, to appoint ambassadors to the imperial court, to set up Christian missions in China, and to import opium legally (!). The Qing government also had to pay them another large indemnity for the trouble they had been caused.

After the Second Opium War, every major event in China would be influenced by the Western presence. European merchants, missionaries, diplomats, and military men arrived in the treaty port cities, bringing with them new ideas and attitudes. The foreign presence greatly disrupted the Chinese economy, and many laborers found themselves out of work. The country was once again besieged by foreigners, but these threatened the traditional way of life more than either the Mongols or Manchus had ever done.

The Taiping Rebellion

The Manchus were very worried about the loss of face caused by their huge concessions to the West. They feared that if their subjects believed the government was weak, they might be encouraged to rise up and overthrow it. As it turned, their fears were justified. The Taiping rebellion would become China's most destructive civil war.

The leader of the rebellion, Hong Xiuquan, was a brilliant but erratic scholar. He failed four times to pass the civil service exams in Guangzhou. but during the time he spent in that city, he was exposed to the Christian ideas taught by local Protestant missionaries. In 1837, while he was very ill, Hong had a vision in he was presented with a sword and instructed to use it to attack all demons. He became convinced that he was God's Chinese son, the younger brother of Jesus Christ, entrusted with the task of destroying "pagan idols" and bringing Christianity to all Chinese people.

Hong's preaching attracted a fanatical army of followers from among the peas-

---

The Convention of Beijing also gave permission for Chinese to emigrate on British ships, and thousands of Chinese laborers began immigrating overseas to North and South America, Hawaii and Australia.

ants, unemployed workers, and bandits. As thousands more became followers, he established footholds in many areas of northern China. In 1851, he declared the establishment of the *Taiping Tianguo* ("the Heavenly Kingdom of Great Peace") and assumed the title of Heavenly King.

The Taiping (as they came to be known) sought to establish a new order that went counter to China's Confucian traditions. They envisioned a society in which peasants would own and farm the land in common and share money, food, and even clothing. Women would be equal to men, and many harmful practices would be eliminated, including concubinage, arranged marriages, footbinding, opium smoking, and torture by government law officials (which was more common that you might think). Women held positions in Hong's government and even fought in battle.

When the Taiping were banned by the Qing government, their movement turned against the Manchus. Hong claimed that were "the Devil Incarnate," the evil force whom God had commanded him to destroy. Now added to the list of practices banned by the Taiping was the odious queue the Manchu required to be worn by all Chinese men.

In 1852, the Taiping swept through the country, seizing cities, destroying Buddhist and Daoist temples (all religious sects were considered alien), and smashing Confucian ancestral tablets. As they marched into the south, thousands more joined their numbers – mostly members of the lower classes. The following year, the Taiping captured Nanjing and established their headquarters there. They renamed the city *Tianjing* (Heavenly Capital). The Taiping now numbered more than one million.

After the signing of the Convention of Beijing, the British had chosen to support the Qing in their fight against the Taiping. They feared the rebels' strength and fanaticism, and they much preferred to have China run by a government they could manipulate. From 1860 to 1864, the Taiping fought many bitter battles against the combined forces of the Qing and the Europeans. They were defeated in Shanghai, Suzhou, and Hangzhou, and in July, 1864, Nanjing was retaken. By then, Hong had committed suicide. (Hong was not greatly missed by his cohorts. He had long since wavered from the standards he imposed on his followers, living a life of lux-

---

The Taiping Rebellion would be a major source of inspiration for the 20th century Communist leader, Mao Zedong.

ury in the palace in Nanjing, surrounded by dozens of concubines!)

Because none of the Taiping would surrender, they were all executed or burned to death in fires set by the government troops. During the 14 years of fighting, more than 20 million people died. Although nothing had been accomplished by the Taiping, their rebellion was another sign of faltering state of the Manchus.

Cixi Enters the Scene

Despite its weakened state, the life of the Qing dynasty was prolonged by a half-century through the efforts of an extraordinary woman. Her name was Cixi (Chuh Shee). She had entered the imperial palace in 1851 as a sixteen-year-old concubine. Five years later, she provided the emperor, Xianfeng, with his first son. When the emperor died in 1861, the five-year-old boy (Tongzhi) succeeded him. As mother of the little emperor, Cixi was given the high rank of empress dowager. (Xianfeng's wife, Xiao Cian, was known as the empress consort.) The government was placed in the hands of eight men, who were appointed to rule as regents.

But Cixi was an ambitious woman, and she was not satisfied with her new title. She wanted power! She cunningly plotted the downfall of the eight regents, one by one, until she and Xiao Cian were able to rule as joint regents. Cixi, of course, played the dominant role in this team. She savored every moment of her elevated position as she strutted through Forbidden City, surrounded by a retinue of fawning eunuchs.

The Self-Strengthening Movement

Do you remember how Xianfeng's brother, Prince Kong, took over for his brother to negotiate with the Europeans after the Second Opium War? Cixi recognized the prince's talents and now made him her chief minister. His visions would have a tremendous effect upon the final years of the Qing.

Unlike most Chinese officials of the time, Kong believed that China had much to learn from the Westerners, and he proposed a number of efforts to break down the Chinese prejudice against them. An important sign of this more open policy was the establishment of a foreign office, the Zongli Yamen, to deal with European diplomats.

Kong hoped to modernize China by adapting Western technology. His efforts to do this resulted in a policy known as the Self-Strengthening Movement. This name comes from a quotation from the Confucian classic, *The Book of Changes*: "Heaven moves on strongly; the (superior) gentlemen therefore strengthen themselves." Supporters of the movement liked to quote these words to show that using

Western technology to build up the country's military and economic strength was in accordance with China's cultural traditions.

Among the projects sponsored by Kong were the building of new shipyards and arsenals and the setting up of telegraphic communications between major cities. He hired Europeans to teach Chinese soldiers the use of modern guns and rifles. Colleges were founded for the study of Western science and languages, and Chinese students were even sent to the United States and European countries for military and technical training .

The Chinese Maritime Customs Service was later created to control the collection of customs dues at Shanghai. It was run by an Englishman. In 1872, Li Hongzhang (another of Cixi's most trusted advisers) founded the China Merchants Steam Navigation Company in Shanghai. It was intended to provide modern steamship transport, which would compete with foreign companies. The Kaiping coal mines in northern China were expanded to provide fuel for the ships, and the first permanent railway was completed in 1881 to transport the coal to the port cities.

Despite these ambitious projects, the Self-Strengthening Movement failed to turn China into a modern power. Why?

Because what really needed reforming was the imperial bureaucracy itself. The civil service exam system remained virtually unchanged in form and content from the early Ming period. Most Chinese intellectuals, with their vested interest in their classical studies, were slow to appreciate the need for change. And since the Manchus had originally justified their conquest in terms of protecting China's cultural heritage, how could they now abandon traditional values, practices, and institutions? Most of the Manchus, indeed, clung to the most conservative forms of Confucianism. It has been said that they had become more Chinese than the Chinese themselves in refusing to give up the old ways in favor of the new. So even when the opportunity for modernization presented itself, China remained fundamentally tied to the past.

Cixi Rules!

In 1872, the young emperor, Tongzhi, married. Two years later, he came of age and Cixi's regency officially ended. But no one was going to push the empress dowager aside! Tongzhi, exasperated by his mother's domineering ways, turned to his eunuchs for support. But these men convinced him to forget his troubles by slipping out of the palace in disguise and find-

In 1873 the Emperor Tongzhi received ambassadors of Japan, Russia, Britain, France, Holland, and USA at court without the traditional kowtow. This was a major concession to Western protocol.

ing amusement in the bars of Beijing. Tongzhi suddenly died of smallpox in January, 1975. (He seemed to be recovering at first, then took a turn for the worse. Many suspected foul play. Could it be that Cixi finished him off?)

Tongzhi's wife now posed an obstacle, since she was pregnant with possibly the next heir to the throne. Cixi convinced her to commit suicide, thereby insuring that no son would be born to interfere with her own plans. Then, overriding the normal rules of inheritance, she installed her four-year-old nephew, Guangzu, on the throne. As the boy's adoptive mother, Cixi again served as a very dominant co-regent. Her control of the court was assured.

For 50 years, Cixi effectively ruled China. Being a woman, she could not appear at official ceremonies, so she "advised" the emperor from behind a screen placed by the imperial throne. She was a savvy politician, who knew how to play her ministers one against the other in order to retain power. Everyone feared tangling with her, since she was known to fall into violent rages whenever she encountered criticism. She once remarked, "I have often thought that I am the most clever woman that ever lived...look at me, I have 400,000,000 people dependent on my judgment."

This powerful woman was small in stature, standing only 5 feet tall, but she

Cixi

wore 6-inch heels to make her appear more formidable. Her imposing image was enhanced by heavy makeup, which gave her unnatural-looking rouged cheeks and a whitened face. (She has been likened to Queen Elizabeth I of England.) She had very long fingernails, which she used to scratch the cheeks of servants who displeased her!

Cixi poured huge amounts of money into her private quarters in the Forbidden City. She also built a lavish new Summer

Palace to replace the one destroyed by the French and British in 1860 (*Yuanmingyuan*). It had a special theater on the site of an imperial park by Kun Ming Lake. She financed this project with funds that were badly needed for modernizing the naval fleet. The only "ship" she had built was a marble pavilion rising from the water in the shape of a Mississippi paddle-streamer.

When Guangxu came of age in 1889, Cixi "retired" to the Summer Palace, although, of course, she kept her hand in imperial politics. (She insisted upon reading all official government documents.) Guangxu was very frail. His voice was described as being "light and thin like a mosquito." But he worked hard to follow the principles of Prince King to modernize the country. He even learned to speak English.

Cixi was preparing to spend huge sums on the celebration of the 60th birthday in 1894 when war broke out with Japan. She reluctantly abandoned her party plans. The navy that she had refused to modernize was easily defeated by the Japanese fleet. It was another unsettling loss for the Middle Kingdom. According to the terms of the treaty of Shimonoseki, China was forced to pay a huge indemnity to Japan, to allow Japanese industries in four Chinese ports, and to cede Taiwan to Japan. China also lost control of several other countries that had been vassal states, including Burma and Korea. This humiliating "unequal" treaty led to a surge of Chinese nationalism.

In 1898, the young emperor, strongly encouraged by two forward-thinking Chinese officials, supported a series of reforms, many of which grew from ideas proposed during the Self-Strengthening Movement. In a period of about one hundred days, Guangxu issued 40 reform decrees. Some were intended to revise the structure of the government bureaucracy and modernize the legal, postal and military systems. Others would have led to an important shift in Chinese educational standards by promoting the study of practical subjects such as economics over the present emphasis on the Confucian classics. Predictably, these reforms were not supported by the Manchu officials, who preferred more gradual changes, if, indeed, any at all. Cixi felt the same way, but Guangxi fiercely defended the need for the reforms. For a short time, everyone waited to see what would happen.

The dam broke when Yuan Shikai, a Chinese military commander, informed Cixi of Guangxi's supposed plans to curb her influence by imprisoning her. On September 21 (1898), Cixi led a coup and had Guangxi placed under house arrest in the Summer Palace. She then canceled all of his reform edicts and had six of his advisers executed. Cixi was back in the saddle again. The young emperor remained a virtual prisoner for the rest of his life. His aunt even walled up the windows of his quarters in the Summer Palace.

China Stumbles On

After the failure of the reforms, all hopes of modernizing China began to fade. The traditional values, with their emphasis on the classics and veneration for the past, left little room for the flexibility needed in a changing world. Meanwhile, the Qing dynasty was growing weaker and weaker. The requirements that all major decisions have imperial approval and that all documents be copied in Manchu and Chinese made the government both top-heavy and inefficient. Many officials had become so demoralized that they left the government, and those who remained tended to be corruptible. And the population had grown to over 300 million. The bureaucracy was so understaffed that a single district manager often governed 300 square miles and ¼ million people. Taxes were often gathered by the local gentry, who exempted themselves from paying anything at all by raising those of the peasants.

Most devastating of all was the presence of the Europeans. Missionaries now competed with Chinese scholars for moral and religious leadership in the countryside. The preached against many local traditions, condemned the worship of "idols" and the practice of sacrificing to ancestors, and built churches that ignored the rules of *feng shui*. Western merchants had begun selling manufactured goods that competed with local Chinese industries. China's military power was woefully outmatched by Western weaponry. As the Europeans acted more and more as though they owned China, and the anti-foreign feelings within the country began to grow stronger.

The Boxer Rebellion

The Boxer Rebellion began in 1898 in Shandong Province, a peninsula close to Beijing. The area had recently experienced a severe famine. This aggravated the economic hardships caused when machine-spun yarn, imported from the West, lowered the demand for the cotton grown there. The local people were further incensed when coastal cities of Shandong were ceded to the Europeans. Masses of peasants, laborers, and craftsmen gathered to shout their protests, attributing China's misery to all foreigners, a category that now included Chinese Christian converts.

The growing rebellion was spearheaded by "The Society of Righteous and Harmonious Fists," an offshoot of the White Lotus. Members of the society practiced Daoist rituals involving movements mimicking those of animal predators, often in slow motion. (Some claimed that by controlling their breathing and muscles they could withstand bullets.) Westerners likened the movements of these rituals to shadow boxing, and for this reason the rebels came to be known as the Boxers.

When government forces in Shandong began taking action against them, the Boxers moved to other regions of China. Before long, their numbers had grown dramatically. They even found support among the disgruntled Confucian bureaucrats. Soon, groups of Boxers could be seen on the streets of many major cities. In 1900, they began moving into the outskirts of Beijing, where they burned churches, killed Chinese Christian converts, and destroyed electric and telegraph lines. The British and American diplomats immediately demanded that the Qing government send troops to the capital city to stifle the uprising.

Cixi, however, had decided to use the rebellion to her own advantage, naively hoping it would help her rid the country of the intruding Europeans. She appointed a pro-Boxer Manchu prince as head of the Foreign Office. When the rebels, chanting "Support the Qing, destroy the foreigner," entered Beijing, they were met by government troops, who helped them besiege the city's Foreign Legation Quarter. On June 16, a secretary of the Japanese Legation was killed there. Three days later, Cixi ordered all foreign legations out of Beijing within 24 hours. The next day, Germany's minister was killed as he was making his way to negotiate with her ministers. On June 21, Cixi took matters a step further, declaring war on all foreign powers that had diplomatic contacts with China. (These were Britain, the USA, France, Germany, Austria, Belgium, Holland and Japan.)

The siege of the foreign delegations lasted 55 days. Some of the worst fighting took place around the Roman Catholic Cathedral, where the Bishop Favier and 43 French and Italian sailors defended the over 4,000 Chinese Christians who had sought refuge there.

Each of the eight Western powers that had a diplomatic staff in China now sent troops to Beijing. A force of over 20,000 soldiers from the various nations lifted the siege on August 14 and rescued the foreigners and Chinese Christians. (This happened almost exactly 40 years to the day after the British and French had entered Beijing at the end of the Second Opium War.) The rescue was accompanied by a

In 1907, the U.S. government decided to take the funds paid to it by China after the Boxer Rebellion to fund Chinese students. Hundreds of them took advantage of the opportunity to study in universities in the United States.

great deal of looting and assaults upon the civilian population by the foreign troops. Even the Forbidden City was broken into, and the wife of the British minister was later observed taking her pick of its lavish offerings!

With Beijing in foreign hands, Cixi slipped out of the city in a small cart, wearing the blue cotton garments of a peasant woman. Guangxu, also disguised as a peasant, rode in a cart behind her. (The emperor's favorite concubine had urged him to remain and face the enemy, but Cixi had her drowned in a palace well!) Followed by a retinue of high officials, who had exchanged their fine silk robes for cotton tunics, they fled to the ancient city of Chang'an (Xi'an).

Cixi's top minister, Li Hongzhang, negotiated with the Western diplomats, and on September 7, 1901, the "Boxer Protocol" was signed. It was yet another "unequal treaty." China had to pay a staggering indemnity — 450 million ounces of silver over the next 40 years. Officials who had supported the anti-foreign movement were punished, and some were executed. (Many had already committed suicide.) Missions of apology were to be sent to Japan and Germany, whose diplomats had been killed. Chinese fortifications built along the coast protecting Beijing were destroyed, and foreign legations were given the right to station troops in the capital city (for self-protection). These terms hastened the collapse of the now-staggering Qing dynasty.

In January 1902, the Qing court returned to Beijing. Cixi, determined to hold on to her power at any cost, turned on the charm, making numerous gestures of reconciliation with the foreigners. She invited the wives of Western diplomats to tea in the imperial palace and posed with them for photographs. Finally accepting change as inevitable, Cixi initiated a number of reforms, similar to those attempted during Guangxu's ill-fated Reform Movement of 1898. These included modernizing Chinese education and establishing a modern police force. And steps were finally taken, with British cooperation, to control the use of opium. Three years later, the traditional examination system was abolished.

Today, the Forbidden City is known as the Palace Museum. In addition to the majestic halls and palaces themselves, it contains smaller museums, which are filled with artifacts, paintings, porcelain, clocks, furniture, and many other objects of Chinese culture dating back to very earliest times. The Wen Hua Hall houses more than 10 million official documents drawn up by central and local government officials during the Ming and Qing dynasties. This is the largest collection of historical records in China.

Cixi died in 1908 at the age of 73. It was then announced that the emperor, Guangxu, had died the previous day. Many believe she poisoned him, since she had already named her three-year-old great-nephew, Puyi, heir to the throne. The boy would rule as Xuanzong for a very short time. He was China's last emperor.

A Hero of the People

The failure of the Reform Movement of 1898 and of the Boxer Rebellion caused many educated Chinese to believe that a genuine revolution was necessary to remove the old imperial system and establish a new form of government.

Sun Yatsen was a Chinese intellectual who had founded the Society to Revive China in 1894. Sun's plan was to start several local revolutions at the same time in different parts of the country. His goal was to remove not only the Qing government but all foreign powers in China. In 1895 his followers staged an uprising in Guangzhou. It was unsuccessful, but it marked the beginning of this very significant movement in China.

With Qing officials anxious to arrest him, Sun Yatsen fled to Japan, where he founded the Revolutionary Alliance in 1905. From Japan, he traveled to Europe. When he was kidnapped in London by Qing supporters and held at the Chinese legation, he was able to get a message to a British doctor, who had been his teacher in Hong Kong. The Foreign Office was alerted, and the Qing legation was obliged to release Sun. The publicity he gained from this incident made him world-famous virtually overnight. This gave an unexpected boost to his campaign.

Sun remained in Europe for two years, studying Western political and social trends and developing his revolutionary philosophy. He then traveled extensively in other parts of the world, gaining support among Chinese communities in the United States, Japan, and elsewhere, and organizing smaller revolutionary societies. His followers even drew the support of disaffected elements within the units of the Qing army. By 1910, the Revolutionary Alliance had nearly 10,000 members. Many of these were young Chinese who had studied in Japan and had returned to China to fight for their ideals.

The Fall of the Qing

The revolutionary movement gained even greater momentum when the Qing nationalized the Chinese railroads in 1911, an action threatening the autonomy of the Chinese provinces. A strike was called in the railroad companies in Sichuan, and this sparked general rebellions in other provinces. On October 10, Sun's followers attacked the governor's office in Wuchang, forcing the governor to flee. News of the

Wuchang uprising spread quickly, and soon rebels were organizing attacks upon the governments in other cities. In many cases, the Qing officials changed their allegiance to the revolutionaries. By November, 15 of China's 24 provinces had claimed independence from the Qing government.

Sun Yatsen had been in the United States raising funds while all this was happening. Now that the Chinese Revolution had actually begun, he began seeking support among foreign governments. The British and French received him favorably. He then returned to China. On January 1, 1912, Sun was elected provisional president of the Chinese Republic in Nanjing. The Chinese Nationalist Party replaced the Revolutionary Alliance.

Meanwhile, General Yuan Shikai, commander of the Qing Imperial Army, still held power in Beijing. Yuan demanded that Sun make *him* president of the new republic, so that China could be united under a government based in Beijing. Sun agreed to this, on the condition that Yuan persuade the Qing emperor to abdicate.

On February 12, 1912, Puyi (Emperor Xuanzong) officially acknowledged that the people had expressed their displeasure with his rule and that he had lost the Mandate of Heaven. Once officially dethroned, he was allowed to remain at the Forbidden City with a stipend of $3 million per year to maintain his residence.

If the pattern of China's long historical past were followed, a powerful rival would emerge from among the population to claim the Mandate of Heaven. He would reestablish order and create a new dynasty modeled upon those of earlier times. But the old patterns had been broken and the long, long cycle of dynastic rule in China had come to a halt.

On February 15, 1912, Sun Yatsen returned the Middle Kingdom to the imperial ancestors in a ceremony at the tomb of the first Ming emperor, Hongwu (Taizu), at Nanjing. Then he resigned. Yuan Shikai became the first president of the New Republic of China.

Puyi lived in isolation while officials sold of a substantial part of the dynasty's priceless historical relics and works of art. In 1924 warlords forced Puyi to leave the Forbidden City. He was made puppet emperor of Manchuria under the Japanese in 1934. A prisoner of the Soviets in 1945, after years of reeducation under the Communist government, he ended his life as Henry Puyi, a gardener and citizen in the People's Republic of China, dying in 1967 at the age of 62.

Review Questions:

1. In what ways did Dorgon demonstrate his desire to continue the ways of the old Ming dynasty?

2. What new rules did Dorgon impose on the Chinese?

3. What did the Literary Inquisition show about the attitudes of the Manchus?

4. What was unusual about the paintings of Zhu Da?

5. How did Kangxi's policies differ from those of Dorgon?

6. How did Kangxi draw the literati over to his side?

7. What was the purpose of Kangxi's Grand Tours?

8. How did the Jesuit, Matteo Ricci, deal with the issue of ancestor worship among Christian converts?

9. What were the Sacred Edicts?

10. In what major ways did Yongzheng differ from Kangxi?

11. Who ruled China for most of the 18th century?

12. What were Qianlong's greatest interests?

13. In what ways did the palace designed by Castiglione resemble Versailles?

14. Describe the imperial robe worn by Qianlong.

15. What was the basic plot of *Dream of the Red Chamber*?

16. Why was Monkey sent on the quest for Buddhist scriptures?

17. How did the importing of tea throw off the British balance of trade with China?

18. What were the major requests in the letter from King George to Qianlong?

19. Was Macartney's mission a success?

20. What was the White Lotus?

21. Why did the British begin importing opium to China?

22. What were the terms of the Treaty of Nanjing?

23. What were the terms of the Convention of Beijing?

24. What were the goals of the Taiping?

25. How did Prince Kong try to bring China into the modern world?

26. Why did the Self-Strengthening Movement fail to modernize China?

27. Why did Cixi have to stand behind a screen?

28. Name a few complaints the Chinese had against the Europeans.

29. Why did Cixi support the Boxers?

30. Why did the Europeans fight the Boxers?

31. What were Sun Yatsen's original goals?

32. Who was China's last emperor?

PROJECTS:

1. During the 17th century and first half of the 18th, European powers treated China with enormous respect. Admiration for Chinese principles of government filled the writings of the Enlightenment, while its arts

gave birth to two waves of *chinoiserie* (a European fascination with the art, clothing, furniture, gardens, and other areas of Chinese culture). Find out more about either a) European philosophers of the Age of Enlightenment who were influenced in their writing by the Chinese form of government or b) *chinoiserie* in Europe. Consult at least three sources. Then write a short report.

2. Wang Yuanqi (1642-1715) was the greatest of a group of painters of the Qing known as the "Six Masters of the Qing." Kangxi often requested him to paint a landscape in front of him. The emperor appointed him as one of the editors of an anthology of painting and calligraphy that he commissioned in 1708. Wang's style was more abstract than typical Chinese landscape paintings. He seems to separate the rocks and mountains into their individual forms, which has caused some Western critics to compare him to 19th century French Impressionist Cezanne. Find out more about this artist and make a report to your class. Be sure to have copies of his paintings as illustrations for your presentation.

3. Make a detailed timeline indicating the phases of a typical (but mythical) Chinese imperial dynasty from its founding to its fall. Consider such things as the creation of a government, establishment of a capital, efforts to deal with disruptions that might have occurred in the downfall of the previous dynasty, improvements to roads, canals, and other forms of communication, and so forth. Think about what usually causes a government to lose its effectiveness. Don't rule out natural calamities.

4. Adam Schall von Bell was a Jesuit who remained in China after the Manchus overthrew the Ming dynasty. Find out more about him and write a short report.

5. Read *Dream of Red Mansions*. Then write a report on the book or write a play based on some of the episodes.

6. See the movie, *The Last Emperor*. It tells the story of Puyi. Much of it was filmed in the Forbidden City.

7. The Jesuits compared Qianlong to Louis XIV, the "Sun King" of France. Both men dominated the 18th century. Find out more about both men. Then write a report comparing and contrasting their characters and their periods of reign.

8. During the 19th century Shanghai emerged as a major center of artistic production. Ren Bonian, one of the city's most distinguished painters, had a vibrant style inspired not only by Chinese popular art but also by the new bold and restless spirit

of the Western-influenced treaty port. Find out more about him and his work. Then present your findings to the class.

9. Read *Mountain Light* by Laurence Yep. This is a novel set during the Qing dynasty. Members of two Chinese families struggle against the Manchu regime until the son of one of the families departs for California. But that's not the end of the story.

10. In October, 2000, Pope John Paul II announced that 87 Chinese Roman Catholics killed between 1648 and 1930, most of them during the Boxer Rebellion would be canonized (made saints). They were the first Chinese people to be raised to sainthood. The Chinese government did not support the move and issued statements that stopped just short of saying the Christians deserved to die, noting that they had committed "monstrous crimes against the Chinese people." Consult the archives containing newspaper articles from recent years about the present relationship between the Chinese government and the Catholic Church. Write a report based upon your findings.

11. Find a copy of the recent translation of *The Mustard Seed Garden Manual of Painting*, edited (and translated) by Mai-Mai Sze. Select several sections to read, and then enjoy the illustrations of Chinese art.

Important Happenings Elsewhere in the World
(1644-1911)

Louis XIV rules France — 1643 -1715

Age of Enlightenment in Europe — c 1660 – 1750

Steam Engine patented by James Watt — 1769

Outbreak of Seven Years' War between British and French —1756

British control India —1758

American Revolution begins —1776

French Revolution begins — 1789

Lousiana Purchase —1803

Napoleon Marches to Russia — 1812

Queen Victoria —1837 -1901

First Modern Olympic Games in Athens — 1896

Commonwealth of Australia formed — 1901

Russo-Japanese War — 1904 - 1905

EPILOGUE

After 2,133 years, the story of imperial China had come to an end. But, of course, that wasn't the end of Chinese civilization. The rich culture that you have been studying survived the turbulent years of the 20th century, and now, as the 21st century begins, constraints are slowly loosening and ancient traditions like Confucianism are reclaiming a dominant role in Chinese society.

It has been said that to understand China one must understand the past. This is true, not only because of the great emphasis the Chinese have always placed upon historical precedents but also because so many long-held beliefs and values continue to mold their everyday life. So before concluding our study, let's take a moment to review a few of the major themes running through Chinese imperial history.

First and foremost is the all-pervasive emphasis upon order and stability. Shi Huangdi established the first imperial bureaucracy to bring an end to political chaos. As it evolved in later centuries, certain built-in features, particularly the central role of an educated elite, enabled it to become the most enduring — and stable — political system ever devised. Even as dynasties rose and fell, the bureaucracy continued to function iin some form, holding Chinese together in even the worst of times.

The concept of the Mandate of Heaven was an ingenious safety valve, justifying the removal of an "unworthy" ruler. Linking political power with virtuous behavior was something most unusual in world history. The Confucian belief that the well-being of a society depends upon the morality of its members continues to motivate the Chinese people to strive for the common good. And the central role of the family remains as important today as it did in ancient times.

Daoist views about the patterns of nature and a harmonious universe are reflected in the cyclical structure of imperial history — one dynasty rising, flourishing, then falling due to internal decay, to be replaced by a new one. The duality of yin and yang lie at the heart of social pyschology, medicine, landscape painting, astrology, and many other aspects of traditional Chinese culture. The love of balance and symmetry is reflected in the design of buildings, parks, and gardens. If a line were drawn through one of the courtyard houses of the literati of imperial times, the rooms and walls on one side of it would have been a mirror image of the other. And didn't the Middle Kingdom lie in the very center of the square earth?

The Chinese have been avid chroniclers since earliest times, and their written record of the pre-modern era surpasses that of any other nation in the world. Their recorded history even stretched back further, merging with the mythical times of the Yellow Emperor. And the full story still hasn't been told, since archaeologists are continually finding new troves of bamboo strips and ancient scrolls.

Reverence for the past enabled the Chinese to live more fully in the present. The ancient classics provided plentiful guidance for achieving peace and harmony in the here and now, and the ideal of self-cultivation encouraged thoughtful people to find ways to make the most of their own potential. The high value placed upon the refinement and creative skills of the model courtier reflect the important role education has always had in Chinese society.

And then there are all those symbols — dragons, peonies, lotus blossoms, carps, goldfish, pine trees, bamboo, plum blossoms, bats, mountains, and water-falls. So many aspects of the natural world have become metaphors for the Chinese. Not to mention colors and numbers. Even the characters of the written language are symbols that represent ideas and images rather than simply sounds.

The emphasis upon the humanities did not prevent more scientifically-minded people from coming up with all sorts of ingenious inventions — the compass, paper, book-printing, gunpowder, silk cloth, porcelain, the wheelbarrow, kites, playing cards, to name only a few. Imperial engineers contributed greatly to society by building roads, bridges, and canals, as well as those extraordinary ships. Throughout history, the Chinese have been amazingly resourceful.

These are a few of the major themes we have studied in this book, but you can probably think of many more. And now that China is emerging as a major power on the global stage, Westerners will have many more opportunities to learn about and appreciate this rich and fascinating culture.

Emperors of China's Later Dynasties

Northern Song

Taizu (960-976), Taizong (976-997), Zhenzong (998-1022), Renzong (1022-1063), Yingzong (1064-1067), Shenzong (1068-1085), Zhezong (1086-1101), Huizong (1101-1125), Qinzong (1126)

Southern Song

Gaozong (1127-1162), Xiaozong (1163-1190), Guangzong (1190-1194), Ningzong (1195-1224), Lizong (1225-1264), Duzong (1265-1274), Gongzong (1275), Duanzong (1276-1278), Bing Di (1279)

Yuan

Kublai (1279-1294), Temur Oljeitu (Chengzong) 1294-1307; Khaishan (Wuzong) 1308-1311; Ayurbarwada (Renzong) 1311-1320; Shidebala (Yingzong) 1321-1323; Yesun Temur (Taiding) 1323-1328; Tugh Temur (Wenzong) 1328-1332; Khoshila (Mingzong) 1329; Toghon Temur (Shundi) 1333-1368

Ming

Hongwu (1368-98), Jianwen (1399-1402), Yongle (1403-1424), Hongxi (1425), Xuande (1426-1435), Zhengtong/Tianshun (1436-1449, 1457-1464), Jingtai (1450-1457), Chenghua (1465-1487), Hongzhi (1488-1505), Zhengde (1506-1521), Jiajing (1522-1567), Longzing (1567-1572), Wanli (1573-1620), Tiachang (1620), Tianqi (1621-1627), Chongzhen (1628-1644)

Qing

Shunzhi (1644-1661), Kangxi (1661-1722), Yongzheng (1723-1735), Qianlong (173-1795), Jiajing (1796-1820), Daoguang (1821-1850), Xianfeng (1851-1861), Tongzhi (1862-1874), Guangxu (1875-1908), Puyi (1909-1911)

Provinces of Modern China

Modern China has 21 provinces and 5 autonomous border regions, such as Inner Mongolia. Some people think that country's shape resembles that of a chicken! Can you see it?

Chinese Symbols

A Chinese word can mean many things, depending upon the tone with which it is pronounced and its context in a sentence. The Chinese have always enjoyed puns (plays on words), and, perhaps for this reason, they have adopted certain plants and animals as symbols for concepts that sound similar to them. In English, an example would be using a doe (female deer) as a symbol for dough (a slang term for money). The grammatical term for words that sound alike is homophone. Here are a few examples.

A bat, *fu* in Chinese, is a symbol of good luck.
A butterfly, *die*, is a symbol of longevity.
A fish, *yu*, is a symbol of abundance, or wealth.
A goldfish, *jin yu*, is a double pun, meaning gold (*jin*) in abundance.
A carp, *li*, sounds like the word for advantage and so symbolizes success in the exams.
A chrysanthemum, *ju*, sounds a lot like *jiu* (a long time), so it means longlasting. It also is a symbol of autumn.

Other plants and animals symbolize concepts suggested by their physical characteristics, unique activities, or their role in a well-known myth. (The carp also falls into this category.)

bamboo (*zhu*)	resilience
a carp (*li*)	success in civil service examinations
a cicada (*guo-guo*)	immortality
a crane (*he*)	longevity
a cricket (*xi shou*)	fighting spirit
a dragon (*long*)	masculine vigor, the emperor, east, rain, good luck
a lion (*shi zi*)	a guardian
a lotus (*lian, he*)	binding, concord, unison
a magnolia (*mu lan*)	a beautiful woman
mandarin ducks (*yuan-yang*)	they live in pairs and symbolize marital happiness
an onion (*cong*)	cleverness
an orange (*ju-z*)	good luck
an oriole (*ying*)	friendship
a peach (*tag*)	immortality
a peacock (*kong*)	beauty
a pearl (*zhu*)	purity, precious, wisdom (when shown with dragons)
a peony (*mu dan*)	beauty, spring, young love and happiness
a persimmon (*shi*)	business
a pheasant (*ye ji*)	a golden pheasant symbolizes the educated elite
a phoenix (*feng huang*)	female, yin, south, harbinger of opportunities
a pine (*song*)	longevity, steadfastness
a plum (*mei, li*)	promise of spring, winter
a quail (*an, chun*)	courage
a rat (*da shu*)	money
a rhinoceros (*xi-niu*)	a scholar, sound character
a toad (*ha-ma*)	longevity
a tortoise (*gui*)	steadfastness, immortality, north
a unicorn (*qi lin*)	an omen of good things

Selections from *The Analects*

Do not do to others what you do not want others to do to you.

In education there are no class distinctions.

It is only the wisest and the stupidest who cannot change.

Silence is a friend who will never betray.

The way of a gentleman is threefold – being humane he has no anxieties, being wise he has no doubts, being brave he has no fear.

Judge others by what you know of yourself.

The mind of the superior man is occupied with righteousness; the mind of the inferior man is occupied with gain.

A person of true wisdom knows what he knows and knows what he does not know.

Everything has its beauty, but not everyone sees it.

If you know a thing, say it; if not, admit it.

Moral force never dwells in solitude; it will always bring neighbors.

To have faults and to be making no effort to change them is to have faults indeed.

If a man is correct in his own person, then there will be obedience without orders being given; but it he is not correct in his own person, there will not be obedience even though orders are given.

He who rules by virtue is like the polestar, which remains unmoving in its mansion while all the others stars revolve respectfully around it.

By nature men are pretty much alike; it is learning and practice that set them apart.

He who learns but does not think is lost; he who thinks but does not learn is in danger.

By extensively studying all learning, and keeping oneself under the restraint of the rules of propriety, one may thus likewise not err from what is right.

If the people are led by edicts and adherence enforced by punishments, they will try to avoid the punishment but they will have no sense of shame. If they are led by virtue and adherence is accomplished by the rules of propriety, they will have the sense of shame and will reform themselves.

Suggested Reading

Beguin, Gilles and Dominuque Motel, *The Forbidden City of Imperial China*. New York: Harry N. Abrams, Inc., 1997.

Birrell, Anne, *Chinese Mythology: An Introduction*. Baltimore, Md: Johns Hopkins Press, 1993.

Birrell, Anne, *Chinese Myths*. Austin, Texas: University of Texas Press, 2000.

Clayre, Alasdair, *The Heart of the Dragon*. Boston: Houghton Mifflin, 1985.

Dawson, Raymond, *The Chinese Experience*. London, Phoenix Press, 1978.

Eberhard, Wolfram, *A Dictionary of Chinese Symbols*. London: Routledge Press, 1986.

Ebrey, Patricia Buckley, *China: An Illustrated History*. Cambridge, England: Cambridge University Press, 1996.

Ebrey, Patricia Buckley, ed., *Chinese Civilization: A Sourcebook*. New York: Free Press, 1993.

Editors of Time-Life Books, *What Life Was Like In The Land Of The Dragon*. Richmond, Virginia: Time Life Books, 1998.

Fairbank, John King, *China*. Cambridge, MA: Harvard University Press, 1992.

Haw, Stephen G., *A Traveller's History of China*. New York: Interlink Books, 2001.

Hinton, David, transl, *Tao Te Ching*. Washington, DC: Counterpoint, 2000.

Hoff, Benjamin, *The Tao of Pooh*. New York: Penguin Books, 1982.

Hoff, Benjamin, *The Te of Piglet*. New York: Penguin Books, 1992.

Huang, Roy, *China: A Macro History*. New York: M.E. Sharpe, Inc., 1997.

Major, John, *The Silk Route: 7000 Miles of History*. New York: Harper Collins, 1995.

Michaelson, Carol, *Ancient China*. London: Weldon Owen, 1996.

Morton, W. Scott, *China: Its History and Culture*. New York: McGraw-Hill, 1995.

Mote, F.W., *Imperial China*. Cambridge, MA: Harvard University Press, 1999.

Murowchick, Robert, ed., *Cradles of Civilization: China*. London: Weldon Owen, 1994.

Paludan, Ann, *Chronicle of the Chinese Emperors*. London: Thames and Hudson, 1998.

Roberts, J.A.G., *A Concise History of China*. Cambridge, MA: Harvard University Press, 1999.

Saunders, Tao Tao Liu, *Dragons, Gods, and Spirits from Chinese Mythology*. New York: Peter Bedrick Books, 1980.

Spence, Jonathan D., *Emperor of China: Self-portrait of Kangxi*. New York: Vintage Books, 1975.

Steele, Philip, *Step into the Chinese Empire*. New York: Lorenz Books, 1998.

Sullivan, Michael, *The Arts of China*. Berkeley, CA: University of California Press, 1999.

Sullivan, Michael, *The Three Perfections*. New York: George Braziller, 1999.

Temple, Robert, *The Genius of China*. New York: Simon and Schuster, 1989.

Thorp, Robert L. and Richard Ellis Vinograd. *Chinese Art and Culture*, New York: Harry N. Abrams, 2001.

Tregear, Mary, *Chinese Art*. London: Thames and Hudson, 1997.

Watson, Burton, *Chinese Rhyme Prose*. New York: Columbia University Press, 1971.

Williams, Brian, *Ancient China*. New York: Viking, 1996.

Wilker, Josh, *Confucius: Philosopher and Teacher*. New York: Franklin Watts, 1998.

Glossary

Alchemy — The pseudo-science of changing base metals into gold. Daoist alchemists mixed together potions hoping to produce gold as part of an elixir that would make a person immortal.

Buddhism — A religion that was introduced into China from India. Buddhists believe that suffering is caused by the desire for material things and that this suffering can be ended through enlightenment.

Bureaucracy — A form of government divided into departments and manged by appointed (or elected) officials.

Calligraphy — The fine art of writing Chinese characters with a brush dipped in ink.

Censorate — A "watchdog" branch of government that oversees the operating the other branches.

Concubine — A woman who lives with an emperor, king, or noble, and has his children, but does not have the rights or rank of a wife.

Daoism — The Chinese philosophy based on contemplation of the natural world. It later became a religion and is associated with a belief in magic.

Eight Immortals — Eight ordinary people who, through good works and prayer, achieved immortality according to Daoist belief.

Eunuch — A man who had been castrated so that he could live among the wives and concubines of the emperor without the danger of fathering children.

Feng shui — The ancient Daoist art of designing a house, garden, or city according the directions of the compass and the situation of such natural features as mountains, rivers, and trees.

Filial piety — Obligations owed to one's parents and ancestors according to the social ethics of Confucius.

Five Confucian Classics — *The Book of Changes*, *The Book of Documents*, *The Book of Songs*, *The Book of Rites*, and *The Spring and Autumn Annals*.

Four Books of Confucius — *The Analects*, *The Book of Mencius*, *The Doctrine of the Mean*, and *The Great Learning*.

Hanlin Academy — A learned association of scholars formed during the Tang dynasty to aid the the emperor with written documents. In later dynasties, members of the Academy were imperial advisers.

Jinshi — A scholar-official who has passed the highest level civil service examination.

Kaolin — A special white clay found in southern China used to make porcelain.

Khan (khanate) — A khan is a Mongol ruler. His realm is his khanate.

Lacquer — The sap of a tree used as a varnish to coat wood, metal, leather, or paper.

Legalism — A philosophy according to which people are considered weak and so must be forced to act properly by rigid laws and strict punishment.

Li — A Chinese unit of length. One li equals 3/10 of a mile.

Literati — The educated class of imperial Chinese society.

Mandate of Heaven — The ancient concept that Heaven gave authority to a ruler with the priviso that he govern in a virtuous way.

Neo-Confucianism — A philosophy in which the basic tenets of Confucianism were blended with certain beliefs and principles of Daoism and Buddhism, giving it a more spiritual quality.

Pavilion — A light, open building placed in a scenic spot.

Qi — The life force existing in animate and inanimate objects, which needs to be harnessed correctly to avoid imbalance and disharmony.

Silk Road — The overland network of trade routes stretching from Chang'an to the Mediterranean.

Three Perfections — The arts of calligraphy, poetry, and painting.

Three Teachings — The ethics and religious beliefs associated with Daoism, Buddhism and Confucianism.

Yin/yang — The two dual forces of nature, according to Daoism, which must be balanced to achieve harmony. Yin is negative, feminine, and dark, while yang is positive, masculine, and bright.

INDEX